GOTTA FIND A HOME

Conversation with Street People

Book 1

The beggar, engraving by Alphonse Legros (1837-1911)

GOTTA FIND A HOME

Conversations with Street People

Dennis Cardiff

Published by Dennis Cardiff

Gotta Find a Home: Conversations with Street People by Dennis Cardiff

© *2014 Dennis Cardiff All rights reserved.* Ontario, Canada

Published by Dennis Cardiff

The author has tried to recreate events, locales and conversations from his memories of them. In order to maintain anonymity names of individuals and places have been changed.

Cover Illustration Copyright © 2014 by Dennis Cardiff

Cover Font is called DJ Gross and the license can be found at: *http://www.fontsquirrel.com/license/DJ-Gross*

Book design and editing by Karen Silvestri, Karenzo Media

ISBN-10: 0993979904
ISBN-13: 9780993979903

Dedication

To my wife Daisy, for her love, patience and understanding; allowing me to spend hours at my computer, when she would have preferred that I spend them with her.

How It Began

My lungs ached as frost hung in the bitterly cold December morning air, making breathing difficult. I trudged in the falling snow toward the building where I work, in one of the city's grey, concrete, office tower canyons. I dodged other pedestrians, also trying to get to work on time. I noticed a woman seated cross-legged on the sidewalk with her back against a building wall. A snow-covered Buddha, wrapped in a sleeping bag, shivering in the below freezing temperature. I guessed her to be in her forties. Everything about her seemed round. She had the most angelic face, sparkling blue eyes and a beautiful smile. A cap was upturned in front of her. I thought, 'There but for the grace of God go I.' Her smile and blue eyes haunted me all day.

In the past I've been unemployed, my wife and I were unable to pay our mortgage and other bills, we went through bankruptcy, lost our house, my truck. Being in my fifties, my prospects looked dim. It could have been me, on the sidewalk, in her place.

I was told not to give money to panhandlers because they'll just spend it on booze. I thought to myself, What should I do, if anything? What would you do? I asked for advice from a friend who has worked with homeless people. She said, 'The woman is probably hungry. Why don't you ask her if she'd like a breakfast sandwich and maybe a coffee?'

That sounded reasonable, so the next day I asked, "Are you hungry? Would you like some breakfast, perhaps a coffee?"

"That would be nice," she replied.

When I brought her a sandwich and coffee she said to me, "Thank you so much, sir. You're very kind. Bless you." I truly felt blessed.

This has become a morning routine for the past four years. The woman (*I'll call Joy*) and I have become friends. Often I'll sit with her on the sidewalk. We sometimes meet her companions in the park. They have become my closest friends. I think of them as angels. My life has become much richer for the experience.

Table of Contents

How It Began ....

Flashback to 1968 1

Introduction 5

2010-2011 7

Rain Dog 7

Girl Stuff 9

Just Trying to Survive 10

Volunteering 12

A Shitty Christmas 12

At Home Here 13

No Place for a Woman 13

I Can't Fix Anything 14

Double, Double 14

So Called Friends 15

A Place for Now 15

Dialysis Again 15

Dodging Rain Showers 16

Kind Gestures 16

Fed Up With Being Sick 17

Better Spirits 17

One Day He's Going to Kill Me 17

If It's Not One Thing, It's Another 18

Beaten for No Reason 19

Keep the Change 20

Suicide Watch 21

Mentalpause 22

Will You Be Drunk? 22

Some Parents Shouldn't Be Allowed to Have Kids 23

January 2012..24
   Court 24

February 2012 25
   I Don't Like You 25

   Bella Bella...26

   Cinderella 29

   He Chopped My Leg! 31

   Why Do They Have to Be So....? 34

   Some Kind of Scum...37

   I'm a Greeter 38

   How Dare You! 39

   I'm Not an Angry Person 40

March 2012 42
   Lost Brave 42

   The Oven..46

   Crazy in the Head 47

   Come Back Home 49

   You Can't Break the Circle 51

   Candy Kids...54

   Boxing Days...56

   A Clean, Quiet Place..58

   Life is Good 60

   Helping Each Other Up 63

   The Urban Angel 65

   The Choice is Yours 66

   When the Weirdos Come Out 67

   Kicked in the Knee...70

They're My Family 71

Must Have Jumped a Bus 73

Pizza and Pears 74

Sitting on the Sidewalk 77

Thank You to You Too 79

Now I Got Two Dogs 80

A Place to Go 83

April 2012 84

She Bites 84

I Don't Want to See That Stuff 85

Easter Dinner 88

Some People Only Take 91

You are My Sunshine 93

I Don't Know Any Dale 95

Men Are Better With Numbers 97

Old Friends 98

Stabbing 101

A Mean, Nasty, Inuit Woman 103

Stories 107

Protest 109

Bad Shape 110

Picky Person 113

Anger Management 116

Pink Bandana 121

When the Natives Get Drunk 125

May 2012 128

Jumping the Bus 128

It's a Small World 129

Police and Paramedics 133

Are They Going to Mow Us Down? 136

Luther and His Demons...141

Women Rule...144

Up on the Lawn 150

Silver Concerned About Cure.....................................153

Rain on the Street 158

Playing Risk 159

Methadone..162

Wild Night at Bingo 168

There's Something About the Number Five 171

New Shoes for Shakes...175

Hippo...181

Shaggy Goes to the Spa..187

Shark is Robbed 192

Ride to Remember 195

June 2012..199

The Usual Suspects...199

A Brand New Start 202

Daimon Released from Prison 207

Panhandlers Feeding Panhandlers 211

War Memorial...214

Little Jake Gets Charged...218

Chicken Man..221

Barbecue 224

Hobophobia..226

Millhaven Penitentiary 229

Algonquin Land 232

Chili Beaten 234

Psycho 236

No Matter Where We Go, They Tell Us To Move 240

Saint Nick 244

Weasel in Hospital 248

Silver and the coffee shop 252

Daimon Gets Stomped 258

Okay, hire me! 261

July 2012 264

Fish Sticks 264

Staggering Somewhat Straight 266

Bellydancing on YouTube 266

Wolf Rants 269

Sleeping Rough 272

No Dogs Allowed 276

Conversations With God 277

Bear Gets a Ticket 279

Ian The Mooch 282

'Shrooms 284

Serge Beaten Again 287

Little Jake Ticketed Again 292

Gene Goes to Prison 294

Poster Boy 298

Cops Go Easy 302

Gravy Stains 305

One Week Sober 309

Cirrhosis 313

Trading Pants 316

Part of the Family ....

Ottawa Innercity Missions, Street Outreach Program.................

Interview With Dennis Cardiff ....

The Usual Suspects ....

(Alphabetical listing of Dennis' street friends) ....

Flashback to 1968

My first encounter with a panhandler was when I moved to Toronto in 1968 to live with Jack, my brother. Being a storyteller himself, he viewed panhandlers as follows: If they present you with an interesting, unique story of why you should give them money, that story has value and should be rewarded accordingly.

There was one certain corner I had to pass each morning on my way to work. There was no way around it. Standing there every morning was Sam, a panhandler. He wore slippers; his clothes were ragged, but neat and clean. I'd guess his age to be in the late seventies. Each morning, Sam had a different hard luck story to tell me.

"Good morning, could you spare a quarter so that I could buy something to eat? My stomach is rumbling. Do you hear it? I'm diabetic, so it's imperative that I eat on a regular schedule, or I could go into diabetic shock."

How could I say no?

At that time, bus, streetcar and subway fares were a quarter. By comparison, an adult fare is now three dollars. I always made sure that I had an extra quarter for Sam.

One morning, just for fun, I ran up to Sam and said, "Can you spare me a quarter? I've been late for work twice this week; if I'm late again I'll be fired!"

Sam reached both hands into his pockets and they came out full of quarters. "Here, take all you need," he said. I graciously accepted a quarter.

From then on, I just gave Sam a quarter every day and asked about his life. "What time do you come out here, Sam?"

"I'm here for the six o'clock morning traffic, people walking to work. When rush hour is over, I work my way along two streets and then have lunch at the Mission. After that, I go to the bakery. I have my cart, so I pick up bottles along the way, anything I can find a use for. I'm good at fixing things. I get a lot of good things on garbage day. I look for cigar butts. Once a week I'll treat myself to a new cigar. I work my way north, then turn west and arrive at the other Mission for supper. I follow the same route every day. I've gotten to know a lot of people, so there are plenty of opportunities to stop and chat for a while. A friend of mine owns a restaurant, so I stop there for tea."

Through our discussions I learned that Sam had his own room. He didn't drink. He had a woman friend, but he liked his independence. He earned a living, but he worked hard.

Introduction

Throughout the past four years I have met many people, now friends, who for various reasons are, or were, homeless.

- Antonio slept on a park bench and was beaten; he had his teeth kicked out for no other reason than his choice to sleep outdoors. He is a small, gentle man who has a phobia about enclosed spaces.

- Craig slept on the sidewalk in the freezing cold. I saw him every morning and was never sure if, when I lifted the corner of his sleeping bag, I would find him dead or alive. Sometimes, he confided, he would have preferred never to awake.

- Joy fell on hard times. She slept behind a dumpster in back of the coffee shop. I saw her with blackened eyes, bruised legs, cracked ribs, cut and swollen lips. I usually see her sitting on the sidewalk panning for change.

I can't do much for these people except to show them love, compassion, an ear to listen, perhaps a breakfast sandwich and a coffee. I want to do more. To know them is to love them. What is seen cannot be unseen.

When I'm with the homeless, I don't judge. I ask a minimum of questions, only enough to keep the conversation moving. I don't interrogate or ask about their past. Mostly, I listen and try to understand. I am often asked why I am there. Although the reasons are deeper, I usually answer by saying, "The conversations here are more interesting than where I work." I visit these people on the streets, on the way to my place of employment, and at noon hours.

What I have learned over the past four years has changed my life. These people, who I consider to be my friends, are alcoholics, drug and other substance users. Some work as prostitutes, some have AIDS, most or all have served time in jail for various offences. All of them I would trust with my life. They have welcomed me into their street family. I am honored to be considered a member.

I have heard sickening stories of abuse as children and babies born with drug dependencies. Most have mental and physical illnesses, suffer beatings, broken bones, stabbings, and have a fear of abusive partners and the police.

Authority in any form is seen negatively, as a means to control their lives. The homeless shelters are noisy, infested with bedbugs, the scene of fights and a place where personal items are stolen. Many homeless people prefer to sleep inside common areas such as bank foyers, outside under bridges, or behind dumpsters.

I have recalled conversations from memory and recorded them on these pages. I've attempted to be as accurate and truthful as possible. I haven't used any recording devices, so recollections may be faulty. I leave out details that I think may incriminate, but I don't interpret, explain or edit.

What they say is what you read. I have changed names and locations for purposes of privacy. My friends don't choose to be addicts. It's a disease and should be treated as such. They need help. They can't do it on their own, but they want it on their own terms.

2010-2011

Rain Dog

8 December 2010

I was accepted for an orientation session for volunteers at the Shepherd. I trained for the Drop-In Program from five until nine. This is the evening meal open to everyone without charge. First I had to learn the *Rules for Food Handlers*.

They served a very good meal with choices of roast chicken, mashed potatoes, peas, gravy, barley soup, salads (*green, couscous and pasta*), muffins, cakes, donuts and sandwiches (*some to go, if they wished*).

I wiped tables, gathered dishes and served soup. It was five hours on my feet after a long day at work, but I enjoyed it. There was a sweet lady from England who served beside me. She was full of stories and was worried about her son who is an alcoholic. She loves peanut butter and was very interested when I told her that for breakfast I eat toast spread with peanut butter, covered by scrambled eggs (*mostly whites*). This lady seemed to know most of the guests and said to them how much she had missed them, worried if some didn't show up, worried if they were sitting all alone and not smiling as usual.

The guests and the staff were very nice. The dishwasher, who sings in a choir, sang Christmas carols as he sprayed the dishes, and everyone joined in.

A native man gave me two drawings. I didn't want to accept them, but he insisted. He said that he likes to pay his own way. He showed me his biography that indicated he had exhibited widely and had many gallery exhibitions of his work. The drawings were signed *Rain Dog*. I was truly blessed by the gift of these drawings.

In response I wrote a poem for him:

Rain Dog
What brings you to the shelter?
Where will you sleep tonight?
Where will you wander tomorrow?

You have blessed me with your gifts,
giving of your art, your soul.
Blessing others with your smile.

I'd love to hear your tales
of places you have traveled,
of things you've seen and done.

I hope to see you again
so that I may learn from you.
Rain Dog, you write on my heart.

Rain Dog - People who live outdoors, people who sleep in doorways, loners knit together by some corporeal way of sharing pain and discomfort. (The Urban Dictionary}

Girl Stuff

22 December 2010

Joy's eyes were blackened and she had a gash across the bridge of her nose. She was weeping. I asked, "What happened, Joy?"

"My boyfriend punched me in the face. I'm covered in bruises, my ribs are in bad shape and I've been coughing blood."

"Did you phone the police?"

"No, if the police come again, we'll be kicked out of the place we're staying. It's not the first time he's beaten me. I've had broken bones, cracked and separated ribs. We've been together four years now. He's okay when he's sober, but when he drinks he gets crazy. I've kicked him out for good, but he always comes back saying he's sorry and that it'll never happen again. Also, I'm on probation. I served time at the Prison for Women for assaulting this same guy. I shouldn't have been charged. There was a lot of blood, but it was all mine. Another time in prison, I was raped by a male guard and gave birth to his son. My probation officer is trying to arrange an appointment with a mental health counselor because, as a child, I was molested by my father, grandfather and uncle. Depending on the results of this interview, I may be eligible for better assisted housing."

"I wish there were something I could do."

"What I need is some girl stuff. I'm just starting my period."

"I'd love to help, but I'm already ten minutes late for work."

"It's okay; I'll ask one of my regular women friends who will be dropping by."

Just Trying to Survive

23 December 2010

"Hi Joy, your eyes are looking better."

"Right now I have a headache, a cold, a sore throat and I can't seem to stop crying. On top of that, yesterday, going down the stairs, I tripped over my roommate's dog, Harley, and broke my tail bone. The pain is unbearable.

"It's not just that. I was thinking about one of my friends, Leanne. She was murdered three months ago on September 5th. She lived at the Shepherd. She was a prostitute. They found her body, with her pants pulled down, between a fence and the hydro substation. Who does that kind of thing? He didn't even have the decency to cover her body.

"Six women, prostitutes or drug addicts, have been murdered here since 1990, and the cops think it may be a serial killer. In 2006, Jennifer, who was 36 years old, a native, a mother of four who worked the streets for 20 years to pay for her crack habit was found in a parking lot. She was face-down, lying in the dirt, naked and bleeding. She died in hospital and an autopsy showed she had been stabbed at least a dozen times while trying to fight off her attacker. She had stab wounds to her head, legs and wrists.

"Pamela was 39. She was murdered in 2008. Her body was found partially nude and beaten, near a bicycle path in the park. They found a pair of men's reading glasses at the scene. It's believed that they belonged to the killer and that he's over forty.

"Carrie was 32 in 1995. She was last seen in her apartment in the early morning with a man in his late 20s/early 30s — he had short brown hair, tattoos on both arms, wore a light-colored kilt. I've kept all the newspaper clippings. You'd think a guy dressed like that would be easy to spot. She was found strangled.

"In 1993 there was Sophie; she was 24, she turned to prostitution to support her children and unemployed boyfriend. She was last seen alive getting into a white van. She was found strangled, her body found stuffed into two garbage bags in a parking lot.

"Melinda was only 16 in 1990. She was beautiful and had only been working the streets for three weeks. It was a Saturday night; she'd been in a cafe. People saw her jump into a car. She was found strangled, her body in a parking lot dumpster. One snake-skinned stiletto heel was missing. Over twenty years later, it's still missing; so is her killer.

"I don't think the cops are even trying to catch the guy. Prostitutes are considered scum. The cops are more likely to beat them than to help them. The women are just trying to survive from day to day. They do what they do for food, drugs or alcohol. Most of them don't see any way out. Just because they're prostitutes, or addicts, is no reason to kill them. None of us on the street are safe. I used to do that, but I no longer have an expensive habit to maintain, so I don't do it anymore."

I hugged her and said "I'm glad you don't do it anymore."

As I sat with Joy, some ladies in a nearby office building bought her a large frozen turkey. She also had a bag of presents. I could see crackers, to go with the turkey, and a pair of socks. A lady stopped by and dropped her $20 since she wouldn't be seeing her again until after the holidays.

"I'm going to cook this turkey, freeze some and share it with my neighbors who aren't doing very well."

I said, "If you're interested, you're welcome to come to the Shepherd on Christmas Eve. They're putting on a turkey dinner with all the trimmings."

"Thanks, I won't promise that I'll come. I don't do well in crowds. I'm agoraphobic, but I'll see. Thanks again for inviting me."

Volunteering

25 December 2010

I spent this evening at the Shepherd. I was wiping and clearing tables, then I was assigned to wash dishes. It involved placing the cups, plates and cutlery in the stacking tray, so they could be rinsed with the pressure sprayer before sliding the tray into the washer.

I didn't see my favorite people there, but all the guests were helpful and polite. They brought their trays to the counter, scraped their plates and said, "Thank you very much sir, have a merry Christmas."

The volunteers were also very nice, much nicer than the people I work with on a paid basis. I was asked if I was doing okay, if I wanted to sit down, if I wanted a drink of juice, or something to eat. At the end of the shift I was thanked for the work I did.

All in all it was a very pleasant evening.

A Shitty Christmas

1 January 2011

This morning I saw Joy for the first time since Christmas. I was so glad to see her. When I sat down beside her, I noticed that she had a black eye and other bruises on her face. I put my arm around her and said, "I guess your boyfriend came back?"

"Yeah, Big Jake came back, he always does, but he's in jail now. I had a real shitty Christmas. Pardon the language."

"Are you hungry? Do you want a coffee or anything else?"

"No thanks, I've eaten breakfast and have had three cups of coffee. I could use some girl stuff."

"I'd be glad to help you with that, Joy, but there aren't any stores close by."

"That's okay, I'll make out."

At Home Here

13 February 2011

Last night at the Shepherd, I was washing dishes *(not what I particularly enjoy, since there is not much interaction with the guests)*. I heard a tapping behind me *(that I ignored)*; it continued so I turned around. Some of the regulars help sporadically with kitchen duties, although I haven't been there long enough to know who does what. I turned around and J.P. was standing at the pass through where I stack the trays. He pointed at a tray of cups.

I said, "Oh, you want a cup?" and commenced to hand him one.

"No, I want the whole fucking tray, sir."

It was so incongruous that I couldn't take offense. I smiled and said, "Here you go; thank you very much for your help."

This seemed to surprise him, since he is usually the first to start fights, but he brought more dishes into the kitchen, for which I thanked him, and he grunted, which is probably the closest to a positive response that he is capable of. I am feeling more and more at home there. These people truly need friends who will help and encourage them.

No Place for a Woman

23 February 2011

"Hi Sweetie," Joy greeted me, "it's good to see you. I've been sick lately due to this cold. The guy who sometimes sleeps here told me that he's been staying at the Shepherd, but he finds it very rough and noisy. Still, I'm happy that he isn't sleeping on the sidewalk. I stayed there once, but never again. It's no place for a woman."

When we finished our conversation she said, "Bye Sweetie." It made me feel so good seeing her again, knowing that she was uninjured and relatively safe.

I Can't Fix Anything

24 March 2011

Her eye blackened and her voice hoarse, Joy greeted me, "Hi, Dennis, I'm feeling sick this morning. Even though it was cold last night, Craig slept on the sidewalk. He had said that being drunk helped him through the night."

She told me that she has never had a job, a legal one, anyway. While she was incarcerated, her mother ran up $6700 of bills in her name, including fines for drinking in public.

Whenever Joy talks about money, I get nervous. She's a sweet person, but she has made her choices and will never change. I bought her breakfast and left it at that.

I don't know why it hit me so hard today. I know I can't fix anything and it's going to keep happening. I gave her a hug. She said, "God bless you."

Double, Double

14 April 2011

Crying and having trouble speaking this morning because of a fat lip, Joy said that she'd been beaten again. She didn't know that her ex had a key to her apartment. He let himself in and that's when the trouble began. She called the police and they took him away (*again*).

Joy has lots of friends. This morning I had to stand in line to talk to her. A word of encouragement, my attention, a sausage and cheese on an English muffin, steeped tea *(double, double)* is the best I can do.

Her smile is reward enough for any kindness that I can offer.

So Called Friends

13 June 2011

It's been a month since I've seen Joy. She's been in hospital and has lost a lot of weight. She is now on kidney dialysis and uses a cane to help her walk.

She was evicted from the place she was living because while in hospital, she couldn't pay her rent. Her furniture and other belongings were all put on the lawn. She tried some of the shelters, but said that they were disgusting.

She is staying with, as she called them, 'so called friends'. They told her that she had to bring home thirty dollars today or they would throw her out. She had been sitting on the sidewalk since six this morning, in the rain, and only had ten dollars in her cap.

I bought her tea and breakfast. There is only so much I can do.

A Place for Now

14 June 2011

The good news is that Joy has started to pee again. She thinks that she will only be required to have dialysis for another week.

Her biggest fear is infection from some of the shelters where she's had to sleep. She has a place for now.

Dialysis Again

15 June 2011

Joy was feeling more cheerful today. Her blood pressure is low, so they aren't able to warm the blood that they circulate through her system. She feels very cold during the five hour process. She goes again this afternoon from 1:00 to 6:00 pm.

Dodging Rain Showers

24 June 2011

This morning Joy had to keep dodging rain showers. She has found a place to stay until next week. A social worker helped her to complete forms for assisted living.

Her dialysis is going well with the next appointment being this afternoon. She is peeing more and tests on her kidneys indicate that they are functioning. There's hope that her problem will clear up in a few weeks.

Kind Gestures

14 July 2011

Yesterday, my boss noticed me with Joy. We were both sitting cross-legged on the sidewalk. Her cap with change was in front of her. Her arm was around me and I was pouring my heart out to her. I explained to my boss that I occasionally buy her a sandwich and tea. She accepted that and said it was a kind gesture.

Yesterday, Joy had no shoes. A friend of hers noticed this, asked her size, and then came back with a hundred and fifty dollar pair of women's leather shoes that he'd stolen. Another friend of hers was arrested for stealing a block of cheese. She admitted that her kidney damage was due to alcohol.

After I left her, she was going to the bridge where she could be in the shade and play dice with her friends.

Fed Up With Being Sick

9 August 2011

It nearly broke my heart to see Joy this morning. She was sitting on the sidewalk, wrapped in a blanket, sobbing her eyes out. Doctors have found toxins in her blood which may mean kidney problems. This afternoon she is going to the hospital for a spinal tap to determine whether or not she has meningitis.

She has been kept awake by vomiting and diarrhea. I offered her a breakfast sandwich, but all she wanted was steeped tea, three sugars, one cream. She is losing weight and is fed up with being sick.

The good news is she now has a place, so she is able to shower, have a clean bed and eat good meals. Eventually, she will be able to save first and last month's rent towards a place of her own.

One Day He's Going to Kill Me

2 September 2011

Joy was crying and drinking sherry mixed with water. Her disability check was sent to the wrong address. There is a new resident at her house who is driving her crazy. This woman is eighteen years old and does nothing but talk to herself. Joy is hoping to move to a friend's basement in the near future.

She has cracked cartilage in her nose with a gash across the bridge, two black eyes and pneumonia in both lungs. Her boyfriend, Big Jake, who is six foot, three and weighs over two hundred pounds, punched her in the face when she wouldn't give him oral sex *(she couldn't breathe through her nose because of the pneumonia)*. He left her on the sidewalk in a pool of blood.

A month ago he kicked her to the point that her whole right side was bruised; she had two cracked and two fractured ribs. In both cases she phoned the police, so hopefully this time he will be in jail a long time.

I sat with her, gave her a gentle hug and let her vent.

"I love Jake, but I have to take care of myself. I can't be somebody's punching bag. One day he's going to kill me."

I can't believe that she lets Jake anywhere near her. She even felt bad about phoning the police. Then he stole her phone. I've been hearing these stories since I first met her. I can't figure it out.

Joy's friends have told her that he will kill her one day, and she believes it. Originally, they were to move into their friend's basement together. Now, the friend says that Jake is not welcome. He has been responsible for all the other beatings Joy has received in the past two years.

Joy said, "I'm sorry for venting my feelings to you."

I replied, "You did the same for me."

"Yeah, that's what friends are for, right?"

If It's Not One Thing, It's Another
12 September 2011

"I'm moving into a friend's house," said Joy. "It's really nice; lots of room. We didn't have an exciting weekend; we just spent time organizing the house. Everything seems to be going relatively well." Joy was rubbing her hand and continued, "My roommate was drunk and acting like a bozo last week, so I gave him a shot in the head. I think I broke my hand again. I didn't go to the hospital, but it really hurts. That and the arthritis in my knees. Cops tell me to get up, and I say to them, 'Where would you like me to sit, since I can't stand?' If it's not one thing, it's another.

"I got a letter from Jake, through a friend who lives at the shelter where I used to be. It had a dream catcher inside. I taught him how to make those. He doesn't know my new address, my friend won't tell him. In the letter, Jake apologized and said that he felt badly for nearly killing me. He asked me to appear in court for him and to change my testimony. He wants me to say that we were both drunk and that I don't remember what happened.

"I don't know what to do. I still love him, but I'm not willing to risk a charge of perjury, or obstruction of justice. That would put me back inside.

"Even if Jake does go to jail, he will be getting out some time and will be looking for me. He'll find me because we have the same friends and go to the same places. I don't want to move to another city just to get away from him."

Beaten for No Reason

14 September 2011

Antonio, a mutual friend of ours, was badly beaten as he slept on a park bench. He was punched and kicked for no reason and was left with two broken ribs, a black eye, the side of his face purple and swollen. He also has a concussion. Now, he sleeps in another park with surveillance cameras. He is a tiny man; he probably doesn't weigh a hundred pounds. I just feel sick thinking about him.

Keep the Change

15 September 2011

I was approaching Joy, and was about to enter the restaurant where I buy her sausage, egg and cheese on an English muffin, when she waved and beckoned me to come over.

She asked, "Can I change my order? I'd like a toasted sesame seed bagel with double cream cheese. Would that be okay?"

I returned with her bagel and sat next to her on the sidewalk. She smiled and began eating the bagel, "Lately, I love cream cheese. People ask me if I'm pregnant and I tell them that if I am I'll sue the doctor. I've been having trouble eating sausage. It gives me severe heart burn. It's because I have this wire cage in my stomach — long story short, I used to be a crack dealer. I'd mix the crack with flavored spritzers: grape, strawberry and pink lemonade. I sell this guy a pink one, he gets a buzz, everything is great — happy customer.

"He goes inside for a while then comes out again. He asks for another pink one. 'Look man, I only got purple and red, but it's all the same shit.'

"He goes berserk and says I'm trying to rip him off. He reaches in his coat and pulls out a saw toothed machete. He stabbed me in the stomach, and then pulled it up through my ribs. My stomach was cut up so bad they had to reconstruct it. Now, I have this chicken wire cage holding everything together. They made a small upper chamber and a larger one below.

"Now, food goes into the small chamber where it's predigested. Sometimes it doesn't stay, it comes right back up. I have to be real careful what I eat."

Joy had to pee and asked if I would wait with her stuff. She said, "Any change you make you can keep." When she returned she said that I looked really cool sitting there.

I didn't make any money, but I had a firsthand view of pan handling on the street, the dirty looks, averted eyes, etc. One woman said, "Good luck."

I think she meant it seriously.

Suicide Watch

20 September 2011

This morning, Joy was hyper, tense and a bit drunk. She made a comment to a woman passing by (*I think it was one of our new employees*), "Hey, Sweetheart, you need to get more of a tan!"

The woman replied, "Thank you so much for the fashion advice."

Joy's bedroom ceiling was leaking last night during a rain storm. It was dripping onto her air mattress. She kicked her roommate off the couch (*where he had passed out watching television*).

She is nervous about her court appearance Friday for an assault charge against Jake. Her lawyer expects the case to go in her favor, since he has been charged four times with assaulting Joy. Jake is also well known to the police. He served one year last time, but it's expected that, with this latest charge, he will go to the penitentiary for a long stay.

"I have problems being in confined places with a lot of people. I was in a cell with four women who were very agitated and noisy. I checked myself into the psych ward. I was fine, drawing with colored pencils. Then, another woman was brought in who screamed continually.

"I just lost it, man (*pointing to her head*). I started stabbing myself in my private places with the pencils. Then they put me on suicide watch."

Mentalpause

27 September 2011

Joy was in relatively good spirits. "I've got these abdominal cramps because of my period. Also I think I'm starting 'mentalpause'. I remember when my mom had it. My roommate wants to bring his son to stay with us. He's in grade ten. I don't know how that will work out.

"My court case has been moved up to October 19th. I'm not overly worried about it. It's only a parole violation. There will be a pretrial, then a trial, but my lawyer expects that it will eventually be thrown out of court.

"Jake, on the other hand has been charged with assault, assault with bodily harm and attempted murder. My lawyer says he'll be sent to the penitentiary for a long time.

"A friend of mine says that the next time he sees Jake, he's going to kill him for what he did to me."

Will You Be Drunk?

4 October 2011

Joy said, "I have an appointment this afternoon with my parole officer. She asked me, 'Will you be drunk?' I said, 'I don't know. We'll see.'

"Now we have four adults and four kids, aged five, six, thirteen and fourteen, staying at the house. I end up doing a lot of babysitting, cooking and cleaning. Some of the adults, and some of the kids, and I don't get along. One of the kids said, 'I don't have to do what you say, you can't hit me.'

"I said to him, 'I can't hit you, but I know kids your age who can.' "

I was surprised to see her on the sidewalk one morning when it was raining. She said she had to get away from the house because of the kids.

Some Parents Shouldn't Be Allowed to Have Kids

7 October 2011

This morning I could see my breath it was so cold. I met Joy as I got off the bus. She gave me a big hug and said, "I was freezing my ass off sitting on the sidewalk; I'm going home."

I asked her how things were working out with the kids. She said, "I gave my notice to my roommate, said I was leaving. He asked the other family to move out. It's not like they were contributing anything. Now it's just my roommate and his fourteen year old son. I get along fine with him. I just got tired of the responsibility of caring for somebody else's children. I've raised my family.

"Anyway, I wasn't being paid for it, or even thanked. The parents just neglected to care for them. The five year old girl hadn't had a change of underwear in four days. It's heartbreaking that some parents are allowed to have children."

January 2012

Court

19 January 2012

This morning, in the freezing cold, Joy was huddled in a sleeping bag with only her face showing. Her feet were nearly frozen from sitting on the sidewalk for two hours. She's been in hospital for the past two months due to epileptic seizures. She'd cut back on her medication because she wasn't having any symptoms, then the seizures hit. Her doctor has upped her meds, now she feels *spinny*.

She didn't have a pleasant time in hospital, in fact she went AWOL. The nurses tried to get her to stay, but she'd had an altercation with a woman.

Joy said, "Either I'm out of here, or I'm going to hit her. In which case I'll be going to jail, and she'll be in my hospital bed."

Tuesday, Joy was scheduled to appear in court due to Jake having assaulted her. Jake pled guilty, but they didn't tell her until she appeared in court. She was in a wheelchair. She said, "I wonder what kind of a deal they offered him. I'm not overly concerned as long as he's out of my life."

I spoke to Joy about the possibility of writing a story about her and her friends. She thought that was a great idea. We'll talk more about it tomorrow.

February 2012

I Don't Like You

Today was a learning experience. The weather was what the meteorologists called freezing fog. I walked to the heater (an exhaust fan on one of the public buildings) where Chester and a woman were standing. I'd met Chester the previous day; the woman I had seen, but we hadn't been introduced.

Chester said to the woman, "Debbie, this is … what did you say your name is?"

"I'm Dennis." I shook Chester's hand then extended it to Debbie.

She withheld hers and said, "What are you doing here?"

"I'm here to visit friends. I was hoping Joy would be here."

Chester was very friendly and talkative. The previous day he hadn't said a word. "He's solid, Debbie; he was here yesterday talking with Ian."

Debbie noticed the cloth bag I was carrying. It had the name of one of the shelters printed on the side. She said, "There was a man who was barred from all the shelters. The temperature was minus forty degrees. No place would let him in. He froze to death standing up, leaning against the brick wall of one of them."

"Why was he barred?" I asked.

"It doesn't matter why he was barred! Nobody should be forced to freeze to death!"

"I agree."

Chester, in a kindly voice, broke the awkward silence, "Debbie and I have been friends for a long time — on the wagon and off. I was sober for 10 years. That's when I was with Epeepee, an Inuit woman. When she died four years ago, I fell off the wagon."

"I'm sorry to hear that," I said.

"I don't like your voice!" said Debbie.

"I'm sorry; I won't talk."

"It's not your voice I don't like, it's the tone. It's clinical and condescending."

"I'm sorry. I didn't mean to come across that way."

Chester went on with his stories. He mentioned where he lived, that he likes British Columbia pot, and that he used to be a drug dealer.

"Chester, don't give away personal information." To me she said, "I don't like you!"

"Would you like me to leave?" I said.

"Yes!"

"Goodbye, Chester. Goodbye Debbie."

Today I learned that even the agencies whose sole purpose is to help the poor, the destitute and the homeless can be seen as the enemy. I learned that I will always be an outsider to homeless people. I haven't had their experiences. I don't blend. I am humbled.

I only want to help, but those who don't know me may not always see that. I must show more sensitivity. Tomorrow, I hope to have a more positive experience, but I've learned from today.

Bella Bella

2 February 2012

Shakes was standing near 'the heater' (a warm air exhaust vent on the side of a public building). I asked his, "How's life?" He replied, "I'll be great once I get this drunk on."

I talked to Ian about his birthplace, Bella Bella *(also known as Waglisla),* on Campbell Island. I had researched it on the Internet.

"Yeah man, it's grown since I've been there, but it's beautiful. That's God's country out there. The only way in is by boat or plane. The ferries may run there, but I'm not sure since that one tipped over a few years back.

"When I was a kid we used to have races, through the forest for a mile or so, around things, over things, under things, through the swamp then swim the last part. I was fast. We really had fun."

Trudy, mostly called Mom, mentioned that she had visited Andre in the hospital yesterday. Mom is very sweet and motherly looking with shoulder length white hair.

"He doesn't look good. Besides the heart attack, he has pneumonia. He has a nurse twenty-four hours a day, sitting at his side. She told me all the details of his condition. He died twice, but they brought him back. He's got tubes coming out of everywhere and one down his throat because he can't breathe on his own. He looks like a robot. They have him in an induced coma. They want to bring him back slow."

"I had double pneumonia one time," said Shakes. "That's really bad. You can die from that. My martial arts trainer was with me. He gave me a shot of whiskey every hour. I took karate, taekwondo, kick boxing and boxing. I knew that stuff even before I went to the pen."

"I have a red belt in jiu jitsu," said Ian as he took my wrist and elbow, putting it in a position where he could either throw me or break my arm.

"My hands are considered weapons. Even these steel toed boots are considered weapons. The police told me that. They could see the yellow markings on the sides. A friend got me these boots; he said if you ever need boots, let me know. I went to him and the next day he brought me these. They cost $300 and they're really warm."

Philip, a large man with a beard, reached into his backpack and pulled out two small gift boxes and a heart-shaped tin of chocolate covered toffees. He gave them to Mom.

She opened the boxes and showed everyone. In the first box were a necklace with a silver pendant and two stud earrings with pink stones. In the second box was a necklace with a black rectangular stone.

"Philip!" she said, "How long have you known me?"

"Six years, maybe."

"In all that time didn't you notice that my ears aren't pierced? I guess now I'll have to have them done. I'm going to the Shep (*street slang for one of the shelters*) soon to get my meds. My worker had them sent there."

Ian said to Philip, "You're barred from there, aren't you?"

"I'm barred for life. I hit two staff. They reported me, and I was sent down for sixty days. I'm up on another charge coming to court soon. I hit someone. I don't know who. I was drunk."

Trudy asked, "Has anybody got a comb? I've gone three days without combing my hair."

Philip reached into his backpack and pulled out a comb.

"That's my comb, Philip! Now go easy, start from the bottom and go up. I've got a lot of tangles." Philip gently combed out Trudy's hair.

"Trudy, I went to your place the other night, but you weren't there. I had five bottles of wine with me, so I just stayed there and got pickled. Do you know that your building was raided? If your roommates have any needles lying around, you could get arrested just for being there. I don't think you should go back."

At that point Juanita arrived with two quarts of Molson Ice Beer.

"Where's Andre?" she questioned. "I came all this way to see him, and he's not here."

"Don't you know that he's in hospital?" asked Philip, "I was with him when it happened. We were at McDonalds. We had cheeseburgers and each of us had a bottle of wine with us. We drank it out of McDonald's cups. Then Andre just slumped over in his chair. Somebody called an ambulance."

Trudy said to Shakes, "I had a couple of joints earlier, but I could really use a drink. Will you give me a drink?"

"Not now, maybe later."

"Shakes!" said Ian, "If you don't give Mom a drink now, I won't give you a drink later." He pulled a bottle of Imperial Sherry from his backpack. To me he said, "We always share with everybody. I don't know what's gotten into Shakes." He passed the bottle around and we each took a swig.

"Very good!" I said. "This is what you were telling me about the other day."

Medium amber color; aromas of walnuts, caramel and figs; sweet and creamy along with flavors of brown sugar. The sherry has a slightly impetuous bouquet. I can imagine it served with pecan pie.

Ian opened a bag of Cheezies and offered some to Trudy.

"Are you crazy! You'll ruin your buzz. I'm trying to hang onto my stone. I'm not going to ruin it just because of munchies. I'm allowed back on D. Street now. I was banned for six months. I haven't been causing any trouble. I just get drunk. I woke up at Bernice's place and asked her if I had any money. She checked and said that I still had fifty bucks. That was a relief!"

Cinderella

3 February 2012

I can only describe today as unbelievable. I was expecting to meet with Ian at the heater, so I stopped by the liquor store to buy his favorite, Imperial Sherry. He had shared with me, so I felt it only fair to share with him.

I walked to the heater — it was deserted. I walked to the park benches — also deserted. I started heading back along Queen Street towards work when I saw a slim, beautiful woman waving at me. I can only describe her as *drop dead gorgeous*. I turned around to see if there was someone behind me that she was waving at. She called out, "Dennis!"

The woman's hair was dark in a stylish pixie cut, teased and gelled in the latest fashion. She wore a fitted tweed jacket, slim jeans, designer sunglasses and tasteful makeup. I wasn't wearing my glasses, but when I came closer I realized it was Joy. I said, "You look beautiful! You sure do scrub up good!"

"Well, don't let anybody else know. I'm dressed like this for court. I appeared this morning and Jake pleaded innocent. I was called to the witness stand and said, 'What do you want me to say? You've seen the video, the hospital reports, statements from people who saw me bruised and beaten with broken bones. What else is there?' Anyway, I have to go back at two o'clock. I don't know what is going to happen."

We went to the food court in the building where I work. I found an unoccupied table and asked Joy to wait so I could go to my office and get the pair of boots I had for her.

When I came back, I felt like Prince Charming sliding the boot onto Joy's foot. Like Cinderella, a perfect fit. I went over to the shoemakers to get a pair of thermal insoles, since she had been complaining of having cold feet.

We had about ten minutes to chat before I had to go back to work. Joy had spent the last week in hospital for epileptic seizures, which she admitted were due to her drinking. She hadn't liked the hospital food and had dropped to 123 pounds.

I also learned that the date of her birth is February 12, 1966. She looks surprisingly young for a mother of five. She was born in Toronto. Her mother was French, her father a mix of English and Ojibwa *(or Metis)*. "I'm often told that I'm not Indian enough because of my blue eyes."

I left her with the bottle of sherry. I don't think I will ever be able to look at her the same way again. She is a true Cinderella story — emerging from behind a dumpster, in back of the coffee shop, to the beautiful, confident woman she is today.

He Chopped My Leg!

8 February 2012

When I got off the bus this morning I was greeted by Metro and Two-four, who hands out the free newspapers. "Good morning, Dale!" they both shouted *(They never remember my name)*. "Joy's here!"

I was pleased since I hadn't seen her in four days. I brought her toasted sesame seed bagel, steeped tea with one cream and three sugars.

"How've you been, Joy?"

"My legs are sore from fibromyalgia; apart from that I'm okay."

"How did court go Friday?"

"I don't know what happened. I didn't go back. That's probably why my probation officer wants to see me this morning. I'm also AWOL from the hospital."

"When you were living in Toronto, you were married and had five children, is that right? When did things start to go wrong for you?"

"Well, I was living common law, but it wasn't a happy time for me. I have five sons, the oldest, born in 1984, is now living on his own. Second oldest was born in 1990, the others in

1992, 1996 and 1997. They're all living with family. They all have my telephone number, but they don't phone very often. I don't interfere with their lives. They're settled now. No point me barging in.

"Nothing was ever good between me and my common law husband. The second youngest saw his father come at me with a machete, no, it was a hatchet! He chopped my leg!

"My life has always been messed up. My grandfather was a freak. My father was a freak. I got along really well with my mother; in fact, she was my best friend until I got into drugs. Then she threw me out. I'd finished grade eight and was fourteen at the time.

"When I started making good money, she was friendly enough! I bought her a house. My boys thought of her as their mom until she passed away. God bless her soul."

At that point Chester arrived. I said hello to him. He looked at Joy and rubbed his thumb and fingers together indicating that he wanted money.

"I know I owe Jacques money. This is the first time I haven't paid him as soon as my check came in, but I was in hospital. I signed the check over to Roy, who deposited it in the bank. The landlord took the rent money out and there's nothing left."

Chester said, "Niaut."

Joy replied, "Niaut. That's Inuit for good-bye," she said to me. "Jacques can wait for his money."

Chester then walked away. I asked Joy if Chester was Inuit.

"No, he just seems to hang out with a lot of Inuit women. They go out together. He gets drunk and they dig *(rob)* him. I asked him if he ever gets anything. He said no. Next time he sees them, they're all friends again. I can't figure these guys. They'd be better off with a twenty dollar hooker.

"A couple of them have full blown HIV. Little Jake was drunk and his girlfriend threw him out. He passed out in the snow. Somehow he rolled over onto a fit *(rig or hypodermic needle)*. That's how he got HIV."

It was time for me to leave, and Joy mentioned that she had to pee, so I walked her to the library. I noticed that she was limping.

"I didn't notice you limping on Friday."

"No, Friday it was okay."

Joy said, "Don't forget that Sunday is my birthday."

"I remember, February 12th. Will you be at the heater later on?" I asked as we parted.

"No, after my meeting, I'm going home."

At noon the sun was shining and the temperature was a relatively mild 28 degrees. I walked to the heater and noticed Ian and Chester. I can hardly count Ian, since he was lying on his back, his head on his knapsack, sound asleep. I said to Chester, "He must have had a rough night."

"He's tired, that's all."

A large man with a big smile and a missing front tooth came over. Chester introduced him as Hippo.

"Where you been, Hippo? I haven't seen you for a long time."

"I just got out of jail."

"What for?"

"A Metro store. No more boosting for me. I just got out of jail today."

"You got some money for me?"

"Chester, I already paid you $15. There's nobody around that I owe money to. Not until tomorrow, anyway."

"I was just kidding. I know you paid me. You want to come to my house?" He playfully kicked Hippo's shin.

"No, I'm just going to hang out for a while." Hippo walked to the stairs where other people were sitting. I could hear them talking and laughing.

Chester said, "I came by bus downtown this morning and had breakfast at the Salvation Army. It was a good breakfast. Then I did my butt run, visited some friends — five people. I took the bus home, then came back here. See all the bus transfers I have. I think I'm going to have my last beer." He opened a large can of Old Milwaukee. "I haven't had any beer for three days.

"I was born in old Quebec. I'm 63 years old now, and I've never been in hospital. I wasn't even born in hospital. I was born at home. I nearly drowned though. My brother and I were swimming in a lake. I dove in and hit my head on a rock. I didn't know where I was. My brother reached down into the water and pulled me up by my hair; otherwise, I would have drowned.

"I read cards, you know. My first wife showed me how. I read a lady's cards the other day, and I said to her, 'Someone you love very deeply is sick.'

" 'Yes,' she said, 'my husband has cancer.' "

Chester's eyes welled up with tears. "I hate it. You know Jacques? I read his cards once and I saw three deaths. There was Jacques, Andre and I can't remember the third one. I don't know how it happens, but I hate it.

"Friends are really important."

I said, "I agree, they're the most important sometimes. If we have friends, we have someone who will help us make it through the day, and sometimes through the night."

"Well, I'm off now. I'm going to see my dealer. He has a big bag for me."

Why Do They Have to Be So....?

9 February 2012

This morning as I was walking along the sidewalk, approaching the spot where I usually meet Joy, I saw two feet sticking out from behind a concrete partition. Before I went to the restaurant for Joy's bagel and tea I wanted to make sure it was her. Lately her visits have been sporadic, and if she's not there, another person may take over her spot. I saw a head peek out, then go back. I walked closer. The head peeked out again, then I saw Joy's smiling face and her hand waving. She had been playing peek-a-boo. She had also been drinking.

"Do you like me better when I'm sober, or when I've been drinking?"

"Joy, I like you however you are."

"I'm going to have to move. Roy and I had a big fight last night, mostly over his coke head girlfriend. I could have had some last night, but I said, 'No, thanks.' What does that say about me? There is a word for it."

"It says you have willpower."

"Big Jake will be out of prison in eight months. My parole officer said he was sentenced to eighteen months, but with time already served and time off for good behavior, he could be out in October."

A man stopped, pulled out his change purse and handed us each a quarter.

"Bless you, sir," I said.

Joy said to me under her breath. "What does he expect us to do with this? Make a phone call? That's what it costs now to use a pay phone. I couldn't believe it.

"I miss my boys so much, and I miss my mom. I feel bad that I haven't lived my life the way she wanted. She was happy though when I was making big money, even if it was illegal. I just want to talk to her."

"You can, Joy. Just talk to her. She can hear you. It's not a question of being good or bad, right or wrong, but about choices and consequences. It was choices that brought you here. It was choices that brought me here."

"Sometimes, I just scream at her. I don't look like her or my father. I was the youngest of eleven children. I was born with blond hair and blue eyes; my sisters and brothers are all dark. I got a lot of abuse growing up, especially from my father's side of the family.

"I asked my mom one day if I was adopted, or if I was maybe the mailman's baby or something. She said, 'We found you in a cabbage patch. You were so cute we decided to bring you home and keep you.' I found out later that I was meant to be aborted. My father had the cash in an envelope. My grandfather slit it open and ran off with the money. He came back eventually.

"When I was two years old, my grandfather took me out to the woodshed. There was a cross beam in the shed. He chained me, hung me from the beam, then he punched me and did things to me. It happened again when I was four, with my father and my uncle – they called him Bugless. His real name is Douglas. I hate him so much for what he did to me. One time my mother saw him coming, and she told me to run as fast as I could. I went to one of the tree forts we had built in the forest.

"I can get so cold sometimes. I just hate people, especially men. Why do they have to be so..."

"There's a lot that can be said for dogs," I replied, referring to a quote by Mark Twain.

Silent tears had been streaming down Joy's cheeks, but she started laughing. "Now, I can take care of myself. Since 1995, I've been taking kick boxing. The owner of the studio drives a Hummer to advertise his business."

A lady stopped and offered both of us a chocolate chip cookie.

"Bless you, ma'am," I said.

"She's okay. I'm careful about what food I accept. There was one guy who used to bring me fruit. Fruit's okay. I like fruit. One day he brought me a homemade muffin. After I ate it, I felt a buzz like I'd had four hits of LSD. I was able to make it to the Sally. That was the only place I could think of to go. I was able to lie down and eventually it wore off.

"I miss my boys, but I can't go back to Montreal. I have two outstanding assault charges against me. In 2007, I was pushing a carriage with my two babies in it. A woman ran by and dropped a plastic bag into the carriage. Before I could do anything, one of the babies had the bag and was chewing on the corner. There was white powder all over his mouth. It was cocaine. The woman was running from the police. I caught up with her and beat her unconscious. Can you imagine? Throwing cocaine into a baby carriage!"

I mentioned that I had been to the heater yesterday and had a long talk with Chester. I said that he was really a sweet man.

"He is sweet. All the women take advantage of him except me. I've been here thirty years. I'm not going to turn over a friend. He was drinking with Jacques one time and he fell backwards down fourteen concrete steps. He was in a coma for a while. His memory isn't so good any more.

"He had a nice house off Parliament and he gets pension checks, so he always has money. Four of us were at the Prestige Hotel one time. They know me there, so everything was cool. Roland took Chester's bank card to the beer store. He was gone in the morning and Chester's account had been cleaned out. Some of them blamed me for it, but Chester said, 'I know it wasn't Joy. I saw Roland take my card.' We haven't seen him since, but he'll be back in the summer."

Some Kind of Scum

10 February 2012

I nearly missed Joy this morning. I saw some feet sticking out from behind a concrete partition, so I went into the restaurant for her bagel and tea. When I came back, she was gone. I asked Metro if he had seen her pass by. He said he thought she had entered the restaurant. I waited outside for what seemed a very long time, but eventually she came out.

"Are you stalking me?" she said with mock anger. "I see the way people in there look at me, like I'm some kind of scum."

"Of course I'm stalking you. I have something for you. I gave her a poem written by a friend. When she started reading she said, "Oh, my God...... Oh, My God.........Oh, my God."

Then the tears came. "All this from somebody I've never met. It's so sweet. Thank your friend for me, and tell her I love her."

I hugged her and she started sobbing into my shoulder. She looked up at me and said, "If you start crying, I'm going to kick you."

I said, "My friend has been in some of the places you've been. She understands. There are a lot of people who love you. You've told me of the terrible things that were done to you, about the guilt you feel because you didn't live your life the way your mother may have wanted, but that is the past, it's gone, and you don't have to carry it with you. It doesn't define who you are now.

"I know you're worried about what will happen when Jake gets out of prison, but that is in the future. We never know what will happen tomorrow or next week. You don't have to carry that either."

"I still love Jake, but I can't live with him."

"It helps if you can forgive others who have harmed you, and forgive yourself. The only things you can control are what's happening this moment. Have you ever tried meditation?"

"Sometimes, when I'm alone."

"The next time you get a feeling of sadness or pain or frustration, just concentrate on breathing in and breathing out. Count your breaths. Look at what is happening in your mind and decide if there is anything you can do about it. If not, concentrate on what you see in front of you, what you smell in the air, what you are going to do next. Will you give it a try?"

"Yes."

I hugged her again and said, "Happy birthday, Joy. There are lots of people who love you."

I'm a Greeter

17 February 2012

When I brought Joy her tea and bagel, she said to me, "I was trying to get your attention before you went into the restaurant. Instead of breakfast I was going to ask you to buy me some bus tickets. I got a $150 fine this morning for jumping the bus by the back door without paying."

"What are you going to do about the fine?"

"I don't know. I can't pay it. I still owe money to Jacques and he's mouthing off about it. I won't be able to pay him until my next check comes in. Roy owes me money for the rent. He's staying with his new girlfriend, so I have the house to myself; well, with the dog, the snake and two lizards.

"I've got a sore back because Roy's dog has been jumping up on me. He's a pit bull. Maybe he's missing his master. He's been acting funny lately. I think it's near time to have him put down. I'll have to do it. Roy wouldn't be able to. That dog has trouble going up and down the stairs. He's no good around kids. He's not even a good guard dog. It used to be that he'd bark when someone came to the door, now he just lays there.

"Lizzy, one of the lizards, has been going crazy lately. I thought they were supposed to hibernate or something, but not her. I threw her a handful of crickets and she was scurrying all over the place. She tries to get out too. That's all I'd need.

"Roy doesn't have much in the way of street smarts. His friends, his poker buddies, all have real jobs. I have a real job. I sit on the sidewalk and greet people. I'm a greeter. I could work at Wal-Mart."

How Dare You!

20 February 2012

How Dare You!

Am I not worthy
to be treated
as a human being,
more like yourself
than you would care
to admit?

Am I invisible,
will you not look
me in the eyes?
Must you look away
pretending
I don't exist?

Am I not worthy
of common courtesy?
What is it that you despise
about me sitting here
humbly, silently
on the sidewalk?

How dare you judge me!
You don't know my life!
I've done you no offense!
You treat me as detestable slime,
that you would scrape
from your boot.

I'm Not an Angry Person

24 February 2012

I told Joy about meeting Shaggy and Wolf at the wall the other day. She told me of her own experiences.

"I don't know why he keeps that damned dog. Wolf, Shaggy, Andre and me were in the park, across the way, near the overpass. Andre had a container of chili from Wendy's. We shared it and I fed some, with my fingers, to Shaggy. When we were nearly finished, I tore down the sides of the container so Shaggy could lick the bottom. When I got up, he bit me in the Achilles' tendon. I punched him, and he bit all the harder. I've been bitten by other dogs, and it just left a bruise from their teeth, but Shaggy is the only dog that punctured my skin and caused me to bleed. I nearly had to crawl home after that. Whenever Shaggy is around, he tries to bite me.

"Tom has found Antonio a place to stay. After Antonio was beaten, Tom bought him some clothes and arranged a room in an apartment for him. I looked after his cart when he was taken to hospital. Antonio normally hates enclosed spaces, but since the beating, he's happy to be locked inside where he is safe. He goes out occasionally, but not for long.

"I haven't been to the wall very much lately. I'm trying to manage my drinking on my own. I drink when I want to, not when it's pushed in my face. I drank on Friday, but I haven't had anything else until this morning. Right now, I'm half in the bag.

"My parole officer wants to get me into a home for women suffering from alcoholism, but first she wants me to attend an anger management course. I really don't want to do that. It means three hours a day for six weeks. That really cuts into the time I have for myself. What are they going to do if I don't take the course? Add to my parole? I've already got one parole violation because they didn't tell her I was in hospital.

"I'm not an angry person! Look at me! I'm smiling. The only reason I was charged with assault was because Jake was beating me."

Lost Brave

1 March 2012

a lost brave
leans against a building
(tho he is unwelcome)
beside a busy walk.
everything he owns
fills a pack
upon his back

he is far
from his fishing boat,
an ocean teeming with fish,
from the majestic forest,
from his children,
his clan

his eyes reveal
a story of hurt and pain -
the uncertainty of the city.
a sidewalk for a bed,
charity of strangers
his only grace

a challenge
every day -
a new beginning.
beyond the fire
that tames his demons
the only plan that matters
is to survive

far from home
he can scarce remember.
a lost brave, fighting back tears,
pride in the knowledge
of his ancestry,
his place -
his blood

Wind was whipping the freezing ice crystals, like coarse sand, against my face as I walked to the heater, a warm air exhaust vent on a public building. Ian was standing alone.

"I've made my price already, the price I need to buy a bottle. I've got another in my backpack that Marlena gave me. I haven't even started that one. She said, 'Since you're giving me money, I'll buy you a bottle.' She even offered to carry my backpack, since my back is still sore from being thrown down the stairs. I said, 'Sure, you can carry my backpack, I'll carry your purse.' 'You can't carry my purse!' she said. 'Sure I can! It takes a real man to carry a purse.'

"It was the same when I was in hospital for detox. A nurse told me that if I'd wear a pink hat, she'd bring me a bottle. 'Sure,' I said, 'bring it on! It takes a real man to wear a pink hat.' I wore the hat and she brought me a bottle.

"Before that, I was hallucinating. It seemed that the ground ahead of me was crawling with things. I felt really dizzy. I phoned the pharmacy and told them how I was feeling. They asked if I was taking any drugs. I said, 'Not bad drugs, a little weed now and then.' 'Do you drink?' they asked. 'Yes, I drink.' 'What you've got then is delirium tremens, the DTs.' They said I should get to a hospital right away because it could be fatal.

"I didn't know what to do. I was homeless and didn't have any way to get to the hospital, so I phoned Alcoholics Anonymous. They said they would send someone to pick me up and stay with me in the hospital. I was unconscious for three days.

"The doctor said that my heart rate was one hundred and eighty. He asked if I was an athlete. I said I was. He told me that having a strong heart probably saved my life, because that number was in the heart attack range.

"Marlena and I are still seeing each other, but I don't go to her house. I don't want to cause any trouble between her and her family. When I was there, I'd do lots of things to help out. I'd sweep and mop the floor, carry out the garbage — anything. I was feeling edgy, so I wanted things to do to keep me occupied. Before I have my first drink of the day, I'm hard to get along with. Once I'm fixed, I'm okay.

"Marlena wants to have a baby, but I'm not ready for that yet. I still have to get my life in order. I could get a job. My former boss keeps leaving messages at the Shepherd for me saying, 'Ian, get your shit together and come back to work.' I was a swamper, or what he called a professional furniture handler. He would go in and do all the paper work and I would be in the truck stacking furniture. I was good at that; that's why he wants me back. I was paid $800 a week.

"We did some local moves, some to Ottawa and the smaller cities in between. We'd go to Montreal. The farthest we went was a move to Sudbury.

"We'd have a lot of laughs kidding each other. He'd ask me, 'Ian, do you want a beer?' I'd say, 'Of course!' I didn't do any of the driving. I don't have my license. When I drink, sometimes I get crazy. I might get behind the wheel of a car and kill myself or someone else.

"I was on the alcohol addiction program at the Shepherd, but I messed that up. They would give me a small glass of wine every hour, but I had a bottle stashed outside. They could see that I was getting more and more drunk as the day went on, so they kicked me out.

"While I was there, I mopped the floors, cleaned the tables, operated the dishwasher. One of the managers, a little guy, Albert, came in after I had just cleaned the counter. He made himself a sandwich and left a mess where I had just cleaned. I had a wet cloth in my hand from wiping tables. I wrung it out and handed it to him, 'You know how to use this, so use it! It's not my job to clean up after you!' I've always been hard headed that way.

"When I was on the shelter side, I'd strip the sheets from the beds. Sometimes, a guy would have pissed the bed. I hated that — the stink! I told them if I was going to do that job, I wanted a free newspaper. They agreed to that. It was something. I'm not going to go back on a program. I'm going to do it by myself. I've cut back quite a bit.

"Lately I've been sleeping in the entrance of the bank, where they have the banking machines. There's a bench that I can hide behind. The heater was too hot, so I took a pair of tweezers and adjusted the temperature — now it's just right. Sometimes the cops will find me there and kick me out. In the morning, the manager will tell me to wake up and get out. She's nice though. I tell her, 'Just give me a few minutes to wake up, then I'll be out of here.'

"I don't know why Andre isn't here. I haven't seen him for five days. He's usually the first to come by. Maybe he got a parole violation. That could mean thirty days; of course, he'd only have to serve twenty of that. This is a red zone for me. According to my probation, I'm not allowed to get drunk or to associate with alcoholics."

A security guard, wearing a yellow neon vest approached. "It's time to move along. We used to let people stand around here, but there was too much mess, cigarette butts, cigarette packages, bottles. So, you've got one minute to finish your smoke, then I'm coming back. If you're still here, I'm phoning the police."

To me Ian said, "I should have told him that this building is on Algonquin land. I'm part Algonquin, but I don't know what to do. Maybe I'll contact the Algonquin Chief. He may be able to tell me what can be done."

It's the first time I've been rousted, but now I know how it feels.

The Oven

2 March 2012

Beside the sidewalk, I met Ellen, sitting cross-legged in the snow, her cap in front of her. She was wearing jeans and a brown coat. Her brown hair was relatively short. Her features were pleasant, like someone I may have passed in a grocery or department store. She didn't look like the stereotypical panhandler.

"Have you seen Shakes or the others?" I asked.

"They are usually around here, or across the street at the heater, but I haven't seen them today. Maybe they're under the bridge. That's a place they sometimes meet."

"I'll try there. Yesterday, Ian and I were rousted from the heater. Perhaps Shakes is at his office (*panhandling at the corner*).

Before I left, I gave Helen a Subway card. "This will buy you a sandwich. Do you smoke?"

"Yes." I offered her a cigarette.

"Thanks," she said. We both said goodbye and I walked toward the bridge. No luck there, so I headed down the street to find Shakes. He wasn't there, so I headed to the Oven, well known for their chili.

Rooting through a trash basket across from the Oven, I met Curtis. In contrast to Ellen, if one were to stereotype a homeless person, Curtis would fit the description. He wore a red and black checked lumberman's jacket, khaki work pants, a black toque, a week's growth of beard and looked generally dirty.

"Have you seen Shakes or any of the others?" I asked.

"No," he said with some apprehension.

I gave him a Subway card. "This will buy you a sandwich," I said.

"Thanks."

"Would you like a cigarette?"

"No, I'm good."

We were about to shake hands, but he pulled his back. Perhaps, he remembered that it had just recently been in the trash barrel.

We said good bye. I checked the Oven, but didn't see any familiar faces.

Crazy in the Head

5 March 2012

I wore a scarf over my face to protect from the cold breeze. Ian looked at his watch, joking that I always arrive at the same time, 12:10 pm and leave at the same time, 12:50. He could set his watch by me.

I said, "It's okay, I have an appointment. Am I late?" Ian and Hippo laughed.

Two men, Spike and Brent, came and shook hands with everyone.

"Spike, you're looking great!" said Ian. He was freshly shaved; he took off his cap to show his fresh haircut. He was wearing a red jacket.

"I've got a meeting to go to. When it comes time for panning, I'll put my panhandling clothes on." They left.

"I gave Spike that jacket," said Hippo, "I wish I had it now.

"I saw Chester at the Salvation Army for breakfast this morning. We had bacon, eggs and home fries. I've been staying there for the past week, but I hate it. I'm staying tonight because I get my PNA *(Personal Needs Allowance)* check tomorrow.

"If I stay there for a full week, they give me a check for $28. I hate it there. Everyone is all cracked out. Things get stolen. Last night I just stepped out back to have a drink, and a guy tried to stab me with a knife. It sliced the whole sleeve of my outside jacket and made a three inch cut on my inside jacket." He showed me the cut on the outside of his sleeve. "Luckily, it didn't reach my skin."

"How did the fight start?" I asked.

"I don't know. The guy was crazy in the head, but I took care of him, *biff! bam! pow!* That was the end of it.

"Which shelter do you prefer?"

"I don't know about the Mission, since I've been barred. The Shepherd has the best food."

Ian said, "I don't eat the food at the Shepherd, they serve too many carrots. Sometimes I'll get a plate for Marlena and take it outside, since they only allow women at certain times. It is a men's shelter. I'd prefer to panhandle and buy my own food."

I asked, "How did you get that name, Hippo?"

"I think it was Joy who first started calling me Hippo. My name is actually Nathan. I'm from Oshawa. Those were the days when Rip, Tim and Hobo were still around. They were old guys. They're dead now.

"I'm waiting on an inheritance from my grandma. She passed away. When I get the money, I'm heading to British Columbia. I got a call from my old boss. He said my job is waiting for me, driving a big grapple skidder for hauling logs out of the bush. The tires are this high." He reached above his head. "If you look in Facebook, I have some pictures posted of the equipment I've run. It's great to be out in the bush. I'm by myself, the cab is heated and air conditioned, with a CD system. I get $29 an hour."

Come Back Home

6 March 2012

Spring is gradually approaching, but after standing outside for an hour at the benches, my cheeks were so stiff I could barely talk. I asked Ian, "How have things been going since I saw you yesterday?"

"Marlena and I had a rough night. We started off sleeping at a bank. We were rousted by the police. We moved on to another bank. After a few hours, we were rousted again. I said, 'I know of another bank we can go to.' We spent the rest of the night there. The manager woke us up when she came in. 'Okay Ian, time to move on,' she said. 'Okay, just give me a few minutes to wake up and clear my head. I'll clean up my cigarette butts."

"How does Marlena like sleeping in the bank?"

"She was a bit scared, but I told her, 'You'll be safe. I'll get some shut eye, but my ears will be open. If anybody tries anything, I'll give it to them, believe me.' She also found it too hot. I'll have to get my tweezers and turn down the thermostat again."

Ian introduced me to Ryan who said, "I'm just out of jail. I was coming across the bridge and I said, 'Hey, I know that guy, it's Ian.' So we've been sharing a beer. I grew this beard in prison, but I'm going to shave it off. Ian looks fine with a beard, but I look ugly. I look like a hobo.

"I was talking to my old boss. I can go back to work once I clean myself up. I do events. I installed the Christmas lights at the Eaton Center. I'm also a painter and a carpenter — that's my trade."

"When do you think you'll be going back to work?"

"Maybe next week. I'll have to ease off the booze. I got a friend who will help me out with a place to stay for $100 a week. He's got a few places, but the crack heads he puts in one place. I'll be staying somewhere different. I'm originally from Belfast, Ireland. My parents brought me over when I was nine months old. We lived near the old Montreal Forum. My dad coached hockey, all the teams I played on when I was a kid. He'd see some guy rough me up and he'd say, 'Get back in there and fight him!' That was before they curbed the violence in minor hockey. He was a good coach, but he never learned to skate. Whenever there would be a father and son skate, I'd have to hold him up so he wouldn't fall. He would be all wobbly. I sure miss him. Bless his soul.

"When I was a lad, I was born in 1956, you know. We had a 1969 Volkswagen, a bug, just like in the *Herbie* movies. My mom and dad went to the neighbors one time, and I found the car keys. A friend and I decided we'd go for a ride. I was grinding gears. I didn't know what I was doing. We went up a steep hill and the car stalled. My friend was pulling back on the emergency brake. I started the car, revved the engine, but the car was in second gear. We rolled back down the hill into a bus, smashed the back bumper of the car. I drove it back to our driveway and didn't say a thing. My parents didn't notice the damage for a month or so. They blamed my brother Adam. He got a beating for it.

"I have a twin, you know. My sister, Jessica has breast cancer. She was even written up in the newspaper. When she was first diagnosed, they removed her breast. She was cancer free for seventeen years, then it came back. She doesn't talk to me, but I still love her.

"My brother, Adam, had breast cancer when he was young. He had surgery and he's been fine ever since. They cut out his left chest muscle and even the muscles at the bottom of the arm *(the triceps)*.

"My mom wants me to come back home. I've always sent her money when I had it, and she's helped me out when she could."

You Can't Break the Circle

7 March 2012

I handed Joy a sheet of bus tickets. She said, "Thank you so much. You've saved my life. I got another $150 fine for sneaking on the bus without paying. The guy said, 'So, what name are you going by today?'

"I asked, 'What name was I going by last time? Just give me the paper!' I can't remember what name I gave him.

"I haven't been out much. The weather has been too cold. I was out for a while yesterday, but I had to come into the restaurant to get warm."

"All these guys keep hitting on me! I'm lonely. I miss Big Jake! I was a hooker and bought my mother the house that she died in. If I'm with some guy, I want a long-term relationship. I don't want some fly-by-night stuff. I'd rather shoot myself in the face.

"I haven't had a drink in nearly two weeks, until yesterday. I was over at Jacques', playing dice, when he starts rubbing my back, then my thigh. I said, 'Jacques, are you trying to get it on with me? It's not going to happen!' He said, 'Well, you're in my house, you're drinking my vodka, eating my egg rolls!'

"You're not getting my bod for that! Think again!

"I could tell you some stories that would make your hair curl. When I was about four, my dad and Uncle Doug took me and my sister to the lake. My grandfather had a place on an island. My dad and Uncle Doug decided to take my sister into town. My grandmother made me a sandwich and told me to run as far and as fast as I could. She knew what my grandfather was like.

"One time he caught her sending me off, and he started beating her. I jumped on his back, but he just threw me against a wall. I ran to one of our tree forts. It wasn't even on my grandfather's property. When Mr. Jones saw him he said, 'Bruce, you're not coming on my land with a shotgun!' Why would a grown man be chasing a four year old with a shotgun?"

An attractive couple approached us. The woman, with long black hair, an expensive coat and long black leather boots looked like a movie star. She bent gracefully from her knees and put change in Joy's cap, then kissed her on the cheek.

"So this is your new husband?" inquired Joy.

"Yes Joy, this is Bryce. Bryce, this is Joy."

"This is my friend Dennis. Dennis, this is Katrina and Bryce."

"I'm very pleased to meet you," I said and shook hands with both of them.

Joy asked, "So, how long have you two been married now?"

"It's been two months."

"So, I guess you're still on your wedding thingamajig?"

"We'll always be on our honeymoon. So, how have you been doing, Joy?"

"I still have problems with my fibromyalgia. I'm sore all over. I was in hospital a couple of times. My kidneys shut down. It could have had something to do with my epileptic seizures. It could have been because I wasn't eating properly. You'll have to come over to visit me in my new place."

"We'd love to, Joy." Then they left.

"She's gorgeous," I said.

"Yeah, isn't she? That's the religious lady I told you about. The first time I met her, I was standing up. She gave me a big hug and kissed me on the cheek. I wasn't sure if she was just being kind or if she really liked me."

"What religion is she?"

"Christian."

"Do you know what church she goes to?"

"I don't know. Are there a lot of Christian religions? I was brought up Protestant. I've been to a lot of different churches. I like the ones where they do lots of lively singing, like spirituals. Those are my favorites.

"I have an appointment with Angela, my probation officer. I hate her. I thought I had an appointment with her March first. I went to her office, and she wasn't there. The receptionist checked her book and said that I was supposed to have been there the day before. I said, 'I had an appointment for March first,' She said, 'This is March second!' I had the dates mixed up. I asked, 'So, are you going to breach me because I missed an appointment?'

"A breach would mean thirty days in jail, wouldn't it?" I asked.

"If the judge is an asshole, he could make it sixty, but I'm not going to jail. I still have until November until my probation is finished. Angela wants me to go for anger management counseling. I don't think I need anger management counseling.

The sun was shining, the weather was warm and most of the snow had melted from the sidewalk. There was a large group near the benches. Someone was waving at Toothless Chuck across the street, but he didn't come over.

Ryan came over to me and thanked me for the Subway card I had given to him and Ian the previous day.

I said, "Lots of people have helped me in the past. You can do the same for another person some time."

Ryan said, "I was walking along the street this morning and I met an elder. We talked for a while. He reached into his pocket and handed me a hundred dollar bill, so I bought beer and cigarettes for the guys. I can give you five dollars for yesterday."

I assured him that it wasn't necessary.

"Have a beer then."

"If I came back to work smelling of beer, I'd lose my job, but we'll go for a beer sometime when I don't have to go to work."

Shakes said, "I saw my daughter and my grandson this morning! I have two daughters and seven grandchildren. They've been busy."

Someone said to me, "With your white hair slicked back you look like either a politician or a mafioso. Which is it?"

"Is there a difference?" I asked.

Jacques was lighting his carved stone pipe. He passed it to Shakes, who took a hit then passed it to me. I thought of a dozen reasons why I shouldn't take it. I could be arrested for possession of marijuana. I could lose my job if anyone smelled it on me or if I acted stoned. If things got out of hand, I might not have a place to sleep, like most of the people here.

"Come on, Dennis, you can't break the circle." All eyes were on me. I'd already turned down a beer. Generally people who don't drink aren't trusted. I thought I'd lose all credibility if I was afraid to do what all of these people do on a daily basis, and are doing right now. I took the pipe, inhaled, and passed it back to Jacques.

I was noticing Weasel's hair. It was freshly washed, cascading over his shoulders like a L'Oreal commercial. I could just imagine him shaking his head, his hair flowing in slow motion, *because you're worth it.*

Shark was telling me about the problems he was having with HIV. One benefit is that he gets free marijuana.

Shaggy was walking around the circle of people. Wolf said, "Shaggy, make your mind up. Decide who you're going to bite, and get it over with."

Candy Kids

A woman came by and put two pennies in Joy's cap. She took them out and placed them behind her on the sidewalk. "I'll leave them for Roland, he'll take them. The pennies I left yesterday are still here.

"Do you see that fat guy across the street talking to the security guard? He tried to take my spot yesterday. He said, 'You're only here a few days a week and I'm sleeping on the sidewalk with my dog.' I said, 'That's not my problem. You made your own choices.' Then he punched me in the head. The security guard saw it and raced across the street. He had the guy down on the sidewalk in seconds. I have a lot of friends around here.

"I have to find a new place to live. Roy says he's going to raise my rent. It's just because he owes a lot of money. The electricity hasn't been paid, the heat hasn't been paid and he's probably behind on the rent. He asked me to have cable hooked up for the TV, but I can't. When I was staying with Fat Richard, he ran up a bill of $270, just on porn. What a sicko! He left and I was stuck with the bill. I couldn't pay it, so I can't go back there.

"When I see those young girls at the Mission, it makes me so mad. We call them 'twinkies' or 'candy kids.' I'd just like to slap them and tell them to go home while they still have the chance."

When I arrived at the benches, Shakes was sitting alone with a snow shovel.

"Do you know why I have this shovel? I went to the mission, and they wouldn't feed me, so I took their shovel. I wasn't sneaky about it. I took it right in front of their faces.

"I'm barred there for life. I was sleeping there one time and the staff kicked me. I call them 'the steroid monkeys.' How would you like to be kicked at six o'clock in the morning? They could have said, 'Hey Shakes, it's time to get up,' but they didn't. They kicked me. I said, 'Okay, just wait until I get out of bed. I used to be a boxer. I've sparred with Shawn O'Sullivan and George Chuvallo. It wasn't long before the steroid monkeys were lying, out cold, on the floor.

"I lost one of my mitts. I have a right, but no left."

"Where were you born, Shakes?"

"On the Curve Lake reservation, that's my rez, but mostly I grew up on the streets of Toronto.

"Since time immemorial the Anishnaabeg ancestors of the Mississauga's of Curve Lake First Nation have inhabited North America. Written history, spelling and grammar misinterpretations have led to confusion of what we have been called over the years. To avoid argument, we will go with the fact that we speak the Anishnaabeg language; we are Ojibway by description and of the Mississauga Nation because we resided in the general area of the Mississauga River.

"I'm just waiting for Hippo to come back with my run. He's getting a bottle of wine for me. I hope he doesn't try to boost it. If he does, he'll go back to jail and I won't get my wine. I haven't had a drink for two hours now.

"One time a guy took a photograph of me. He said he'd bring me back a print. What he brought back was a poster. Can you imagine me on a poster? Ha, ha, ha. I gave it to my mom. She loved it.

"My mom still owns a restaurant. I go there for lunch every day. If she doesn't see me she worries."

Boxing Days

9 March 2012

Donny was collecting wine bottles and beer cans from the trash barrel to return for deposit.

"Hey, I got at least a buck here!" He'd stand the beer cans on the sidewalk and stomp them with his foot, so they'd take less space in his backpack.

Jacques and Outcast, without his dentures, were enjoying the sun.

Wolf came over to show Donny how to stomp the cans properly. "We used to do this in my apartment, with a hardwood floor. You should have seen the circles it left."

Outcast asked me, "You're here almost every day. Do you work close by? We were trying to figure out what kind of work you do."

"I come most days, not every day. I work in that tall building down the street. I'm in the mail room. I fetch and carry, do what I'm told. I find the conversations here more interesting."

"Right on, man! I used to work in the mail room at Unemployment Insurance. It was back when they issued those cardboard checks. I worked in the room where they cut the checks. It was really high security. Not even the guards were allowed into the place where we worked. We used to smoke pot, do anything we wanted. Who'd have thought that the people cutting those checks were stoned all the time?"

A boy, who didn't appear to be old enough to shave, came by on a skate board. He stopped and asked, "Do any of you guys want to buy some weed?"

Shakes replied, "We've got our own, but thanks for asking."

He turned to Jacques. "Jacques, dial *Shakes 1*; I want to speak to my daughter." Jacques speed dialed and handed Shakes the phone.

"It's me. If I'm not at my office by three o'clock, I'll be at mom's." He then handed the phone back to Jacques.

Outcast asked, "Hey Jacques, how much are you paying for your phone plan?"

"I pay twenty-five a month. It's the cheapest I could find. I can call anywhere in the city day or night. If I pay another ten a month, I could call anywhere in Canada.

"I was checking some rates this morning. Let me get the brochure out of my pocket." With the brochure, also came his dentures, falling on the sidewalk.

"Don't anybody move! Damn! It looks like I broke a tooth."

Shakes pulled a plastic toy baby out of his pocket. He flicked a switch on the baby's back and held it to my ear. I heard laughing, then, "Time to wake up!"

He laughed and said, "Isn't that funny? It belongs to my grandson."

I said to Shakes, "Tell me about your boxing days in Toronto."

"I learned to box when I was six years old. We had a heavy bag in the barn. My dad taught me, my dad and my uncle. Later, I sparred in the ring with George Chuvalo and there was another guy. I forget his name. Oh, I remember, it was Shawn O'Sullivan."

"Where did you fight?"

"Cabbagetown. I was always fighting."

He raised his hand to some ladies passing by. "Hi ladies! Have a nice day."

To me he whispered, "Nice rump roast on that one. Ha, ha, ha."

To Donny he said, "I got some pot, but I need a cigarette roller. Donny will you roll a joint for me?"

"I'd love to man, but I got the shakes. Your pot would end up all over the sidewalk. Ask Outcast, he's good at that."

"Outcast, will you roll me a joint?"

"I can't, man. I got my hands full. Use Jacques' pipe. Jacques, give Shakes your pot pipe."

A Clean, Quiet Place

12 March 2012

Shaggy came bounding up to sniff my hand and nearly bit my knee. I stroked her for a while, then she ran off barking at someone. Wolf said that she's been going crazy today. He gave her some biscuits; she ate them, and then wanted more. He offered her dry dog food and a bowl of water, but she just barked. Eventually she lay down beside me. She allowed me to scratch her neck for a while, and then indicated that she'd had enough. I thought she was going to bite my hand, but she didn't close her teeth. Little Jake has scars all over his hand where she has bitten him.

Shaggy limps due to a car accident. I asked Wolf about it. He said, "I don't want to go there."

I asked Jake about his weekend. "I had some ups and downs," he said.

"I threw him out of my house Friday night," said Wolf, "at three o'clock in the morning. I guess that would be one of the downs he's talking about."

"Yeah, I got a lot of people pissed off at me that night. I don't know what happened."

I asked Wolf about his weekend. "I had a barbeque. I was eating a piece of steak, and I didn't chew it well enough. Somehow it got stuck in my esophagus. I asked my friend to do the Heimlich maneuver on me. He did it wrong, and I thought he broke some of my ribs. I was in so much pain that we sent for the paramedics. The hospital staff sure had a laugh at one drunk trying to help another drunk. I should say they had a good laugh at me, since my friend didn't stick around. They said the Heimlich maneuver wouldn't have worked, even if it had been done properly, because both air passages would have to be blocked. Only one of mine was blocked. I was able to breathe through the other one. They shoved some kind of tool down my throat and were able to extract the piece of steak. They sure had a laugh.

"It turned out that I didn't have any broken or cracked ribs. A couple have been bruised and separated. It hurts so much I can't bend over to tie my shoes."

Hippo said, "I slept outside last night, under the bridge. There is an exhaust fan overhead, I've got a good sleeping bag, the weather was mild, so it wasn't too bad. I've had it with the shelters. It's really bad there now, mostly crack heads. Things get stolen, it's noisy, fights start, there are bedbugs. I'd like to get a clean place that's quiet, no bugs and a lock on the door."

I mentioned to him that I'd visited his Facebook site. He said, "Then you saw the picture of the D11 Cat that I ran. That's the world's largest bulldozer. I operated that one at the Peace Canyon Dam near Chetwynd, British Columbia. The reservoir is Dinosaur Lake, thirteen miles long."

Shark said, "I've been sick. I've had a lot of pain in my legs, my right hip and my shoulders from my HIV. Morphine makes me sick. I take the pills and sometimes they stay down, most times they come right back up. Marijuana and booze work better than the morphine."

Bettie, Shakes' daughter, came by with her baby. Everyone crowded around and commented on how cute he was, not at all like his grandfather. The baby started crying, so Bettie thought it best to move on.

Life is Good

14 March 2012

Joy was singing her rain dance song, "rain, rain go away / come again another day."

I held my umbrella over her, but she said, "Don't bother; I'm soaked through to the skin already.

"I've been sick since Friday. I was at Jacques' house, cooking him supper and drinking his homemade wine.

Usually it doesn't bother me, but this must have been a bad batch. I've been throwing up ever since.

"I was expecting Trudy and her dog Mitzie to come by today. Mitzie is cute, but I don't touch her. She could be carrying fleas, bedbugs or anything. I even stay clear of some of my friends because the shelters are full of bedbugs. A while back, I invited some friends to stay over because they had no place to sleep. When I next used the mattress, it was crawling with bedbugs. I threw out a $2500 mattress. I won't do that again.

"I saw Angela, my probation officer, Friday. She told me that Big Jake is being sent to Millhaven Maximum Security Prison for assessment. Later, they may move him somewhere else. I don't care, as long as he's not here. They are supposed to notify me when he gets out, but he'll still find me. We have the same friends, but now there are a lot of them who are anxious to beat him up, especially Butcher. He has my permission.

"I'm looking for a new place. There are a couple that I'm going to view Saturday, in Scarborough. It will be close to where I used to live."

As I approached the benches, I saw Hippo rolling a cigarette.

"Have you been sleeping outdoors lately, Hippo?"

"Last night I stayed at the Salvation Army. It was too wet to sleep outside."

"How was it?"

"It was okay, better than sleeping in the rain."

"Were there any bedbugs?"

"I didn't notice any. I'm going back there at 2:00 for my PNA. It's based on how long I've stayed there. I think I should get $28 this time. That'll be good, especially since I don't have any money now."

I told Wolf that Joy had gotten sick drinking Jacques' homemade rice and raisin wine.

"That stuff is powerful, about 28% alcohol. Jacques hasn't been drinking lately, so I think that this last batch has had longer to ferment. I drank four 12 ounce glasses of that stuff. When I was going down the stairs, I slipped and hit the back of my head on one of the steps. I got a big bump. I can still feel it.

"Weasel brought his dog, Bear, to my place last night and he hasn't been back since. At 5:30 this morning, I had two dogs to walk."

Shaggy bit Little Jake's shoe and wouldn't let go. Jake was dancing on one leg trying to get his foot out of Shaggy's mouth.

"She bit my thumb Saturday," said Wolf. "I bled like a stuck pig. You can still see the mark and it hurts like hell."

"How old is Shaggy?"

"She's ten and a half years old, come September. I can't remember her birthday."

"Do you think she is in any pain, perhaps from arthritis?"

"No, she's not in any pain."

"I can run pretty fast," said Jake, "I had Shaggy on her leash and was running with her. She was pulling me the whole way. She's a strong dog."

Wolf said, "I'd better get back home to check on Bear (part golden retriever, part boxer) and Bowser (a full-size stuffed dog that Shakes won at the fair, but he doesn't remember). Maybe, Bowser has eaten Bear."

"Shakes," I asked, "has Shaggy ever bitten you?"

"Only once. For some reason she didn't want me to leave. She bit into the back of my pant leg and wouldn't let go."

"On Friday I saw your daughter Bettie with your grandson. What is his name?"

"Tomorrow. At least I call him that because I can't pronounce his real name. I just say, 'I'll see you, Tomorrow.'"

"How many grandchildren do you have?" Shakes held up his hand with outstretched fingers indicating five.

"What is your other daughter's name?"

"Fran, Francesca."

"So does Bettie have two children and Fran three?"

"Roughly."

"Are you planning to go to work at three o'clock?"

"Around there. Right now I just want to get drunk. I still have a bottle of sherry in my coat pocket; I have ten dollars in my wallet. I'm enjoying myself. I'm contented. Life is good."

Helping Each Other Up

15 March 2012

Joy was covered in a blanket, her hood pulled up, sitting on a piece of cardboard. I mentioned to her, "Yesterday, Shakes didn't want me to go back to work. He wanted me to keep him company. Everyone else had left."

"If you'd stayed, he would have gotten so drunk that he couldn't walk. Then he'd ask you to help him to mom and pop's. That's why his other friends go south on him. The last time I helped him, he fell down three times. I'm not strong enough to pick him up. I had to ask someone to help me to get him on his feet. We got him up and leaned against a wall. We left him there.

"I've been sitting here since 6 am. I'm freezing and miserable. I was so nervous this morning that I smoked a joint before coming here and I've been drinking. I was doing so good before. I don't know what's going on with Roy. I have to find a new place. I've made appointments to see five apartments; three on Saturday, two on Sunday.

"There's been a police car parked in front of our house for the past few days. The cop will look at his computer, then look at the house. He stays there all day. It's really got me freaked.

"I hate kids! I don't hate all kids; I have five boys of my own. I hate other people's kids! Leon, who lived in the house where I am now, had two teenagers. Neighborhood kids would come over and just hang around. They'd want to see the lizards, the snake, and Harley. He's a pit bull. Harley doesn't like kids. He bites them. I don't want to have to take him to the basement just so these neighbors can come in. I don't want them here.

"They still come to the door. I tell them, 'Leon doesn't live here anymore. Go away!' They say, 'Come on, Joy, let us come in for just a little while.' 'No!' I say, 'This isn't a zoo. You can't just come around here anytime you want.'

"I bought groceries yesterday: margarine, chicken, pork chops. I could really pig out. I like to have some food in the fridge for when Roy's son comes over, but he always brings a couple of friends with him. I can't afford to feed these neighborhood kids.

"When I took Harley for his walk this morning, he pulled me face down on the sidewalk. Roy is sixty pounds heavier than me, but even he has trouble controlling him sometimes."

A strange looking man came by carrying a backpack. He said something to Joy. I couldn't make it out. She replied, "Whatever."

"Who was that?" I asked.

"One of the bugs from the Mission."

"What's a bug?"

"One of the crazies. I don't pay any attention to them. All this time I've been venting. I'm sorry." Her attention shifted to the sidewalk.

"Hi handsome."

"Hi Joy," said a well-dressed man with an Australian accent. He bent to put a five dollar bill in Joy's hat.

"Thanks honey! Next time you go back, save some room for me in your suitcase. I'm small; I won't take up too much space."

"I'll keep that in mind," he said as he walked away.

"Well, I should be heading to work," I said.

"I'm finished here too," said Joy.

"I'll get up first, then I'll help you up. Look at us, two old farts helping each other up."

The Urban Angel

16 March 2012

Metro and Two-four, the newspaper vendors, greeted me this morning. "Hi Dale, don't drink too much green beer this weekend."

I said, "I'll be into the scotch whiskey, myself."

"Have a good weekend, Dale."

"You too Metro, Two-four."

In the next block I met Nick, who was sitting cross-legged on the wet sidewalk in his usual place in front of the church. I said, "I guess it's too wet for Joy. She's getting soft in her old age."

"She may have been here earlier. If she was here at six o'clock, her usual time, it was pouring rain. I got here about forty-five minutes later and the rain had stopped. The weather's fine now."

At noon, Hippo said, "I've been sober for two day now. I'm going to stay that way. I'm staying on the second floor of the Salvation Army."

"Is that better?" I asked.

"No, not really. I want to get a place of my own where it's quiet, and I can lock the door and lay down."

"Someplace without bedbugs?"

"Even some of the rooming houses have bedbugs."

"I've heard that they can be killed with heat," I offered.

Hippo shook his head. "No, by freezing. When I had them, they took all my clothes, put them in a plastic bag and threw it in the freezer for twenty-four hours."

It was time for me to return to work. On my way I met Ian.

Dennis Cardiff

The Choice is Yours

17 March 2012

I look into my crystal ball;
your future's looking bleak.
Think of where you want to be
next year, next month, next week.

From what you told me yesterday,
you risk your freedom and your wealth.
How does this fit into your plan?
How does this affect your health?

I know you're trying harder
than you've ever tried before.
Please, leave that place before police
come crashing through your door.

You have friends, you're not alone,
pack your bags and leave the jars.
Even sleeping on the sidewalk
beats staring through prison bars.

The choice is yours, it's always been.
Think of yourself. What's best for you?
I want to see your smile each day;
a memory — it just won't do.

When the Weirdos Come Out

19 March 2012

Joy started crying and buried her head in my shoulder. She said, "I know I need to get out of that place. The police car is still parked in front of our house. There aren't that many people coming to our door, especially now with the police out front.

"I saw a few apartments on the weekend. Some of them were nice. The rent is about $750 a month, about the same as I'm paying Roy.

"I just found out that I'm paying the full amount of the rent. Roy doesn't pay anything towards rent. He's supposed to pay the rest of the bills, but I don't know if he's been paying them.

"Yesterday I was outside cleaning and raking the backyard because of the mess that Harley had made over the winter. He was outside with me the whole time. We came inside, and he crapped in the middle of the kitchen floor and on Roy's CDs, then he peed on Roy's computer.

"I think he's dying. He's ten and a half years old. Roy needs to pay more attention to him, but he's always away at his girlfriend's house. Her name is Christina. She's a coke head. I always call her Christine just to make her mad.

"I left a note for Roy, 'He's your dog, deal with it.' I took a toothpick and pinned the note to the pile of dog turd. When I came home later, the note and the pile were still there and Harley had pooped again, right beside the first pile.

"I have just enough money to pay rent and to buy food. I don't have any extra to buy dog food. Harley doesn't eat the canned food; it gives him the runs. He eats the kibble that comes in big bags. I can't afford to buy that. Yesterday, I cooked pork chops and gave him the bones and some of the fat.

"Tonight I'm having pirogues. I just love the ones with cheese."

A woman stopped and put a dollar in Joy's cap. "Hi sweetheart!" Joy said. "Thanks honey!"

To me she said, "She's lost ten pounds. I told her about the diet that I was on. I don't eat during the week, only on Sunday. I told her to try it and it worked for her.

"I have names for some of the people that walk by. Some of them I see every day. There's one little old lady with skinny legs. She's always rushing. I call her 'the stork.' There's a guy who I'll see here in the morning, then I'll see him again at the park. I call him 'the stalker'.

A strange looking man wearing a trench coat stopped in front of us and just stared. Joy gave him the finger. He just stood there staring at us. "Get out of here!" yelled Joy. The man eventually walked away.

"I have to deal with the twinkies and candy kids. There were some here this morning. I had to kick them out. They said, 'We slept here last night, so this is our spot.'

"I said, 'Look dude, it doesn't work that way. I've been here eleven years and there's no way you're taking my spot. Tomorrow I'm going to be packing, maybe a sharpened screwdriver or a long blade.' "

Later, at the park, Joy said, "Some people say that spring is here when the trees start to bud, but I say it's when the weirdos come out. After Dennis left, this guy came back and kicked me in the knee, knocking me to the ground. That's why I'm gimping. Tomorrow, I'm going to take a sock and put a bar of soap in it. If that guy comes back, I'm going to beat him with it."

"Everybody seems to be fighting!" said Debbie. "I was in a fight with Chester yesterday. He was flashing all this money and when I asked him for a loan, he said no, so I slapped him. He hit me back, but I grabbed him around the knees and pulled him down. I was punching him in the face when somebody pulled me off."

Loretta came over and gave Joy a hug. She said, "I would have brought your pants, but I didn't know you would be here."

After she left, Joy said to me, "A couple of years ago she was hit by a car and left for dead. She had broken arms, broken legs, a broken pelvis. One side of her face was smashed. She lost an eye. Nobody thought that she'd recover. It took about a year before she was able to leave her house. She's been coming here for about nine months now. She's very sweet."

Joy said to Debbie, "You're so skinny, you don't have an ass anymore."

"I'm on the Shepherd diet," said Debbie, "I went there for lunch yesterday and everything tasted like dog food, I couldn't eat it. You should go there and get a take out for Harley."

"How are you doing, Rocky?" Joy said to a man wearing a Metallica shirt. "I'm going to get that shirt from you, just wait and see."

"This has been a good day," said Rocky, "I went for an interview for assisted housing and it was approved. I've been waiting nine months for the interview." Rocky has the deepest voice I've ever heard.

"Congratulations!" said Joy.

I asked her if she could qualify for assisted housing.

"Rocky is Inuit. Where he's going it's for just Inuit people. If I had my native card and the rest of my identification, there are places that I could qualify for, but a lot of my papers and photographs of my kids were lost when I went into hospital. I have a birth certificate, but nothing with my picture on it. I asked Roy to get my papers, but he didn't. He was only concerned about his tools."

"Could Angela, your probation officer, help?"

"My probie? She could, she's supposed to, but I haven't gotten them yet. Angela could help me find a place, but this time I'm doing it by myself. I'm proud of that.

"I think I'm going to be leaving soon. I feel uncomfortable. I have agoraphobia and there are a lot of people here. It's not just the number of people, but some of them I don't know too well and some of them I don't like. Can you spare me some change?"

"I don't have any," I said. "I don't even have my wallet with me."

"That's probably a good idea."

Kicked in the Knee

20 March 2012

Joy wasn't in her spot today. I went to the next block to talk with Nick. "So what excuse does Joy have for not being here today?" he asked.

"She was kicked in the knee by some guy yesterday morning. While we were sitting together, he came up to us and just stared. Joy said, 'Get lost!'

"After I left, he came back and kicked her in the knee."

"What was his reason for that?"

"He was crazy," I said.

"That explains it."

"She also had a problem with some twinkies and candy kids who tried to take her spot."

Nick shook his head. "Joy wouldn't have any of that. These kids come from the suburbs. I don't know what they think they're playing at."

I said, "I'm half an hour early for work because I can't depend on the buses getting me here on time. The service is really poor now.

Nick said, "I guess you heard that they have a new guy in charge of the transit commission. He's only been at the job a month and now he's on a cruise in the Caribbean.

"That shows where our money is going. I've travelled quite a bit. I'm originally from the Hamilton area."

"How is your day going, so far?" I asked.

"I've been here since 6:45. Tuesdays are always slow. I'll be staying until about 10:30. After that, it's quiet, not many people passing by. I'll stay later, depending on how much I've collected."

"What days are the best for you?"

"Friday is always the best. People feel generous because of the coming weekend. Second, would be Monday. I guess people still have some of that good spirit left."

They're My Family

21 March 2012

"Hi Joy," I said, "were you able to see your probation officer yet?"

She replied, "Unfortunately, Angela is away this week. I have an appointment with her next Wednesday."

I asked, "Is there a possibility of seeing another probation officer?

She said, "Maybe I can."

"Promise me that you'll go as soon as you can?"

"I promise.

"The police car is still parked in front," said Joy, "but there's no pot in the house. I told Roy that I'm moving out. He sold his $3000 bicycle for $150 and took some other things, including a plasma TV to the pawn shop. He admitted that he'd really messed up."

Later at the park Joy said, "I'm feeling a bit drunk," said Joy. "I feel all messed up. Things are going around in my head. My mind is going a hundred and twenty miles an hour. I feel like I want to cut myself. There are two reasons why people cut themselves, either for attention or for distraction. I just want to be able to think straight.

"I'm supposed to phone this lady at Millhaven (*Penitentiary*) to find out where Jake is being transferred. I don't care where he is as long as it's not here. They're supposed to send me a letter advising me of when he's going to be released. He isn't supposed to come within a hundred feet of me. So, I could be here and he could be across the street having a beer or something.

"When Jake beat me up, Shakes was there. He tried to defend me, but Jake knocked him down. He tried to get up, but I said, 'Shakes, stay down!' Jake had already broken my nose and I was on the ground. Then he started kicking me in the ribs. That's when I passed out.

"I really love him. We had talked about getting a place in the country, maybe raising a few chickens. I thought we would grow old together and live happily ever after. I'm not going to change my life because of him. We have the same friends. I introduced him to all these people. They're all I have. They're my family. That means everything to me.

"Angela, my probie, isn't so bad. It's just that she gets after me to take a course in anger management. I'm not angry. When I was arrested, it was my blood on Jake. All that stuff you see on TV about DNA tests, that's bullshit. He said in court, 'It's about time that women pay for assaulting men.'

"My snake, Cyprus, shed her skin today. It's the first time it came off in one piece. Some of my native friends make bracelets by weaving strips of snake skin, but I don't want that. It feels rough with the scales."

"Hey, Joy!" called Wolf, "I need a cigarette roller. Would you please roll me one?"

"Wolf, this pot is hard. I've chewed my fingernails and I can't break this up. I need scissors. Hippo, fat boy, get me Little Jake's scissors!" To me she said, "These guys will do anything for me. They've seen me fight. They're afraid of me, and I'm the only woman here that they haven't had."

"Shakes," I asked, "how have you been?"

"This has been a bad month. Yesterday, I gave a runner $15 to buy me two bottles of wine and he went south on me. Then I went to that church where they serve meals. I gave a guy $10 to buy me a bottle and he went south. So far, this month, I've lost $100, that's not counting what I lost previous to this month."

Must Have Jumped a Bus

22 March 2012

Joy doesn't remember meeting me yesterday.

"After I had a joint, I got so wasted that I don't even know how I got home last night. I must have jumped a bus."

She isn't doing well this morning. She said, "I haven't been taking my medication lately because I don't have a health card. I can't get a health card because my picture identification was lost. Angela has copies of my papers, but she won't be back until Wednesday. I have an appointment with her then. No other probation officers can help me. I had two epileptic seizures last night.

"I still miss Jake. I've written letters to him in prison, but he hasn't answered. I just want to find out how he's doing. I worry about him.

"Rodent has gotten letters from him. I think he sends money to Jake. Rodent asked me if I wanted to see the letters that Jake sent him. I said, 'I don't want to see them if they're like the last one you showed me, where he did nothing but call me names like bitch, douche bag and ho.

"I think Jake likes Rodent more than he does me."

Pizza and Pears

23 March 2012

Joy was still feeling down today. "I hate sitting with my legs straight out, but my knee is still swollen from where that guy kicked me. I can't sit cross-legged. My fibromyalgia is causing pain in my legs. I have been having trouble sleeping, so I drink until I pass out. Now, my liver is kicking me. After today, I'm going to stop drinking."

"Joy, what you said yesterday, about incidents that happened in your past. That was a long time ago. You've been carrying that weight and punishing yourself for over eleven years. What you need to know is that you've been forgiven, so now you can forgive and love yourself. Leave the rest in the past where it belongs. You can't change what happened; the only changes you can make are right now. Also, you don't have to worry about what will happen when Jake gets out. That's seven months away."

"I miss my house, I miss seeing my kids. I can never see them ever again. I still miss Jake. I was talking to Rodent yesterday. He got another letter from Jake. He loves to rub my nose in it. I accused him of being him gay. He denied it, but I said, 'Dude, you were in prison 25 years, there's no way you didn't switch sides.' I was in prison more years than Jake will ever be. I got to like women."

"That's understandable," I said.

"I don't know why I keep thinking of Jake, but we did have some good times together. I was going out with Crash, who moved to Vancouver, but when I met Jake, that was it. He's the love of my life. He always will be. Roy doesn't like him and calls him names, but I said, 'When Jake gets out, I may decide to have him over. I have to put up with your skanky girlfriends, so I'll invite whoever I please.'

"I remember about ten years ago, there was this guy who panned across the street. He didn't like pizza. I don't like pears. Sometimes we'd have food fights. He'd throw a piece of pizza across the street at me. I'd throw a pear at him. We'd both be ducking and dodging. I think he's in Calgary now. He got involved with some program to help him straighten out.

"Humans. I look at what some of these people wear and I wonder who dresses them. Look at that guy, his jeans are below his ass. I was sitting here early one morning and a guy in the apartment across the street was in the window stretching. He was stark naked. I don't need that first thing in the morning. I waved at him; he backed away and closed the curtains.

"Jacques is going to help me get a phone. I can't go back to my old plan because I owe them over $800 in charges that Fat Richard billed to my account for porn films. I hate porn. What a loser he was."

Joy gave me a banana that someone had placed in her cap. "I don't like these. Do you want it?" she asked.

"I'll see if Nick wants it," I said.

I had to go to work, so on my way I stopped to talk to Nick. "Here's a banana from Joy."

Nick asked, "Doesn't Joy like bananas? Bananas are a good source of potassium."

"Joy doesn't like bananas, apricots, apples or pears," I said.

Nick replied, "I was talking to her this morning. I was early, so we chatted for a while."

I said, "She's sweet…when she wants to be."

"For a moment there, I didn't think we were talking about the same Joy," Nick said.

I said, "I wouldn't want to be her enemy."

"No."

While I was talking to Nick, about six people dropped change into his cap.

I said, "I'm lucky for you. Joy always says I'm lucky for her. Sometimes when she goes into the restaurant—"

"You mean when she needs to pee."

"Yes, when she needs to pee, I guard her stuff. She says, 'Any change you make you can keep.' "

"I was lucky for her this morning," said Nick, "but she never said that to me."

Shakes pondered, "This morning I woke up," I didn't know where I was or how I got there. I was in Lindsay's apartment. I still had two bottles of wine, so I had some wine, some cigarettes and some mary jane. I started walking. I wasn't looking for trouble, but trouble found me."

"Jake," said Debbie, "you've got girly socks on, and girly pants."

"These are the only things I could find to wear."

"Jake, can you roll me a joint?" asked Shakes.

Jake pulled out his scissors. "Okay Shakes, give me your pot and I'll roll you a joint."

"Dennis," said Shakes, "can you hold my cigarette? I'm running out of hands here."

"Me, Rocky and Silver were stopped by the police this morning," said Tim, "for drinking beer in the park. It's lucky that all three of us were sharing the same can. The cop poured it out, so we lost half a beer. If we'd each had our own, we would have lost three. He just told us to move along and find another place, so we're here."

"Dennis, what time is it?" asked Jake.

"12:15."

"Shakes," said Jake, "we'd better get to work."

"What time are you going to work, Shakes?" I asked.

"I'll go to work at whatever time I feel like it. I'm my own boss."

"And you have your own office," I added (*referring to his spot on the sidewalk*).

"Yes, I have."

"Shaggy!" shouted Wolf, "Find a place, any place and lie down." A boy came weaving down the sidewalk on a skateboard. "Whoa! Did you see that? It's a good thing I had Shaggy on her lead, or she would have taken a chunk out of that kid. She loves to chase skateboards. She nearly pulled my shoulder out of joint."

"Hippo," I said, "you'd better not let Joy see you in that Metallica shirt. She'll want to take it off you."

"No, it's Rocky's shirt she wants."

Sitting on the Sidewalk

24 March 2012

i'm sitting on the sidewalk
as a woman sobs on my shoulder.
i put my arm around her
and say, "it's okay."
knowing that nothing is okay,
it will never be okay.

i'm way out of my depth.
i don't know what to do
or to say.
anything that comes to mind
is shallow and meaningless.
this woman's experiences
are completely foreign to me.

all I can do is let her cry,
tell her that she has forgiveness,
that what saddens her,
what keeps her awake
or gives her nightmares
is all in the past.
it's time for her to forgive herself
and love herself
and live
in the present moment.

she can't go on.
she can't stand the pain.
she can't do this anymore.
drink is the only thing
that numbs her mind
enough to endure,
enough to pass out at night
and do it all over again
the next day.

i can only do
and say so much.
it's always a pleasant surprise
to see her sitting on the sidewalk
knowing that she's made it
through another night;
that she hasn't been taken
by violence, sickness
or the police.
i do what i can.

Thank You to You as Well

27 March 2012

Joy was wrapped in her blanket.

"I didn't come here yesterday — too cold. This is a bad day. I came down late, about 7:00. I have a crawly feeling in my legs from fibromyalgia and have a sharp pain in my hip. I don't know what that's about. I'm only staying here long enough to get enough money to buy some tampons.

"I'll probably come back downtown later to buy some wine. The store I go to doesn't open until 11:00. The only wine store near where I live sells these fancy vintage wines that cost a fortune. They laughed when I asked for Imperial Sherry.

"I don't know what Roy's plans are about the house. He took his computer yesterday. It seems like he's gradually moving his stuff out. I'm still stuck with feeding Harley. I bought some crickets for his lizards and some mice for my python.

"I don't know what I'm going to do, but I'm not giving Roy any money for next month's rent. All of my stuff fits in a bag, except for a few trinkets I made while I was in the hospital. I travel light.

"There's some good news! The police car hasn't been parked in front of our house since the weekend. I don't know what was up with that."

A native man stopped and put two five dollar bills in Joy's cap.

"Miigwech!" said Joy. To me she said, "That means 'thank you' in Algonquin."

The man replied, "Miigwech gaye giin!" (*thank you to you as well.*)

On my way to catch the bus I saw Craig sitting on the sidewalk. We greeted each other then he said, "There's this restaurant —"

I handed him a gift card, "There's enough here to buy a sandwich and a coffee."

"There's this restaurant—"

"I'm sorry, Craig. I'm on my way to an appointment."

"How much is on the card?"

"Five dollars."

"Okay."

Now I Got Two Dogs

29 March 2012

I asked Nick, "You haven't seen Joy today have you?"

"No, Joy is a wuss. Mind you I wasn't here yesterday. I wasn't about to sit in freezing rain and ice pellets."

"Joy's been complaining about a sharp pain in her hip," I said. "It may be arthritis. Sitting on the cold sidewalk wouldn't help."

"No it wouldn't, but Joy has some sort of cushion, doesn't she?"

"Yes, in her backpack she brings a chair cushion and puts a piece of cardboard under that. Then, of course, she has her blanket."

"Yes, Joy always has her blanket. I use a rolled up yoga mat as a cushion. It keeps me from the cold and it's comfortable to sit on."

"Do you ever go to the benches at the Green?" I asked.

"No, I don't go there. I know some of those people, but I don't associate with them much. I've known Joy since she was sharing an apartment with someone *(Big Jake)* in King's Park. A friend of mine had an apartment in the same building."

"I don't seem to be lucky for you today," I said. "Last time I was here, you collected quite a bit of change."

Nick said, "There's no rhyme or reason to it. There are good days and there are bad days. Summer can be slow because a lot of people are on holidays."

Nick was humming a tune. I said, "You have a good singing voice."

"No, I'm no singer," he said. "I'm banned from most of the karaoke bars; not from the drinking part, from the singing part."

"The Ontario government has brought down a new budget. Do you have any opinion on that?" I asked.

"Well, they've frozen ODSP *(Ontario Disability Support Program)* for two years. I'm not on that; I'm on Family Benefits.

We get an increase of about one percent a year. That amounts to a couple of dollars on our monthly check."

"Do you have any suggestions on how things could be improved?"

"I'm no economist."

"I'm celebrating today," said Shakes. "I think I may get corked. I went to court this morning and they stayed the charges of obstruction against me. I've been on bail since November. I was banned from going anywhere near the Village Restaurant. At first I wasn't allowed within 600 feet, then they reduced that to 300 feet, then 50 feet. This morning the judge said, 'Shakes, you're free to go anywhere you want.' I had three bottles of wine with me while I was in court."

Shaggy was barking at everyone that passed. Wolf said, "Now I got two dogs to walk at 5:30 in the morning, Shaggy and Bear. Weasel brought Bear over on Friday and asked me if I would take care of her because he had to go back into hospital. Of course, I complained and said that he should be paying me to look after her, but actually I like having Bear around. In the morning when I take them out, Shag wants to go one way, Bear the other way. Then they get all tangled up around me.

"What do you think of this weather? We have summer one day, winter the next. *(Our temperatures exceeded those of Florida last week; now it is snowing.)* There was no way I was going to bring Shaggy down here yesterday. You see how long her coat is. When that gets wet, she has an extra fifty pounds to carry, and she's eleven years old."

"You have another dog, Bowser, don't you?" I asked.

"You don't know about Bowser? That's Shakes' dog. It's stuffed, but I don't think Shakes knows that. One time he was drunk and he came down the sidewalk with this huge stuffed dog the size of Shaggy. I put it out on my balcony. My apartment is on the second floor over the entrance to the building. The neighbors would see this dog and they'd say, 'Wolf, why doesn't your dog bark anymore?' They thought it was real.

"I like to come down here and visit with my friends, but I don't like too many people around. I never have more than three people at my apartment. I like having the dogs around. I see them communicating together and they communicate with me as well. I'll be in another room and I'll hear Shaggy's bowl banging against the wall. She pushes it around with her nose. When I hear that sound, I know she's hungry. You've been around animals, you know what I mean."

Shaggy knocked over Wolf's can of Old Milwaukee beer, and then commenced to lick the pool that formed. Wolf took a plastic bag, poured beer in it and said, "Okay, Shaggy, if you want to be in the club, you have to drink your beer." Shaggy lapped the beer contentedly. "See, she understands what I'm saying. You saw that."

A Place to Go

30 March 2012

Nick was sitting on the sidewalk in front of the church. Within the church is a drop-in ministry for all who find themselves in need of fellowship, a smile, and some good food. Joy has told me that the ladies who volunteer with this program are always fussing over Nick. They bring him big sandwiches, desserts and mugs of coffee.

Nick is always neat in appearance, his white beard is trimmed, and he has sparkling blue eyes. He is also the most un-talkative man I have ever met. I think of myself as a listener and an observer, but not a conversationalist. Today I was determined to have a conversation with him.

"Good morning, Nick."

"Good morning, Dennis."

"I guess Joy decided that it was too cold for her today," I commented.

"Yes, it's too cold for Joy."

"Do you have any big plans for the weekend?" I tried again.

"It depends on the weather."

"The forecast is for sunshine with temperatures around the freezing mark."

"In that case, I have no plans. How about you?"

"Nothing definite," I said. The next five minutes passed in absolute silence. "Well, I guess I'd better get to work. I'll see you on Monday, Nick."

"I'll see you on Monday, Dennis."

April 2012

She Bites

2 April 2012

"Hey, it's Kenny Rogers!" said Serge, referring to me.

"Yes, that's what you said the last time I saw you. That was quite a while ago."

"Holy lord thunder! Hi Dennis! It's really good seeing you again."

"It's good seeing you, Hippo! It's been a while. What have you been up to?"

"I've been okay. I come by here every once in a while. I got real drunk yesterday. I've been barred from the Mission again. This time for two days."

"What happened?"

"I put a hole in the wall. It happened in the dormitory. I came in at about four in the morning and my bunk mate wrote the time down in a book, as if he was a cop or something. That got me mad. I put my elbow through the wall. It was either that or set fire to the guy. I would have done it too – douse him with lighter fluid, light a match, then *poof*.

"Last night, Jake and I slept under the bridge. It was a little cool."

I asked, "You have a sleeping bag, don't you?"

"No, I used to have one, but not now. Jacques gave me a winter coat. Now, I need new boots. The soles are coming off these.

"I'm just about ready to move to British Columbia. Remember, I told you that I had an inheritance coming from my grandma? I phoned my parents on the weekend to see how things were coming along. I thought I was going to get $10,000. It turns out it's going to be more than that – about $80,000.

"I've got a job waiting for me, working in the bush. I'll buy a mobile home, and I'll be set."

"Joy was here earlier, but she went home. She's in the middle of moving. Roy hadn't paid the hydro, so they've had no electricity. I don't know what's going on with him."

Bear barked at a kid riding by on a skate board. A lady stopped to admire the dog. Jake said, "Don't touch her; she bites, especially kids on skateboards."

"Oh, that's what the fuss was about," she said.

I Don't Want to See That Stuff

4 April 2012

A man was standing in Joy's spot. Middle aged, his hair brown and thinning, cap in hand. I thought, *He must be new in town; otherwise, he wouldn't have been standing in Joy's spot, not if he values his life.*

I introduced myself and gave him a gift card for a sandwich. He seemed truly grateful, not only for the card but for accepting him as an equal. His name is Ghyslain. I'm not good at small talk and didn't want him to think I was just interested in him for information, so I just said, "Have a good day!" If I see him again, I'll be prepared with more to talk about.

At the benches, I said to Joy, "Hippo mentioned that you were in the middle of moving. Is that all settled now?" Joy sat on the curb beside Bruce and I sat on the sidewalk.

"Can you believe it? Roy didn't pay the hydro. I was stuck with no electricity. I'm staying with a friend for the next month. Do you know Toothless Chuck? Well, he has a couple of teeth in front. Anyway, that's where I'm staying. It was fine for the first couple of nights when it was just me and him, but then his friends started staying over.

"I was eating my supper when Mona starts making out with this guy on the living room floor. I don't want to see that stuff while I'm eating. I was ready to kill her. I said, 'Will you take that stuff to the shower? That's what showers are made for.'

"I haven't been back to the other place since I picked up my stuff. My down filled winter coat got ruined in the last rain we had. I put it in the dryer, but I couldn't get the down to go back where it was supposed to be, so I left it behind as a bed for Harley.

"I also had to leave my python, Cyprus behind. That was upsetting. I paid $75 for that snake. I think she was named after the Cuban-American/Latino hip-hop group, Cyprus Hill. I don't know. That's the name she had at the pet store."

Bruce said, "Some of my mates back in Scotland were really into that group."

He continued, "Well, I went to court today and got my resolution. They gave me a hundred and twenty days, so I'll serve eighty. I'll be going in May second. My lawyer told me that I could get probation, but I'm a drinker. I'd pile up violations in no time, better I just go to jail.

"After I get out I'm going out west, near Calgary. A friend phoned and offered me a job as a chef, that's what I studied for in college. I can get work anywhere. When I get out, I'll have everything cleared up — my tickets, everything.

"Ever since I finished college, I've been traveling — a wandering hobo. This is the eleventh country I've been to, but it's time to move on. I've got myself into a rut here. I traveled all over Scotland, England, Wales, Cyprus and North Africa before coming here. Now, I'm sleeping behind the dumpsters in back of the coffee shop. I've stayed there before. They know me.

"I told the manager that I was back, just in case one of the staff saw me there and phoned the police. It's relatively safe there; they have a spot light and a surveillance camera. They're really good to me. Sometimes, the manager will bring me a coffee in the morning. The cardboard I sleep on, I slide under the dumpster, so it's there when I need it at night.

"Sometimes, I'll go to the Oven for breakfast. I can get three eggs, half a plate of potatoes. Being Scottish, I love potatoes. If the fat cook is on, he'll give me an extra sausage and an extra piece of toast. If I go there near closing time, at three in the afternoon, they'll give me an extra bowl of soup. You see this belly? This isn't a beer belly, it's an eating belly.

"One of my favorite places to go is Wendy's. I get their Double Junior Bacon Cheeseburger for $1.89. Since I'm Scottish, I take out one of the meat patties, wrap it up and put it in my pocket. Then I go to the grocery store where I can buy a bun for fifty cents. That really makes a meal."

I said, "You do alright then?"

He nodded. "I do alright. I panhandle. I make thirty to forty dollars, then quit for the day. It's lazy work. I can't wait until summer when I'll have my drinking under control and I can go out west. It's not that the grass is greener; it's just that the grass is different."

It started to rain, then snow, then hail.

Bruce continued, "I hate the rain. Firstly, I don't like getting soaked. Secondly, when people have an umbrella in one hand and a coffee in the other, I'm not going to get any change."

Shakes came over and asked Joy if she had any pot. "No man," she said, "I don't have any pot. The only one who had any was Shark and he's on a liquor run."

Shakes sat down beside me.

"Here Shakes," said Joy, "you can have some of my wine."

"Bruce, can you help me up?" asked Shakes.

"Okay, man I'll help you. Just grab hold of my hand."

Shakes was pulled to his feet and he walked back to the bench to sit down. "I'm surprised that he's able to walk, being as drunk as he is. I don't do babysitting. If someone is too drunk to walk, I just leave them. Let the police do their job."

Joy said to me, "I'll see you tomorrow."

Bruce said to Joy, "I know you're not feeling well, but it's good to go to work, if only for a little while. I try to work every day whether I feel like it or not."

Easter Dinner

5 April 2012

Ghyslain was sitting in Joy's spot. I sat next to him.

"Are you new to this area?" I asked.

"No, I've been on the streets for fifteen years, but the last three years were in Ottawa and Montreal."

"I guess you know Joy then?"

"Yes, I gave her this spot when I moved."

"How is it living on the streets in Ottawa and Montreal, as compared to Toronto?"

"It's much better here. The people are friendlier. In Montreal, I was sleeping in a park. They woke me at four in the morning and gave me a ticket. I said to them, 'If you think I'm paying this ticket, you're crazy.'"

I said, "Jacques has a wall papered with tickets."

"That sounds like Jacques. Do you know Old Andre? He died." He was quiet for a moment. "I'm getting cold sitting here. I'm going inside for a coffee."

I moved to the next block to talk with Nick.

"How has it been going since I saw you last?"

"I wasn't here yesterday. It was too cold, but overall it's been going fine."

"Do you know Bearded Bruce?" I asked.

"Yes, I know him."

"He was telling me that he's visited eleven countries."

"He probably counts Scotland as a country, then England and Wales. He'd count Ireland as two countries. In that case, I've visited eleven countries also, but that was a long time ago."

"Do you have any plans for the weekend?"

"No, no plans. I may phone the Mission and ask when they're planning to have their Easter meal."

At noon Shakes said, "You know, I think I'm starting to get there. It's cold, that's why I have socks on my hands."

"Shakes," said Wolf, "Here's a pair of gloves you can wear."

"These have dog hair on them. Is it from Bowser?" *(Shakes' stuffed dog, standing watch on Wolf's balcony.)*

"I should have been working this morning," said Joy. "What happened is I overslept. Bruce and Jimmy John were at Chuck's last night. Bruce is so funny when he's stoned.

"Jimmy John got up early and stole three of Chuck's beer, leaving him with only one. That's really low. I saw him sniffing around my bag as well, but I kept a close eye on it.

"Mona and Tony left Chuck's place. They were supposed to pay him $75. That's only right if you stay at someone's place and they feed you. I don't know if they would have paid Chuck if Bruce and I hadn't gone after them. When I caught up with Tony, he had a huge wad of bills."

"Are you feeling better today?" I asked.

"After I ate yesterday, I felt better, but I'm on my period now. I don't know why I'm telling you this, but I was off it for the past four months and now it's back. It's heavier than usual. I'm soaking through a tampon every hour for most of the day. Will you walk with me to the mall? I want to buy a bottle of wine and use their bathroom. It'll be warm in there."

We walked.

"I was talking to Ghyslain this morning," I said. "He was in your spot."

"He's a good guy. He'll move on when I go back to work. The Sandwich Lady was by earlier; she gave me a list of all the events at the Mission, the Salvation Army and the Shepherd. You won't see me there – too many people. I'm agoraphobic. Besides that, a lot of people there are pretty sketchy. I'm not that well balanced as it is. I don't need any of them to make it worse."

"How is the food there?"

"The Easter meal is always good. I've liked it when I've gone. During the week, the menu is boring. Each day they have something different, but from week to week, it's the same. On Sundays they have an Indian family come in to make a vegetarian meal. Can you imagine trying to get men to eat tofu? I don't think so!

"I got some chocolate Easter eggs this morning. I don't like eating chocolate, but I've got a gallon of vanilla ice cream at Chuck's place. I'm going to smash up the chocolate and mix it with the ice cream. I think that'll be good."

Some People Only Take

10 April 2012

Standing in Joy's spot was a neatly dressed man named Kirk. He said, "I just got in from British Columbia this morning. It took me four days hitchhiking. I got a lot of rides from truckers. I had been working in a logging camp. It was a fairly large camp with thirty machines. I operated a skidder. The owner died and left the company to his twenty-two year old son, who didn't want to carry on the business.

"I stopped at the Mission this morning. They weren't serving meals. They told me to come back at seven this evening.

"I'm originally from the Kootenay region of southern British Columbia, but I found it too expensive to live there. I was paying $850 per month, plus utilities, for a one bedroom apartment."

I directed him to the church up the street. They serve lunch there. I also suggested he go to the benches to meet some of my friends. They could show him around and give him information.

After leaving Kirk, I walked along the sidewalk and met Ian and Marlena.

"How was the Easter weekend for you, Ian?"

"Easter day was great. I was panning and collected $83."

"How are you, Marlena?"

"I don't know."

At noon Hippo said, "I'm still barred from the Mission, but they let me come for the Easter meal yesterday. It was really good. They served prime rib, mashed potatoes and apple pie. I filled my plate a couple of times."

"I was there too," said Silver, "I forgot my doggy bag. I was looking forward to having something to eat later while I was watching American Idol."

"Are you still sleeping under the bridge, Hippo?" I asked.

"No, I'm staying at the Salvation Army. There are a lot of crack heads there. Someone stole my socks."

"When I stayed there," said Silver, "someone stole my sneakers."

"I should get a cougar to sleep under my bed," said Hippo.

"Maybe you could borrow Bear from Weasel," I said, "or borrow Bowser. He's staying on Wolf's balcony right now. At least you wouldn't have to feed him."

I asked Kenny where he was from.

"I've lived in Calgary, but I've lived here for a while now. Sometimes I work construction or install dry wall, but I prefer labor. I'd never work in an office. I only work outside."

Larry said, "I panhandle like the rest of my friends here, but I don't use a cap or a cup. I just sit on a corner and ask people if they have any spare change. That way I can't be charged by the police."

"Hippo," said Silver. "Do you want to go on a beer run for me? I'll give you a beer and a dollar."

"Can I have a beer?" asked Raven.

Later, Silver said to me, "I don't mind sharing, but some people only take, they don't give back."

You are My Sunshine

11 April 2012

Annie was singing, "You Are My Sunshine."

Debbie asked, "Are you aware of the weird things that are happening with the moon lately?"

"When I was a kid," I said, "we used solunar tables based on the moon that indicated the best times for fishing. They were always right."

"When I was a boy," said Little Jake, "my step dad took us to Rouge Lake in Algonquin Park. In those days, there were no roads into the park. We had to portage with our canoes for ten hours before we got to the lake. That night while all the adults were drinking, us kids were tearing around with the dogs. Next morning, my step dad said, 'When the sun gets to the top of that hill is the time the fish will be biting.' We caught fifty-six speckled trout in one and a half hours. It was amazing! Then the game warden came along and said we had six fish over our limit. He gave my mom a ticket. She had to drive all the way to Perth to pay it."

"When I was a girl," said Debbie.

"Will you shut up!" yelled Jake.

"I should explain," said Debbie, "Jake and I have an off again, on again relationship. Right now it's off. We love and hate each other."

"Hi pretty lady!" said Andre to a woman passing by, **"Will you smile for me?"** It's hard not to smile when looking at Andre, since he has no front teeth. "That's better. That wasn't so hard was it?"

"Andre, keep your voice down!" said Debbie. "We don't want to attract any unwelcome attention." Nearly everyone had open bottles of liquor under their coats, or somewhere out of sight.

"We've been coming here for ten years, but it only takes one incident for us to get kicked out. We're safe now, but we used to sit at some benches up the hill. They took those away. There used to be two benches here. They've just taken one away."

"Hey, you see these sunglasses?" asked Andre, "Do you know where I got them? When I was walking across the bridge, two guys were coming towards me. One was wearing these sunglasses. I walked up to the guy and grabbed them right off his face, put them on, then I said to him, 'Are you man enough to hit a guy with glasses to get these back?' Then I hit the other guy for no reason.

"I was arrested last night. Shenkman came by with his cart, like one of those you pull behind a bicycle, and I asked him to give me a ride in it, so he did. Then he wanted me to give him a ride. I did, but I accidentally went over the curb and Shenkman fell out. We started fighting and that's when the cops came along."

"Andre, you're not going to start fighting here, are you?" asked Jake.

"No, I love you guys. We're all family here."

I Don't Know Any Dale

13 April 2012

After getting off the bus this morning, I was greeted by Metro. "Good morning, Dennis!"

"Good morning, Metro!"

"So, is it Dennis or Dale? All this time we've been calling you Dale!"

"It's Dennis," I said.

"I see. You were having a little joke on us, or you don't care."

"I don't care, Metro, as long as you don't call me late for dinner."

I approached Joy. She was seated on a plastic storage box that she'd taken from behind the hotel. Her hood was up and her legs were wrapped in a blanket. "How are you feeling, Joy?"

"Miserable! I have pneumonia again! I just can't take it anymore! Toothless Chuck doesn't like to see anybody sleeping on the streets, so he'll take anybody in. We had eight adults staying in a bachelor apartment. I'm agoraphobic! I had to step over people to go to the bathroom. You've never heard such snoring! Sometimes I'd drag my bed to the kitchen to try to get away from the noise. Bruce is up three or four times in the night to get something to eat. It's no wonder he's so big."

"Yes," I replied, "he said he didn't have a beer belly; he had an eating belly."

"I really have to get out of that place! I phoned Angela, mostly because I thought she had breached me on account of I missed our last meeting.

" 'No,' she said, 'from the state you were in when we last met, I knew something must be wrong.' So I asked her, 'Are you sure, when I see you Monday, there won't be two cops waiting in your office to take me to jail?' and she said, 'No, you have nothing to worry about.' I told her I had to move. She said she'd help me.

"I'm also having trouble with my friends at the benches or, the bench as it is now. Some of the guys used to loosen the bolts, so when you sat down, the bench would tip over backwards. The main problem is too many people go there. Jake and Debbie were all over each other. It was enough to make me want to gag myself with a pitchfork.

"Raven's been drinking vodka lately. She was so drunk that she'd wet herself. I was sitting on the bench; she was standing beside me, all I could smell was pee! Shakes kept falling asleep and kept leaning on me. It's just too much sometimes!"

As usual, she switched gears quickly, "So, Metro and Two-four have been calling you Dale?'

"Yes, for a long time!"

"I had a real argument with them this morning. They said that Dale had been asking about me. 'Dale,' I said, 'I don't know any Dale.'

"'Sure you do!' said Metro, 'The white haired gentleman with the beard. He walks with a limp.'

"'That's Dennis!' I said.

"'Are you sure?'

"'Of course I'm sure!' I told them."

Joy shook her head. "So, you didn't mind them calling you Dale, you just went along with it, as long as they didn't call you late for dinner — right?"

"Right!" I laughed.

Men Are Better With Numbers

15 April 2012

Curled up, was Hippo wearing sunglasses and his winter coat, with his head on his backpack, sound asleep. Andre had a scab on his lower lip. He had tried to take a drag from the wrong end of his cigarette. His knuckles were still scabbed from fights earlier in the week. He was talking about his last day at the Shepherd before he was barred.

"I came in late and I had four beer tucked into my belt. One beer slipped and smashed to the floor. A security guard came and shoved me, causing another beer to slip. That got me really mad. I grabbed the guy in a headlock and punched him in the face. Now, all the security guards know not to mess with me.

"A month later I went there to visit a friend. I wasn't in the building, just on the grounds. Someone phoned the police and I did sixty-five days in jail for trespassing."

Little Jake interrupted, **"Will you shut up!"** he yelled at Debbie.

"I know you don't mean that, Jake," said Shark. "You two are really close. Admit it, Jake, you love Debbie."

"I don't care for her one iota. Do you know how big an iota is?" He held up his thumb and index finger indicating about a quarter of an inch.

"Jake," said Debbie, "I know what an iota is. I'm a word person. I'm not very good with numbers, but I think women are naturally better with words. Men are better with numbers."

"I loved learning English," said Inuk.

"I'm a numbers person!" said Andre. "Maths, Sciences, Physics – I love to figure things out."

"What's twelve times twelve?" asked Jake.

Andre thought about it for a while then said, "One hundred and forty-four!"

"It took you a while though," said Jake, "didn't it?"

"Sometimes I know the answer, but it won't come out. My head doesn't always work so well. When I had my second heart attack, I was on the ice under the bridge. I've always wanted to be the troll under the bridge.

"I'd been drinking pretty heavily. I was dressed warm, skidoo suit, boots, the works. The last thing I remember, I was hallucinating. I was talking to Frosty the Snowman on one side and Santa Claus on the other. Then I fell asleep.

"Someone phoned for an ambulance. The paramedics had to peel me from the ice. At the hospital, my body temperature was 32 degrees. They packed me with ice, so I'd thaw gradually. I was put into an induced coma. Doctors said I was dead for four minutes."

"I'd like to go to sleep right here," said Jake.

"Don't do that!" said Debbie. "If you want to sleep, go somewhere more private, or you'll ruin it for the rest of us."

Before leaving I spoke to Rocky, "How did the housing work out? The last time I talked with you, it was all settled."

"It didn't work out; they had too many rules. Also, they wanted to charge me extra because I'm native. They thought I'd be eligible for some grants from the government. It didn't help that the superintendent caught Trudy smoking a joint in the foyer."

Old Friends

16 April 2012

Sitting on the church steps was a sad looking man with a suitcase. He was pleasant looking, in his early forties with dark, wavy hair.

I introduced myself and said, "Are you hungry?"

"Why do you ask?"

"I wondered if you wanted a coffee, breakfast, bus tickets?"

"Oh, no, no, you misunderstand. But, thank you anyway."

We shook hands. When I left he was smiling.

"The meeting with my probation officer went okay." said, Joy, I told her I was losing it. She said, 'You don't have to worry. I'm not going to breach you.' That's not it! I can't get my head together, and I feel sick. It was then that I threw up, all over her desk, her papers, everything. To make it worse, all it smelled of was sherry. I've cut back on my drinking a lot. I water my sherry down until it's almost clear, but I haven't been able to eat much.

"She filled out an application for me for housing. She also made an appointment for me, Wednesday morning, with a clinic. They have a drop-in center for people, like me, with mental illness. They have medical staff, counseling and health care assistance. She said I would have a better chance at housing if I am registered with them.

"The main problem I'm having at Roy's is there are too many people. I haven't been sleeping well because of the noise. Chuck is up three or four times during the night to eat. There were a lot of people over on Saturday. Chili drank a 26 ounce bottle of vodka, and then pulled another bottle out of her purse. She was so drunk that when she walked back to the Shepherd, she was nearly run over by a truck. They put her on suicide watch all night.

"Chuck wanted someone to walk with him because he's getting so fat. I said to him, 'Chuck, do I look like someone who needs to lose weight? Take Bruce with you. He could lose a few pounds.' Bruce didn't want to go. Chuck got mad and said he was going to buy a dog. That's all I'd need. I'm already cleaning up after eight people. I sweep the floor, and within an hour it's dirty again. Today, I just refused. I was better off sleeping behind the dumpsters in back of the coffee shop, at least it was quiet. I had Big Jake then. Now I have nothing.

"Bruce took us out for brunch on Sunday. That was a waste. I only ate one sausage and a piece of toast. He and Chuck filled their plates about three times. I've never seen anybody eat so much. It was disgusting!"

I shook my head in commiseration. Sitting on the curb beside me was Luther, who I've met before. He decided to tell me about himself.

"I'm a member of the Dene, First Nations, from near Lake Athabaska, just south of the Northwest Territories," he said.

"Dene means "people" in our language. At home I was studying to be a shaman.

"Lately I've been playing guitar with a punk rock band in Montreal. We dressed in leather, with studs, the whole punk thing. It was rough. After one of our concerts, I was jumped by four guys. I've studied tai-chi, and that helped. You have to look your opponent in the eye and show him you have no fear. I looked around the guys circling me, and I found the weakest one. Then I struck. I beat three of them, the fourth ran away. Even so, I was cut in three places. I've got a scar at the back of my neck and on the left side of my ribs where I was stabbed with a sharpened screwdriver. I've got a six inch scar on my left forearm from being slashed with a knife.

"I also lived in Vancouver for a while. I used to hang around the park at the University. I got talking with a professor. He had three degrees. He was impressed with how much I knew about aboriginal law. He also wondered why I seemed so happy all the time. I told him that if he was looking for happiness, he should get a tent and spend some time in the forest, being alone with nature. He took my advice and couldn't believe what a peaceful experience it was. The next time I saw him, he called me over to his car. He pulled out a new backpack and gave it to me. He'd seen that mine was torn and patched. Inside were three bottles of wine and $1500 in cash.

"I hadn't been home in four years and I missed my mother. I traveled eighteen hours straight, by snowmobile, to visit her. At one point, we were racing along beside a herd of caribou. When I arrived at our village, I was wearing goggles and a ski mask. I asked around where my mother was and a neighbor told me that she was at Bingo. I knew she was a smoker and would be coming out soon for a cigarette. I kept the mask and goggles on, and when she came out, I started asking about her parents, brothers and sisters. She couldn't figure out who it was, so I took off the mask. She was so happy; she couldn't believe it was me."

Stabbing

17 April 2012

Shark was passing around a bottle of Fireball. Loretta was asleep on the grass. Serge was sitting off by himself.

Shark said, "I took a Demerol earlier; later I have to go to the doctor to get a morphine shot for my liver. I wonder how that's going to mix with the Fireball?"

I was standing next to Al, who has long blond hair and a guitar slung on his back. "I can't believe that this still hurts so much," he said to me. He lifted his sweater to reveal a partially healed, two inch, stab wound in his side. "This happened over a month ago. The blade went in six inches, and just missed my vital organs. I saw the x-rays. I've got another up higher, but it was deflected by my rib cage.

"A crack head named Tom did this. He lived downstairs in the same building as me. He knocked on my door at ten in the evening. I'd been sleeping. I answered the door and he said, 'I'm going to buy some weed. If you give me five bucks we can split a gram.'

"I said, 'Since I'm awake now anyway, I might as well.' He never came back.

"The next morning I heard him trying to do the same thing to my neighbor. He was even bragging about ripping me off. I argued with him and said, 'Since you ripped me off, I want ten bucks or a gram of weed.' He refused and went into his apartment. I walked away, he came up behind me and hit me twice in the side. At first I thought he'd punched me. Then I felt something warm running down. My neighbor handed me a hammer and I started chasing after him, but then thought better of it. I decided to go to the hospital.

"Because I was a crime victim, there was a cop posted in my room. I was hooked up to an IV. I said to the cop, 'Watch this!'

"I pushed the bedside button and a nurse came in. 'It hurts!' I said. She gave me a shot of morphine. I saw a doctor walking past, and I said, 'Doctor, it hurts!' He gave me a shot of morphine. The cop said, 'If you do that once more, I'm going to have to report you.'

"The cop drove me home. Just as we were leaving the parking lot, I said, 'I forgot to get a prescription for pain medication.' He said, 'You're probably going home to smoke pot anyway. I think you can do without a prescription.'

"Since then, Tom has been evicted from our building. There's a sign by the front door saying he's not allowed to enter. He's being held in jail, pending his court appearance. I don't know what's going to happen next."

"That's some story!" I said. "So, what kind of music do you play?"

"A bit of everything: Bob Dylan, the Beatles, Cat Stevens. If you mention a band, I probably know at least one of their songs. If you mentioned the Eagles, I could play *Lyin' Eyes*. If you mentioned Creedence Clearwater Revival, I could play *Proud Mary*. I can play for about six hours without repeating myself. As I get older, my memory gets shorter. If I learn a new song, I forget an old one.

"Today I've been busking at the Square. I had to sing over the noise of the buses. My throat was getting dry, so I stopped here for a few beers. I'm going to try a mall down the street later on."

Al had to rescue his bicycle from Shakes, who could barely walk; riding a bicycle wouldn't have been a good idea.

A Mean, Nasty, Inuit Woman

18 April 2012

Metro greeted me with, "Good morning, Dennis, Dale, anything but late for supper. Have a good day!"

"Have a good day, Metro, Two-four!"

When I arrived at Joy's spot, I saw her plastic storage box (*that she borrows from behind the hotel*), a newspaper folded on top of that, her cap was in front of the box with a bit of change (*jingle, as Ian calls it*), her jacket was lying on the sidewalk beside her box; but no Joy. A tall man wearing glasses and a red short sleeved shirt was standing there, holding a large coffee.

"Is Joy coming back?" I asked.

"She's indisposed at the moment."

"You mean she went into the restaurant to have a pee."

"Yes, that's what I mean. I'm just standing here watching her stuff, but if you're going to be here, I'll be on my way. I'm getting cold."

"I'll take good care of Joy's stuff. She knows me."

Before long I heard, "Hi, Sweetie!" I turned and saw Joy. She was walking stiffly toward me from the direction of the restaurant.

"How are you feeling?" I asked.

"I've had to go pee a lot of times and when I get there, not much comes out. It's dark too, kind of an orangy color. I'm afraid it's my kidneys again. I may have to go back into hospital."

She continued, "I just lost it with my probation officer the other day. Besides throwing up all over her desk, I told her, 'I don't care if you breach me! I don't care about anything!' She said, 'You told me that you couldn't do any more jail time.' I said, 'If it happens, it happens. I just don't care.'

"Today I go to support services from three to seven o'clock. I'm really not an afternoon sort of person, I'd rather go in the morning, but I wasn't the one making the appointment.

"I'm not getting enough sleep. Bruce brought his girlfriend of three years to stay with us. Inuk is her name. She's a mean, nasty, Inuit woman who's been with every man in town. I don't know what Bruce sees in her. She'd have to hang a pork chop around her neck for even a dog to want to play with her.

If Bruce wants to stick his stuff in there knowing where she's been, he'll have to deal with the consequences.

"Last night she even tried to sleep in my bed. 'No, no,' I said, 'Bruce sleeps on the floor, so you sleep on the floor.'

"I even had words with Bruce about her. 'Bruce,' I said, 'You made a mistake crossing me. You just lost a friend.'

"Tony is sleeping in the kitchen now, right in front of the refrigerator, so Bruce isn't able to get up in the night for something to eat.

"Last night there were five people sleeping in Chuck's bachelor apartment. Chili came over, but only long enough to get drunk, then she went to the Shepherd.

"I paid Chuck three hundred bucks to stay there and another two hundred for groceries. With just me and him, that should last three weeks, but we went through them in two. I told him it wasn't working out, so he talked to everybody.

"I just sat back, quiet as a mouse.

"Sometimes I drink until I pass out, but then I wake up in the middle of the night and can't get back to sleep. Sometimes I'll buy a morphine pill from Shark. I break it in half -- if I take a whole one, I'll puke. That usually gives me a good night's sleep.

"When I was in hospital last, the only ones to visit me were Chuck and Shark. I don't care about the rest of those guys."

I said, "If you go into hospital again, I'll visit you."

"If I do have to go in, I'll leave a message with Metro and Two-four.

"It's getting too cold sitting here. I'm going to leave. I'm not going to bother with the guys at the bench, just go straight home. There won't be too many people there, so I'm going to take a long, hot shower. With so many people sharing the one bathroom, I can usually only take about ten minutes."

At noon I was surprised to see a group of my friends, sitting on a low concrete wall, in front of the park.

"Is the bench full?" I asked, "Is that why you're sitting here?"

"Four police were by earlier," said Jacques. "They charged five of us with having alcohol in a place other than a dwelling. Me, Irene, Silver, Mary and Serge were each given a ticket for a hundred and twenty-five. I've got them here in my pocket. I'm going to take them home and stick them on my wall with the others. The thing that makes me really mad is they poured out my wine. Now I'm going to have to get some more."

"How many tickets do you have now, Jacques?" asked Little Jake.

"Well, the first wall is full and the second wall is about half full. With these, I have maybe forty or fifty."

"I started a new batch of my rice raisin wine. It's very simple. The rice and the raisin give it the flavor. I use Sultana raisins, they're the best. I go to the store and buy a big bag of their cheapest rice, unflavored. I add some sugar and yeast. Don't use the little packets of name brand yeast, go to a natural food store and buy a bag of fresh yeast, it's cheaper. Me, I make four gallons at a time, but if you're just starting out, you may want to make just one gallon. In that case, it's two pounds each of rice, raisins and sugar. The recipe calls for one tablespoon of yeast, but I add about a quarter of a cup. I leave it for two weeks and it's ready. They say the alcohol content is 13%, but I'm sure mine is about 20-30%."

"They treat these like parking tickets," said Irene. "We don't have to go to court, we won't do jail time, but if we ever need to buy car insurance these will have to be paid. There's not much chance that any of us will get a car. They can't garnish our pay because we're on ODSP."

"I'm glad I was on a liquor run," said Jake. I already have a six month probation order for panhandling. Here I've got it in my pocket. See for yourself, it says 'soliciting in an aggressive manner.' I'm not aggressive, but if I get another one, or a liquor violation I could go to jail.

"Shakes was charged with vagrancy, even though he has a place to stay and had money in his pocket. I don't know why they would charge him with vagrancy. The charges have been stayed for now. We'll have to wait and see what happens."

Buck came along with Dillinger, a beautiful Golden Retriever, German Shepherd mix. He is four months old and very well behaved. On command, he sits and is rewarded with a doggy treat for his effort.

At various times people came and went. Chuck Senior stopped by on his motorized wheelchair. He gave Jake a baseball cap

"I think I'm going to go to the beach," said Jacques. On the way, I'll stop at the beer store for a six pack. Then I'll get some smoked oysters, a big bag of chips and some Clamato juice to go with my beer. Sometimes, I take my fishing rod."

"Do you ever catch anything?" I asked.

"No, it's just for show, so they won't suspect me of drinking.

"I don't want to catch any carp. It doesn't have much taste and has a lot of bones. The best way to prepare it is to boil it until the bones are soft then put it through a food processor. I usually make patties to fry, and have some sauce on hand to give it some flavor."

Stories

19 April 2012

Hippo said to Trudy. "I'll go for the beer run."

"Hippo, we gave you our money yesterday and you didn't come back. Do you understand how serious that is?"

"I know, I screwed up, but it won't happen again."

Chester came over. "I'll go for the beer run. I have to go to the pharmacy (*a euphemism for going to see his drug dealer*) and do some other errands."

I turned to Mary and asked, "Have you lived around here long?"

She replied, "Trudy and I have lived here about ten years."

"Where were you born?"

"I was born in Manitoba. I don't remember it very well. We only stayed there until I was four years old. My dad was a carpenter and a plumber. He got a job with the government doing maintenance on some of their buildings. For three or four months at a time he would be away working. My mother's health wasn't very good and she needed to be near a doctor. When my father would be away, we would move in with relatives.

"The Inlet was especially beautiful. We saw lots of icebergs and we'd fish for Arctic Char. Have you ever tasted Arctic Char? It's so good.

"My dad even worked on the Legislative Buildings. When I was in Girl Guides, they brought us there on a trip and I got to see my father. He also did a carving that was presented to the Queen on one of her visits. The carving was of an igloo, with a dog team and sled outside. The igloo could be lifted, and you'd see the people inside. It was very detailed."

Mary started waving her arms and got up from the bench. "I have to be very careful about certain types of flies. I'm allergic to them and have a strong reaction when I get bitten.

"Raven's coming over. I used to be friends with her, but she throws tantrums. She's always drawing attention to herself. I've got a beer under my jacket. The last thing I want is to draw the wrong kind of attention. She uses a lot of bad language and it upsets people who are just out for a walk after lunch."

I asked Raven, "Have you lived in the city long?"

"About fifteen years."

"Do you like living here?"

"I'm here. If I didn't like it I'd move, but I'm tired of moving. I have a lot of friends here. My sister also lives here.

April is a bad month for us. Our mother died last year. Her birthday was April 17, and she died ten days later.

"Sometimes my sister has to go into the bathroom she cries so hard. I call her my little sister, but she's taller than me. I've taught her some things. Let's say she's followed my example.

"I've got a husband, but he's not getting out until 2026. I just hate my sister's so called boyfriend. I hate him so much." She pounded the palm of her hand with her fist.

"I like sex, a lot. I have a room. My neighbor is always knocking on my door wanting sex. I tell him, 'Go away, I just want to sleep.' Then he'll come back later."

"I've just been sitting here chatting with Serge," I said. "He's been talking my ear off."

"I bet Serge has lots of stories," said Raven, "if he ever chose to tell them."

Protest

20 April 2012

Shark asked me, "Are you going to be at the park at 4:00? They're expecting about 2000 people to turn out to protest the prohibition of marijuana."

"No," I said, "I don't think I can get leave from work for that, but best of luck. I think they should decriminalize all drugs like they've proposed in British Columbia. In Vancouver they have a safe injection site. Drugs are available by prescription from doctors. There is a guarantee of high quality. Another benefit is that there aren't as many hypodermic needles discarded in parks, where kids or other people can become accidentally injected or infected."

Shark said, "I get medicinal marijuana, but if I run out early, I have to pay five bucks per gram. The street cost is ten. "I'm on ODSP; it covers my basic expenses, food and rent.

This month I bought a new television, so I'm going to be short until the 30th when my check comes in."

"How much does ODSP pay?" asked Inuk.

"The basic is about $600 per month to cover food and rent. Then there are other perks you can apply for. A friend of mine gets $200 as a diaper allowance. He doesn't need diapers, but he went to his doctor, looked sheepish, said he kept having accidents about four or five times a day. The doctor wrote a note for him to get a diaper allowance."

"Jake," I said, "you're quiet today."

"I'm still on my first bottle. I was sitting at the corner for the last hour trying to get a buck ten to make the price."

Shark said, "It took Buck and I an hour in front of the liquor store to make fifteen cents."

Bad Shape

24 April 2012

Joy was cheerful and sober. She said, "Only four people stayed at Toothless Chuck's last night: me, Chuck, Ronny and Chili. See this scrape I've got on my nose? We have this broom with a broken handle. I was sweeping under the sofa, and I hit my nose on the coffee table. I thought I'd broken it again. Chuck was ready to push it back in place. 'No!' I said, 'Don't touch my nose.'

"Chili is really in bad shape. She's smashing cocaine again and has sores and track marks all over her arms. She's on antidepressants, and I think she's taking more than she should. After just a few drinks, she gets falling down drunk. She's all over the place. Last night she wet Chuck's bed. He was really ticked off. Chili's adopted parents want her to come home.

"I said, 'What are you going to do about your arms?' 'Wear long sleeves,' she said. Another time she told me, 'My mother used to slap me every time I swore.' I told her, 'You better get used to having a sore face, because every second word that comes out of your mouth is a swear word.'

"I didn't go to support services last week. I was too messed up. I'll go tomorrow. Angela gave me all the papers I need for housing, except for my picture ID, the one from prison that says I'm on probation. Angela says I'm a really good candidate for the housing program because of my mental condition. It's the first time in my life that being crazy has been a help to me.

"I have an appointment with her on May 2nd. I have a court appearance on the 29th, because of my breach when I was in hospital. I told her, 'I better not get any more time for that!' I'm supposed to be finished probation in November, all except for my anger management program.

"In the last year, I've lost two houses and Big Jake. Jake I'm still working on. The last house I had with Roy was really nice. I have to go back there to get my check. Some things I'd like to pick up as well. I'm hoping that Roy won't be there because there's sure to be a fight, but it's all his fault. He and his girlfriend were just snorting too much. He was working too. He may have lost his job. If he wants money from my check, he's not getting it.

"I saw Clark scooting around in his wheel chair. I was surprised to see that both of his legs have been amputated. When I first met him a few years ago, he'd only lost a foot. He may have diabetes, but he's awfully skinny. Usually people with diabetes are heavier. It probably has to do with all the drugs he's taking."

Betrayal

I look into your eyes,
grey with tears and sorrow
from the Arctic Ocean.

I feel your hurt deep inside,
hear your thunder,
see your rain.

With your fist at your chest
you open your heart,
tell me of hardship,
betrayal and pain.

I listen
with my heart
as one who has been there.

With my arm around your shoulder,
as a brother,
I urge you, to act with patience
and with love –
to be love.

"Hi, bro! Remember me?"

I nodded. "Yes, of course, Alphonse! I met you and your
girlfriend a few months ago at the heater. There was snow on
the ground."

I sat on the curb with him. It started raining, so I pulled up
my hood.

"That's right. Magdalene was here just twenty minutes ago.
'It's cold out, Maggie!' I said, 'Wear my jacket. It will keep you
warm.' Do you think she would wear it? No, she was worried
about her image. 'Why are you concerned about your image?

You have a man. I'm right here.' She wants to look cool, like some of those gangsta rappers she sees on television.

"She's only 22 and I'm 40. She still wants to live the party life. It's the alcohol that makes her that way. She drinks until she passes out. Just this morning I said to her, 'Maggie, you've had enough to drink. Who are you dressing to impress?' She stormed off! I know where she's going and who she's going to see. This has been going on for about a year now. I know exactly where she's going. She's going to sleep with him, and he's going to give her money. She'll stay with him for three or four days until he runs out. Then she'll want to come back to me. This has happened about ten times in the past year. I'll take her back, but it hurts deep inside.

"What hurts most is that she's carrying my child. At least, I think it's my child. I don't even know if it's my child. She doesn't know — she's been with so many men. This morning she said that she was going to the nurse to see about an abortion. She was too drunk. Anyway, it's too late, she's three months pregnant. She's had abortions three times before and has a four year old boy who was taken away by the Children's Aid Society.

"I don't want her to have an abortion. I would raise the child as my own. I'd like us to be a family together. I would take care of her, but she wants to be in control.

"I never had a childhood. I had to raise my siblings. My mother was alcoholic. She was never around. When I was five years old, I looked after a six-month-old baby and a toddler, one and a half years old. I failed kindergarten two times because I was never there. I was looking after my siblings.

"Last night I told Maggie, 'We have to get out of this city.' I said, 'If you want, we could live near your family.' But she doesn't want that because she wouldn't have any control. She was raised by her grandparents; her parents were dead. They gave her everything. I suggested that we live where I come from. She didn't want that either.

"You're the first person I've told this to – that it may not be my child she's carrying. I feel better having told someone. I want to see that child born and, if necessary, I'll raise it myself. She has to stop drinking. One beer a night would be alright, it has nourishment, but she drinks Imperial Sherry, and never just one drink."

Picky Person

25 April 2012

I asked Joy, "How is your pneumonia?"

"It's getting better. I'm still coughing up stuff, my chest is tight, and I sleep with my head elevated.

"Toothless Chuck cooked breakfast for us this morning. Chili was too drunk to go to the Shepherd, so she stayed at our place. Chuck took her to the airport for her flight home. She said, 'I'll be back soon.' I said, 'You'd be better off staying there and entering a detox program.' Her arms are covered with track marks and scars."

A woman stopped to give Joy an orange, and later a man stopped to give her an apple. "I'll save the orange for Jacques. I can't eat them because I have a cage in my chest. The best I can do is suck the juice out and throw away the rest. Do you want the apple? In order to eat it, I'd have to peel it, then it gets brown and yucky. I'm picky, aren't I?"

"Joy, you should be a rich person, then you could have someone to peel your grapes for you."

Joy laughed. "Bruce got sick because of getting soaked in all the rain we had lately. Big Nick offered to take him in for free until he gets well. He offered me the same deal when I lost my last place. The only problem is that where Nick lives, it's infested with bedbugs. They're really hard to get rid of. I invited a couple of people to sleep over at my place. A few days later, I woke up and felt something warm and sticky on my arms. I lifted the sheet, and I was covered in blood. I was crawling with bedbugs. I had to throw out a mattress and rip out my carpeting before I could get rid of them. I'm really careful about who I hug now. They can lie dormant for up to five months.

"I'm going to visit the boys at the bench this morning, and then I'm going to my old place to check for mail. The postman usually gets there around ten. I'm hoping to get some of my stuff. I've still got two keys. One key locks and unlocks the door, the other only locks it. I should be back downtown around noon.

"I've been trying to phone Roy on his cell phone, but I don't get an answer. Where he's staying, with his girlfriend near the airport, he doesn't get good reception. I don't know what's happening with Harley or his three lizards. I don't care about the snake. Roy can give him back to Leon."

Silver was walking up and down the sidewalk. He had hidden his backpack in the bushes because he had beer in it. After getting a liquor violation last week, he didn't want to chance the police showing up again. On the other hand, he didn't want anybody stealing his backpack.

I was sitting on the sidewalk near Don. "I'm thinking of getting a part time job," said Don, "Maybe as a dishwasher or in maintenance. I've done that before. It won't pay very much, not like I used to get. When I lived in Montreal I used to bring in about fifty thousand a year. I knew the city really well and worked for most of the big courier companies. When I started with one company, they had just moved into Canada from the U.S. They weren't very well organized – too few trucks and drivers for the number of shipments they had going out. Even when my manager came with me — he'd drive, I'd deliver — we still couldn't make our quota.

"The run I had was in the industrial section. I had shipments of pipe and heavy machine parts to deliver. The truck was overloaded. Soon, the clutch burnt out. I told them what the problem was, but they still kept overloading my truck. After I'd burnt out the third clutch, they said, 'Don, we think you should move inside the warehouse.'

"I was feeling pretty burned out myself, so I took my severance pay and went on vacation for a while. Then I got into sales. I was really good at sales – everything from real estate and new cars to standing on a corner, with a table and speakers, selling all kinds of stuff. I was making about a thousand a day for a while. I had forty thousand in the bank; then my girlfriend left me. I started drinking, going to the casinos. I couldn't believe how fast I went through that forty thousand.

"This morning a guy saw me collecting bottles. He said, 'I got four cases of empties in the back, if you want them.' I said, 'Sure!' I traded in the bottles and got ten bucks."

Joy arrived with Jacques. "Hi Joy, how did things go at your old place?"

"It was fine. I didn't know what to expect, so I brought Jacques with me. I figured, if nothing else, Jacques could talk French to Roy, but he wasn't there. The locks had been changed. The whole place was cleaned out. It was a lot cleaner than when we first moved in. At that time, we had a disgusting mess to deal with. It was a lot of work just to make the place livable.

"I checked the mail. It's been piling up for a while. My check wasn't there, but nobody else has received theirs yet either. Now that I know Roy won't be there, I can go back tomorrow or anytime."

Anger Management

26 April 2012

Joy confided in me, "Everything's all mixed up. It's doing my head in. When I got the mail yesterday, there was a letter — here I'll show it to you. It says I was assaulted by Raphael Hernandez. I don't know any Raphael Hernandez! Look at the date, it says April twelfth. That was just a couple of weeks ago. Maybe, it's about that crazy guy that kicked me, but I didn't report anything. It could be that the security guard, across the street, saw what happened and phoned the police.

"If I do a victim impact statement, that will keep him off the streets for a while longer. He hasn't been around lately. I guess that's the reason. I'm going to take all these papers, drop them on my probie's desk, and let her sort them out. Angela has filled out the housing application for me; she said I would be an ideal candidate for the program.

"I really flipped at our last meeting. She wants me to take this anger management program. I told her, 'I can't be in a classroom with a lot of people. I'm agoraphobic.'

"She said, 'Can you explain that to me again?'

"I said, 'Look it up on your computer! Being in this office with you is okay, but if the door is closed, I may have a panic attack!' "

I asked, "Do you have an appointment with her?"

"My appointment isn't until May 2nd, but I have to arrange to see her before then. I need my picture ID and a temporary medical card. This pneumonia is really making me feel weak, and I'm coughing up some nasty stuff. It feels like my lungs are half full of fluid. I had seizures last night. I was shaking in bed; I got up, and was wandering around like a spaz. Chuck didn't know what was going on. He thought I was just drunk and told me to lie down. I really need my meds.

"I have to get out of that apartment. I went to look at a place in the market for $650. I could handle that. I told the guy I was on ODSP and that I would turn my check over to him.

115

He wanted first and last month's rent. I don't have that. I told him I'd pay him an extra hundred and fifty a month. That would really leave me strapped for cash.

"I'm not good at dealing with things like finding a new place. Big Jake used to do that. I'd be the one they'd see. It would be my name on the lease. I'd be the one to go out panhandling or whatever, but there'd always be someone else around to sort things out.

"Jacques helped me to get this telephone. I wanted one that played music, but that one was $200. Then you have to download music from a computer, upload it to the telephone; all that's too complicated for me. I decided to take the cheaper one for a $147. I've spent the last two hours trying to figure this thing out. The only thing I have been able to do is to change the picture on the front. See, now I have a kitty cat!"

A woman stopped to talk. Joy introduced her to me as Jenna. She was very attractive with short blonde hair, blue eyes and a beautiful smile. Joy said, "I still have that poem you gave me. The one about how to survive living on the streets. It's here in my pocket… No, maybe in my backpack… Here it is!"

"This is beautiful," said Jenna, "but I didn't give this to you. This is from my friend, Allison. I know this poem. We share things like this. We're both in the same kind of work. Take care. Here's some money for you to have a coffee or anything you like."

We both said goodbye to Jenna. "I'm so bad with names," said Joy. "They go in and I don't know what happens to them. They get lost, then every once in a while they'll pop out. It reminds me of something funny. It was while I was prostituting in Toronto. I was standing on my corner, a police car pulled up and the cop said, 'Tamara, come over here!'

"I said, 'Oh, you've mistaken me for my twin sister. My name's Joy. I just came here to tell Tamara that our mom is sick. We have to go visit her.' They'd believe it every time.

"There were lots of names I used, one was my sister-in-law's, and she's black. My sister got mad at me for using her name, but if anyone ever checked our picture ID, they'd see the difference in our sizes. I was really heavy then — 300 pounds and change.

"You see that woman in jeans that just walked by. When I was fat like that, they didn't have jeans that would fit me. I was the polyester kid. It was horrible the things I had to wear. Now, I weigh 110. I buy the skinny jeans, and they still don't fit. I don't have enough ass and hips to hold them up."

Sitting cross-legged, in front of the store, holding an empty paper cup was Alphonse.

"Alphonse, it's so good to see you. How have you been? Are you and Magdalene back together?"

"She's just down the block. We're back together, but it's not the same. She's still drinking. I told her, 'You can't drink while you're carrying a baby,' but she doesn't listen. I can't control what she does. No person can control what another person does."

Later, at the bench, I overheard Toothless Chuck talking to his dog, "It's okay, boy. I'll take good care of you. No, no, no, Daddy's not going back to jail. No, he isn't."

"I may have a place soon," said Little Jake. Those people who were by the other day were from the Salvation Army. They have three places for me to look at, but I was drunk. I don't know when they're coming back. That's the way it goes!

"Apart from that, things are going well. I didn't have to pan yesterday. I had enough money to have meals at three places."

Shakes pulled a woolen, peaked cap and a lumberjack shirt out of his backpack.

"Those are nice, Shakes," I commented. "Where did you get them?"

"I don't know where I got them. When I woke up this morning, they were in my backpack. I don't know how they got there."

Joy came up the sidewalk with Jacques. She had tears in her eyes. She said, "My check wasn't in the mailbox. I phoned, they said that everything had been mailed. Yesterday, when I took my mail, I left Roy's in the box. Today everything is gone."

"Have other people received their checks?"

"Almost everyone else gets theirs by direct deposit. I'll check again tomorrow, but if it isn't there, I don't know what I'll do. Today, I made $7 panning. I know that Chuck won't throw me out, but he's been talking with Bruce, who might come back.

"Now Chuck has a dog. I know exactly where that dog is going to be sleeping – right beside me. There's a space between the end of Chuck's bed and the closet. That's Joy's territory. If anybody tries to take that, they'll have to fight me. for it.

I was going to spread myself buck-ass-naked on the bed, flip through the channels on the TV, then hop back into the bath."

Two ladies pulling carts stopped by, the sandwich ladies from the Inner City Ministry.

"Would anybody like a sandwich? We don't have enough for everyone, so if you don't absolutely need one, please leave them for those who do. We weren't expecting so many people.

"Jake, would you like a tuna sandwich?"

"No, I'd probably just sit on it and squish it. Then I'd have to throw it out."

To me he said, "I have to get my first bottle down before I can even think of food."

The sandwich ladies also had socks and underwear. Joy got a pair of pink, bikini style panties and a pair of grey socks.

Joy said, "She first brought out this green pair with purple flowers. She said, 'These will look nice on you.' I said, 'I don't think so.' The only time I'd wear something like that would be during my period. If they got really messed up, I could just throw them away. Usually, I wear either boxers or go commando." She held the panties above her head and said, "Okay guys, have a good look. This is the last time any of you are going to have a chance to see these."

Shark introduced me to Spike who had just been released from hospital.

"I was in there for two months with double pneumonia. It started with a blood infection. It took four days for the doctors to figure out what antibiotic would stop the infection. By that time, it had affected my heart valves and caused growths in my lungs. They said that I nearly died."

Pink Bandana

27 April 2012

This morning was bitterly cold and windy. I wasn't expecting to see Joy, but there she was in her usual spot, sitting next to Curt.

"So, are you wearing your pink panties today?" I asked Joy.

"I had forgotten all about them. I was down here setting up, rummaging through my pockets, when they fell out on the sidewalk. The wind took them, and I went chasing after them. The cab driver across the street was watching me. When I caught up with them, I held them up and said, 'See, underwear!' He laughed."

Curt was asking Joy, "So when did you last talk to Big Jake?"

"November. Rodent has been sending him money and been getting letters from him. I don't even know where he is. Last I heard he was in Millhaven, but he may have been transferred by now. The last thing he said to me was, 'You're the reason

I'm in here!' I said 'No dude, you're the reason you're in there.'

"So is it over between you and Jake?"

"No, that story's not over yet, but we'll just have to wait and see what happens. He'll come looking for me.

"This weather reminds me of Winnipeg. Like that Randy Bachman, Neil Young song, *Prairie Town*, with the line 'Portage and Main, 50 below.' "

"I remember how I met you," said Curt. "I was panning once and I asked someone where I could get some weed. They said, 'Go to the park and see the woman with the pink bandana. She'll fix you up.' "

"Yeah, that pink bandana was my signature. I used to buy ten grams of pot and split it into three bags. I'd sell each bag as five grams. That worked pretty well for me."

Chantal stopped to talk for a few minutes. She asked how Joy had been feeling, shook her hand, put some change in her cap.

"I haven't seen Outcast lately," Chantal said.

"You're not likely to, either. He's either hiding out or he's left town. When you rip off a friend like Jacques, who's giving you a place to stay and feeding you, that's pretty low. I remember being at Jacques' place when Outcast was there. He was drunk and said some things I didn't like. I chased him down the stairs, across the park, then clotheslined him — straight arm across the throat. He fell back into the mud of the canal. If I knew then what I know now, I would have jumped on his head and drowned him in that muck.

"He was only at my place once, before I knew what he was like. Roy had his drugs and money there. I'd been responsible for bringing Outcast over, so if he'd taken Roy's' stuff, I would have been in big trouble. I would have had to kill him. That would have been unfortunate."

At noon it was still bitterly cold and windy. The bench was deserted, but across the street I saw people at the heater. I greeted everyone and Shark said to me, "We were here earlier when the security guard chased us away. We stood on the island in the middle of the street until he left, then we came back. We haven't seen him since. He's probably on his lunch break. We're on Candid Camera now."

"He chased Ian and me away," I said, "He allowed Ian to finish his smoke, then he kept checking back every ten minutes."

"I was talking to Joy on the phone," said Jacques. "She won't be coming here. She says she's not feeling well. She got her check today and was supposed to pay me the money she owes me. If she wants something, she wants it right away, now! If somebody wants something from her, it's maybe later, maybe tomorrow."

Shark said, "That's why I don't give her credit, but I have a lot of respect for her. I knew her from a long time ago. She's the one who told me about my first wife. She had thrown herself in front of a train. Our fifteen-year-old son is living with my parents.

"I don't see him very often because I still know too many people there. I'd be back on the freight train, as I call it. I'd be back in *the life* again."

Little Jake asked, "What day was it yesterday?"

Curt answered, "What do you mean? It was yesterday. What do I look like, a calendar?"

"The only date I remember," said Jake, "is Mother's Day. That's the 13th day of May. Am I right? I also remember my brother's birthday and my parent's anniversary, because I was just up there.

"Us kids had a really good time at the anniversary party. It was held in the barn. I say us kids, but I'm 41. My brother has three kids of his own. He did a lot of drinking at that party.

"When we were kids, I remember my brother and me going down to the creek and catching tadpoles. We'd use them for fishing."

"When I was kid," I said, "I used to catch sea lampreys. They'd be a foot or more in length. I had a long stick and would flip them out of the water onto the beach. Sometimes, I'd have half a dozen of them coming towards me at the same time. If they attach themselves to you, the only way to get them off is to burn them with a cigarette, or a lighter."

"Those are really good to use as bait," said Curt, "especially for pike. You cut them up, put them on a three pronged hook, throw them out in the water and jig with them. Now, I want to go fishing.

"Jake and I grew up in the same town. I moved away before he did. It's grown some since then. The last time I was there, I wanted to get some beer. The beer store is right beside the grocery store. It was still open, but I decided to go to the liquor store to get some single, king size cans. I arrived six minutes after they closed. It wasn't far away and I had directions, but I still missed it. I went back to the beer store. I thought it was open for another hour, but it was closed. I was so angry. Where was I going to get a beer?

"I asked a cop if it would be okay for me to set up my tent behind the beer store. They had some school busses parked back there. This was summer so they weren't being used. The cop said, 'It's fine with me. You should be okay there.'

"I was at the beer store as soon as it opened, and I was the first person at the cash. There was an old guy who is usually the first customer. He was really pissed off that I beat him.

"Jake, do you remember that old guy who was always the first one at the beer store? I can't remember his name."

Curt shifted gears again, "Irene, have you seen Miss Vickie lately? I haven't seen her for about two years. She had a bubbly personality, really fun to hang out with. She was pretty and had store bought tits. I remember how nice they looked in a sweater."

"We paid for those tits," said Irene. "She was working for me, so I got a percentage of everything she brought in. Curt, you wouldn't have been able to afford her. You would have had to pay for a hotel room. It would have cost you your entire monthly check."

"Well, we paid for the implants," said Shark. "The nipples she had already."

"Shark," asked Curt, "Did you ever get a look at them, since you paid for them and all?"

"No, Irene wouldn't let me."

"Remember when Weasel tried to carry her up to his bedroom?" said Irene. "He was so drunk that he dropped her. That was as far as he got."

Irene was pestering Shark, trying to get him to leave. She was pulling the strings on his woolen hat (*beneath which he wore a leather Maple Leafs cap*). She moved his backpack, so he couldn't reach his beer.

"I'm waiting for Buck," said Shark. "I have some business with him. You go! Leave me alone! I'll catch up with you later! What is it about women? They're so like... women."

When the Natives Get Drunk

30 April 2012

Today was check day, so everyone at the bench had money and had been drinking heavily. Outcast was sitting alone. He was still ostracized for ripping off Jacques. I sat next to Irene. I asked, "Have you seen Miss Vickie lately? She sounds interesting — pretty, bubbling personality. Curt seemed to have been really taken with her."

"Miss Vickie?" questioned Irene. "I haven't seen her since she moved to the townhouse." She used to phone me and say, 'Irene, do you want to come out and play?' She had no interest in Shark, just me. Sometimes he would get upset if I stayed away too long, but he gets upset anyway. This morning he was upset about something. I asked him, 'Is it because I took a beer out of the fridge? Is it because I took one of your packs of smokes? Is it because I took some weed out of the freezer?' I'm still not sure what he was upset about.

"Vickie and I used to do some drug deals together. The whole idea behind dealing drugs is to make money, not to become a user. She became a user. One thing led to another and she spent two years in jail. I switched to alcohol. It's a lot safer.

"When I got out of high school I went to college. I took my first year and was either going to go into legal or medical. It seems funny now, thinking that I would have gone into law, since nearly everything I do is illegal.

"I drove a cab for quite a while. I know the city really well. I also got to know people. A lot goes on in the back seat of a cab. I learned not to judge and to mind my own business. My dad had my car fixed with GPS tracking, so they always knew where I was. If I detoured off my expected route, they knew about it. If I ever had a problem, all I had to do was signal 88 and cab drivers from all over would come to where I was. I also carried pepper spray and weapons, but I never had to use them.

"The money I made was really large. At income tax time I'd sit down with my accountant and we'd go through my receipts. We'd burn most of them, and we'd pretend some days didn't exist. When I went back to college, I studied accounting so I could do my own income tax."

Shakes and Blaine were upset with each other because of a debt of $50, about which they disagreed. Blaine had been drinking a lot of vodka and wasn't very coherent, but he was LOUD.

"Okay guys," said Bearded Bruce, "let's keep the volume down. If you've got a problem, deal with it tomorrow. Today, is my last day before going back to prison, so I want it quiet and peaceful. Understood?"

Shark said, "That's what happens when you get natives drunk, you get a lot of noise. I used to go out with Blaine's aunt. Every time he'd see me he'd say, 'Where's my aunty? Where's my aunty?' He was an annoying little brat. He always wanted to hang out with us. His mother would come looking for him, and we'd hide him under a pile of dirty laundry. We must have done that three or four times. His mother would say, 'I saw him come down here.' We'd say, 'He was here, but he left a while ago.'

"Tomorrow, I run out of my HIV meds. They'll cover me for a week, but I haven't been able to contact my doctor to have my prescription renewed. The prescription is good for a year. It'll work out."

Shark was eating pistachio nuts and throwing the shells on the sidewalk. People walking by would be startled hearing the shells crack underfoot, or they'd think they'd stepped on a pebble.

Under two jackets, Blaine was wearing a Corona tee shirt. "I'm going to get that shirt from you," said Bruce.

"How are you going to do that?" asked Blaine.

"I'm going to wait until you finish that bottle of vodka, then I'll sit on you and peel that shirt off. You're going to end up in the emergency ward half naked."

Blaine pondered that.

May 2012

Jumping the Bus

2 May 2012

Shakes said to me, "Last year we were watching some people exercising in another area of the park. There were some military guys - cadets, I guess you'd call them. They were doing calisthenics. That's what they called it then. I joined in with them. I was able to keep up. My daughter yelled at me, 'Dad, get away from there!' I was hitting on some women, so they made me leave."

He held out a bottle to me. "Dennis, can you help me with this? My hands are shaking." Shakes handed me his drinking bottle and a bottle of sherry.

I asked, "Do you want it filled right to the top?"

"Yes, please. Could I also have some bus tickets? Sometimes I can hop on at the back door; sometimes I can't. Last night I put a handful of change in the ticket box and the driver said, 'That's not enough.' I said, 'It must be enough, I put over two bucks in there (*fare prices are now $3.30*).' He wouldn't move the bus. Some of the other passengers were getting perturbed. They said, 'For Christ's sake how much does he owe?' A couple of guys put some money in for me. Then the bus driver started moving the bus."

It's a Small World

4 May 2012

"Hi Joy," I said, "did Shakes tell you that he and I were panhandling yesterday?"

Shakes turned to Joy and said, "Yes, we went to my office."

"Shakes," said Joy, "do you mind turning your head in the other direction? Your breath is foul. It smells like you've been chewing on a dirty sock all night. You really should consider brushing your teeth once in a while."

"Okay, if you say so, Joy. I'll turn my head." He laughed.

"It's not funny, Shakes, you should start taking care of yourself, and change your clothes."

He got up and sat next to his daughter, Fran. Before long he was laying on the grass. "Dad!" said Fran, "Don't go to sleep here!"

I asked Joy, "How's everything? Are there still a lot of people staying at Chuck's?"

"Jeff is moving out today. Bearded Bruce signed himself into prison Wednesday morning. He and Inuk have been together three years, and she didn't even come home to spend their last night together. She owes Chuck money. She saw him Wednesday and didn't mention anything about paying him back. She said she's coming over tonight, but Chuck may have something to say about that.

"V, Chuck's dog, is going as well. He's a biter. I reached under the bed to get my bottle of water, and he chomped on my hand. I didn't even know that he was under there. With my free hand, I punched him right between the eyes.

"Barry, what was V's name before Toothless got him?"

"Star," said Barry.

"When I get home I'll see if he responds to that. He doesn't pay attention to anything else, especially V. I think that dog has been abused. He's only six months old. He shouldn't be vicious like that if he had been well treated. Chuck doesn't have the patience for him anyway.

"Yesterday he was talking to some guy from Scarborough. Chuck is asking $100. If the guy is at all interested, but can't afford the price, I think he should drop it to $50. It would be nice if the dog could go there. He needs fields and a place to run."

She pointed at me, "You'd better be careful spending time with Andre and Shakes. That's a sure way to get into trouble."

"I'll be careful, Joy."

"So, this weekend Chuck and I may have the place all to ourselves. I have to go to court next week about my breach, but my lawyer says it will be thrown out. I have all the medical records showing that I was in hospital.

"I saw my 'probie' this morning. She arranged for me to take the anger management course with a counselor one on one. That's the only way I'd be able to take it. Angela knows I can't do another prison term. The last time they had me in the psych ward, in solitary, under suicide watch.

"You may have noticed that I can be a bit mouthy sometimes. When I go through alcohol withdrawal, it's worse. You don't want to be around me then; I'm not a pleasant person. That would also cause me problems in prison."

"How is your pneumonia?" I asked.

"It's still there. I've been procrastinating about going to Public Health, but I need to go there to get my medical card. I could go to my old doctor. He'd give me a prescription for antibiotics, but I have a hard time dealing with him. He's one of those guys under a turban. Half the time I don't know what he's saying.

"He also checks my blood. If I go there after I've been drinking, my levels are normal. If I go there when I haven't been drinking, my levels are high. Go figure.

"My kidneys have been kicking me, so after I finish this bottle, it will be a dry weekend. Either that or I go back to hospital for dialysis. I don't want that. As it is, my sherry is so watered down, nobody else will drink it. Chuck calls it 'goof.' He and Shakes drink it straight. I couldn't do that now.

"When Big Jake and I were drinking beer, we got along fine. We used to drink Labatt Blue, which is 5% alcohol. Then we switched to Maximum Ice at 7.1%. That's when our problems began. It was even worse when we switched to Imperial Sherry at 20%. I could drink any of these guys under the table, but Jake just got mean and nasty. That's when he started beating me.

"We'll probably get together again. My 'probie' said, 'He's not allowed within 100 yards of you, or he'll go right back to jail.' I asked, 'When has a restraining order ever stopped him before?

"I don't want to be in a relationship with anybody. To have Jake as a fuck buddy would be okay, but I don't want to live with him again."

After work I caught my usual bus. I was surprised to see Shark and Irene. They were going to Irene's place, about four blocks from where I live.

Shark said, "I guess you missed all the excitement this afternoon. Shakes and Seamus were passed out on the lawn and somebody phoned the police. They sent three squad cars and the paramedics. They let Shakes go, but they took Seamus away. He couldn't even walk. They'll probably take him to the Shepherd to let him sleep it off.

"Joy has been after Shakes not to panhandle at the bench, since it attracts attention. When he lay down, she told him to sit up. His daughter, Fran, was sitting beside him. I thought she'd take care of him. I guess Fran went shopping. Everyone else just stood around, pretending like they didn't know what was going on. I've known Shakes for fifteen years, since we both lived near the Gardens."

I said, "That's my old neighborhood too. We used to be neighbors and didn't know it."

Shark said, "Shakes is slowly killing himself, but he doesn't care. It's his choice."

I said, "I spent my noon hour yesterday with Andre and Shakes. They were both staggering in different directions. Andre was saying things like, 'Drunk man walking,' and 'White man on a program' and 'Don't get in the way of my staggering.' We went to where Shakes calls his office. I sat with him for a while, then went across the street and sat with Andre. He sure is a character. I don't think he repeated himself once."

Shark said, "He must have had his rubber legs on. He's been staying up in Chinatown lately. Probably into that Chinese cooking wine. It's 37% alcohol. It's great for stir frying, but it's powerful stuff to drink."

"Do you miss living in Montreal?" I asked.

"Montreal has changed so much I wouldn't even recognize it. I'd prefer to live in the country. I studied horticulture for four years. I didn't do well with the chemistry, all those symbols. I like to grow things. Spike, a friend of ours has a place in Quebec on a lake. You met Spike the other day. His double pneumonia has cleared up, but he's still feeling very weak. He was looking white as a ghost. His mom is keeping a close eye on him. Anyway, he's invited us to stay for the summer. There is a row boat, a boat with a small motor for trolling. The only problem is we couldn't get any liquor up there. Maybe it would be good to dry out for a while. We'd still have our pot. We haven't decided.

"When I grew up in Montreal, my grandmother had a farm a few miles out of town. If any of us kids misbehaved, my mom would threaten to send us to the farm. We preferred to stay in the city."

By this time we had reached Irene's stop. It turns out that we're neighbors, living just five blocks apart. It's a small world.

Police and Paramedics

7 May 2012

On a low concrete wall near the park sat a large group of my street friends. This was unusual. A short distance away, someone was lying on the grass. Jake, Chuck and V were standing near the person who appeared to be incapacitated.

Shark said, "Do you see what they've done? Our bench is gone. We're stuck with sitting here in the sun. Even our wrought iron garbage container is gone."

Joy said to me, "Nick passed out due to insulin shock, so Chuck phoned 911. The paramedics should be here shortly. That's why we're here; nobody wants their bags searched, so we stashed them behind the wall. Nick should carry extra insulin with him, but he doesn't. Also, he hasn't eaten. He was more concerned with having a joint. The same thing happened at the barbecue Saturday. He has cancer and has pretty well given up on life. I'd never do that, no matter what condition I was in. I'm too much of a bitch."

The paramedics arrived. They loaded Nick onto a gurney, into the ambulance, then away.

A squad car pulled up to the curb near where Jake and Chuck were standing. Two officers got out. One said to Jake, "What's this garbage doing on the ground?" There was one plastic soft drink container and a plastic bag.

Little Jake said to the officer, "For one thing, it's not our garbage. For another thing the garbage container has been taken away and there's nowhere for us to put the garbage." The officer responded by pushing Jake across the sidewalk. He staggered and nearly fell.

Chuck was talking to the other officer. Joy said, "That dude has verbal diarrhea. It starts first thing in the morning and doesn't end until he goes to sleep. I'm going to get his dog.

131

That's all I need is for Chuck to go to jail and I'll be stuck with V. Did I tell you how he got that name? Chuck was drunk when he bought the dog. He couldn't remember what the previous owner had called it, so he just picked a letter from the alphabet. I don't even like him."

Joy walked over to get V. She said to the officer, "Look dude, my friend is on a lot of pain medication for AIDS. That's why he's staggering. He's very sick."

"And how would you know that?" said the officer.

"Because he's my friend, dude. I know the medical histories of all these people."

"Why is it you're not messed up like this guy?"

"Because I choose not to, dude!"

Joy returned to the group with Chuck and V. Chuck said, "I'm not going to jail!"

Chuck phoned 911 again and said, "Officer D pushed my friend, and I'm scared he's going to hit me with his billy club. I wish to make a formal complaint. Yes, I'll stay on the line."

Jake was forced to walk to the opposite end of the bridge.

Outcast said to me, "You should complain to the city about the removal of the bench and the garbage container. As it is, the closest place to put garbage is at the far end of the bridge. Also, the remaining benches are all in direct sunlight. You should tell them that you work in the area and like to sit in the shade to eat your lunch."

"I could do that," I said. I turned to Rocky.

"How are you, Rocky? Where are you sleeping now?" I asked.

"I'm staying at the Mission."

"You've really got a great voice. Has it always been like that? I wish I had a deep voice like yours. Do you sing?"

"A lot of people have said I should be a blues singer, but I don't sing that well. I just sing for fun, when I'm alone."

I asked Joy, "How was your weekend?"

"It was good. Saturday, at Chuck's place, we had a barbecue for Jennifer's birthday. She's Inuit. We didn't know that her birthday wasn't actually until Sunday, but it didn't matter. Her boyfriend came and Chuck's dad. Chuck cooked some delicious pork chops. We had macaroni salad and regular salad. I can't believe how much I ate. Usually I just pick at my food, but this was so good that I licked my plate.

"I have a real bed now. Saturday, Chuck will be leaving for a few days and he'll be taking V. I'm looking forward to having the whole place to myself. I'm looking forward to the quiet.

"On the 29th of this month, I have a court appearance for the breach I got while I was in hospital. My PO (*probation officer*) wants to meet with me after court, but she's going to be the Duty Officer that day. I could wait forever to see her. I said to her, 'Why can't you tell me in court what it is you have to say?' I'm going to phone her and say I'll come in the following day.

"I'm going to the Women's Center to have counseling for my anger management. I'll be seeing a counselor one on one. It's the place where chicks go for addiction treatment."

"Good evening, sir," said Alphonse.

"Alphonse, it's so good to see you! How've you been? How's Magdalene?"

He put his fist to his forehead. Lines appeared between his eyes that welled up with tears. "I'm so agitated! Not frustrated, agitated! Maggie is four months pregnant and tomorrow she's going to see about an abortion.

"That's why I'm drinking. That's what we do where I come from when things get to be too much."

"I understand, Alphonse; drinking helps to numb the pain."

"It doesn't though. I hurt so bad inside. I don't know how she can do that to my child. I'm hoping that tomorrow they tell her she's too far along; they refuse to give her an abortion."

"Alphonse, perhaps that will happen. I'm sure that will happen."

"I'll take care of the child myself if I have to."

"I'm a father myself, Alphonse, but I can't even imagine how much pain you are feeling right now. I'll say a prayer for you that everything works out as you wish it to. You're a good man, Alphonse. You'll make a good father."

"It's helped a lot being able to talk to someone about it. Thank you, my friend."

"Take care, Alphonse. My heart goes out to you. Perhaps, I'll see you tomorrow."

Are They Going to Mow Us Down?

9 May 2012

"Hi, Joy, I didn't know whether or not to expect you today because of the rain forecast."

"Yeah, it did rain a little bit earlier. I did my little rain dance, you know, 'Rain, rain go away, come again another day.' I brought Bruce's raincoat, just in case, but it was nothing to be concerned about. I don't mind light rain, it's those huge raindrops that I hate."

"How are you feeling?"

"Last night my stomach was doing flip flops. When I got out of bed, I threw up. I try to eat a bland breakfast, so I had a poached egg on toast. As soon as I got it down, I puked it up."

"Have you heard anything from Nick since the paramedics took him away?"

"He was fine once they got some insulin into him. Yeah, he's back. He's really pissed off with the cop, Officer D. He even tried to prevent Chuck from phoning 911. Nick is in bad shape with his diabetes and cancer. I'm not sure, but I think it's all through his internal organs. He's on massive doses of

OxyContin. The cop apologized, asked if there was anything he could do and handed him his card. Nick just flicked it back at him. He's going to press charges.

"Jacques told me that yesterday the RCMP (*Royal Canadian Mounted Police*) rousted everyone from under the bridge. They'd gone there to get out of the rain. Everyone was given liquor violations. I'm glad I wasn't there. That's the first time I've heard of the RCMP getting involved. I've always acted like, 'Nya, nya, nya, can't touch me.' I guess they can.

"I have an appointment on the 15th at the Women's Center to meet with an anger management counselor. It's better than going to the other place and being in a classroom full of women. I'd probably go nuts and kill someone. I don't like being around a lot of women, especially Inuit women like the ones who used to hang around the bench. The yapping would never stop. And they'd keep asking me for a drink out of my bottle. I had to learn to say, 'No, get your own. This is all I've got.'

"Chuck and I were talking about getting an apartment together, but the more I think about it, the more I think I should get a place of my own. Chuck has a heart of gold, he'll help anyone, but it costs a lot in groceries. Like the barbecue we had on Saturday. I can't believe the amount that Chuck eats. That's why he's so fat. He says, 'I have a big appetite.' I say look dude, that doesn't mean you have to eat fifteen times a day. When he serves me a plate of food, it's enough to keep me going for three days.

"We've got a problem with mice. Chuck keeps bugging the landlord about it. I said, 'Make sure he knows that you've got a dog.' V gets into everything. He's supposed to bring some traps over. He said to Chuck, 'If you keep bugging me, I'm going to throw you out.' Chuck said, 'I'm not going anywhere. I'm staying right here.' We'll see what happens.

A man stopped and put an apple in Joy's cap. Joy asked me, "Do you want an apple? I usually give them to Jacques, but he's getting too fat. He doesn't need any more to eat."

"Sure, thanks, I'll take it."

"I've made over forty bucks today. That's more than I've made for a long time. You must be good luck for me."

A tall, good looking black man passed by, smiled and said hello to Joy.

"Hi, handsome, gimme five," she said.

He slapped Joy's hand and mine. "One day he threw some folded bills in my cap. I spread them out. It was four twenties. I said, 'Hey man, this is too much.' He just kept walking and said, 'You keep it.' That's the most money I've ever got at one time.

"I talked to Jacques on the phone this morning. He said, 'So, little one — he calls me little one, because I used to be a lot bigger — are you going to come down and visit us today?' I owe him thirty bucks, but he's going to have to wait until the end of the month. That's what I was talking to Little Jake about. He's owed me seventy for about a year. I asked him about it and he said, 'I thought you said to forget about it. 'Dude, I didn't say forget about it, I said, shove it up your ass. That's not the same thing.'"

"Do you go to the library?" I asked.

"I used to go there to use the washroom. My eyesight is not so good any more. I'm farsighted, I can see things far away, but up close everything is blurry. Jake is nearsighted. When we'd be waiting for the bus together, he'd ask, 'Is that our bus coming?' 'No,' I'd say, 'not that one, the one further down the street.' "

"Did you get to spend a night in the motel?"

"No, I should have. Maybe I will next month, but who knows what's going to happen next month?"

"Hey, can you spare two bucks? That's all I need," asked Larry.

I said, "I don't have any cash, but I can give you a Subway card worth five bucks."

"Would you be offended if I sold it for two bucks?"

"Do whatever you like."

"It's tempting, but I wouldn't do that to you, bro."

Sitting or standing were about a dozen people. Handshakes all around.

I said, "We can all just pretend there is a bench here."

Jacques said, "They take away our bench; we're still here. They take away the garbage container; we're still here. They mow down our trees; we're still here. What are they going to do next? Are they going to mow us down?"

I sat between Jacques and Joy. "I'm really buzzed," said Joy. "Look at all the people here. Some of them I just can't put up with any more. Shakes was a good friend a couple of years ago, but he can't even speak sense now. He'll be asleep before you know it. Makes us all look bad. The last thing we need is to attract attention.

"This is one of those days when I'd rather not be alive." Joy was crying and started coughing. "Tomorrow I'm going to the Women's Center to get my forms filled out. They say it will take two or three weeks for me to get my medical card. They'll want me to quit drinking."

"What kind of symptoms do you get with alcohol withdrawal?"

"I throw up a lot, lose my appetite — what little I have — get the shakes really bad, sweats, nausea, headache, anxiety, rapid heartbeat, increased blood pressure, hallucinations. Last time it looked like the ground beneath my feet was crawling with bugs."

"I smell something burning," said Jacques. "Has Ellen fallen asleep with a cigarette? Maybe her clothes are burning."

Joy checked. "No, she doesn't have a cigarette."

Jacques said, "I smelled something, but maybe it was over there. I don't know. There is something falling. Is it snow? No, it's coming from the trees. It's green. Is that what they call pollenization? These green things fall on the earth and they grow. If they fall in the leaves over there, there's not enough light. If they fall on the grass, they get mowed. Is it the maple leaves that fall like helicopters?"

Ellen awoke and said, "Did somebody mention something about maple bacon?"

"That sounds like something that Chuck cooked the other day. Maple anything is just wrong. I don't even eat pancakes any more. French toast I'll do, but with only a tiny bit of syrup."

"They've got Honey Jack Daniels now," said Ellen. "That's good."

Joy whispered to me, "I'd like to kill her."

She held up her hand. "See my rings? This one on my thumb is a spinner ring. The inside stays still and the outside spins. On my other thumb is Big Jake's twelve step ring. Well, it's mine now. When we were in the jewelry store he asked, 'Do you see anything you fancy?'

"I said, 'No, not really.'

"He said, 'I saw you looking at a ring over there. Do you want it?'

"I said, 'Okay.'

"They're so big; I have to wear them on my thumb. Jake wanted me to put it on the fourth finger of my left hand. This other one was given to me by a girlfriend, Joanne. She's passed on." Joy crossed her heart. "It's my birthstone, amethyst.

"When I've been panning people have said to me, 'If you want money, sell your jewelry!' These are only silver. They're not worth anything to anybody else."

"I was talking to Outcast the other day," said Silver. "He feels like he's being pushed out of the group."

"Well," said Joy, "if he'd quit stealing from us…there's nothing worse than someone who would steal from his friends. Well, a jailhouse thief is worse. Everybody has their tiny ration of coffee or toothpaste. It really sucks when somebody takes it off you. If they get found out, they end up a pile in the corner, beaten by somebody's bitch."

Shark said, "Outcast was at Irene's the other day. He drank six of her beer, and every time he went through the kitchen he took some of my pot and put it in his cigarette pack."

Joy said, "I was at Jacques' place when Outcast was there. Jacques went to the bathroom and Outcast grabbed a stack of DVD's and was going to put them in his pack. I said, 'No, you don't!'"

Jacques said, "It was the next night that he stole pot from me."

It was time for me to go. I said to Joy, "They're forecasting rain for later on."

"I'm okay, I've got Bruce's raincoat. It even covers my feet. When I pull the hood up, I'll stay nice and dry. He's so big that it fits me like a tent.

"Before he went to prison, I told him to ask for the high protein diet. He's going to really gain weight there. That's what I've asked for whenever I've been inside. You get a lot of different kinds of meat and peanut butter. I used to put that in my pocket and save it until later, when I was back in my cell."

Luther and His Demons

10 May 2012

Joy was sitting with Bruce's raincoat wrapped around her knees. V was tied to a gas meter mounted on the library. Neither Joy nor V looked happy.

"Chuck has an appointment with his dentist and his probation officer, so I'm dog-sitting V. I'm not happy. V chewed a hole in my sleeping bag and generally wrecked the house. Right now, I'm ready to kill her. She's driving me insane with her barking. I told Toothless he should get rid of her. She's a biter."

Joy's telephone rang. "Chuck, your dog is driving me nuts. She's eaten all her dog food, all her treats and she's just knocked over her water dish for the second time... Oh, you find that funny, do you? She's scaring people away. I've only made two dollars this morning. So where are you now, and when will you be back? Hurry up, will you? You're still laughing! Oops, she ran away. She pulled the knot loose and she's running down the block. How do I know where she's going? Okay, she didn't run away, but she's your dog! You walk her! You take care of her!"

Joy wasn't wearing her spinner ring today. I asked her why she didn't have the ring from Jake resized, so it would fit her finger. She said, "I'm not ready for that. I think I'm better off living alone.

"I'm going to the Women's Center today, to have the forms filled out for my medical card. Perhaps I'll see you at lunch."

Ian said to me, "How are you doing, man? It's been a long time. My best friend just died; that's why I'm messed up like this." Marlena was concerned about the time, so they left.

I've met Luther at least three times before, but he mistook me for a priest, a judge, a radio talk show host and someone who ignored him at a bar. He is alcoholic, but he seemed fairly sober.

"I have ADHD, that's what they tell me. My mother is in hospital on a ventilator. I lied to her. I said I was coming home to visit her. I tried, but I was thrown off the bus because I was drunk. She wants to die naturally, like my grandmother did, but they have her hooked up to all these tubes.

" Do you see the police across the street? They're just waiting to arrest me for something." (*In fact, they were there to supervise an anti-abortion rally*).

"I'm a demon, I'm the devil himself. Will you hear my confession?"

I said, "Luther, I'm not a priest, I'm not even an expert on Christianity; I practice Buddhism. I'll hear your confession if you want. I've heard lots of confessions."

"Father, I don't know how to start. It's been such a long time. I've killed people."

"Luther, that's in the past, it's a memory. It's time to forgive yourself. I can see that you're a good man. You care for people. Now, is the time you can do the most good for others."

"I can't forgive myself. I want to be an artist. I am an artist. I made a dream catcher and took it to a store to sell it. The owner said it was no good, so I spat on it and left it. The next night his front window was kicked in. The owner thought I did it. The police came over and checked my shoe size. They said, 'No, it wasn't him.'

"I have spiritual powers, I've studied to be a shaman for my people, but I've lost my way. I need to be on the radio for an hour to explain my theories about how the system should be changed. Can you arrange that? We need a school for aboriginal children. Do you agree?"

"I agree with you, Luther, but I don't know anyone in radio. I'll do some research. I'll try to come up with some names. You take care, Luther. You're a good man."

I approached Shakes. "How are you, Shakes?"

"You know me. I'm always the same."

"Where did you sleep?" I asked. "Do you have a regular place where you go?"

"I sleep wherever I choose. If I feel tired, I lay down and sleep wherever I am."

I gave him some bus tickets. "Make sure you share those with Fran."

Fran said, "If he doesn't, I'll just wait until he's asleep and take them."

"You know your father well," I said as I left.

Women Rule

11 May 2012

I said to Joy, "I see that you don't have V with you today."

"This morning, Chuck said to me, 'V needs to go out for a pee.' I said to him, 'Dude, she's your dog. It was you that wanted exercise, so you walk her, you feed her, you train her, or you get rid of her.' I was so angry yesterday that I didn't say more than five words to him.

"I've got to get away from Chuck. He woke me up at 12:30 in the morning with the sound of him smacking his lips as he ate. He's always swearing, it's pussy this, asshole that, blow job something else. I said to him, 'Dude, if you want any woman to come anywhere near you, you need to do something about your hygiene, and brush your teeth.'

"He's a redhead, as you've noticed. I've never liked the smell of redheads. Even after he showers, he has an odor about him.

"I talked to Luther yesterday. He was acting weird. That's what happens when you drink Listerine and rubbing alcohol. The smell stays with you for days. He came on to me. He said, 'Joy, I've always found you attractive. Since Big Jake is in prison, do you think we could get together?'

"I said to him, 'Dude, I'll tell you the same thing I told you last time you asked me that. No, never, nada, it's not going to happen.'

"I saw Shakes, Fran and her asshole boyfriend yesterday. Did you see her eye? It was bruised and nearly swollen shut. That's why she was wearing the shades all day. She said, 'I fell.'

"I said to her, 'You're talking to a woman who was beaten on a regular basis. Don't tell me that you fell. I know what a bruise from a punch looks like.' Then she admitted that he'd hit her. It's a shame; she's such a sweet girl."

I said, "I've heard people say that they ran into a door knob."

Joy laughed. "Yeah, you'd have to be on your hands and knees for that to happen.

"I have to see Buck, so I may see the guys this afternoon, maybe not. Lately, I'm turned off with all of them. The only one who doesn't try to touch me is Chuck. Jacques is the worst. He said, 'Little one, why don't you come over to my place. You could even spend the night.' I said, 'No, dude, I'm not interested.'

"I have to pee again. That's another reason I can't have a dog here. I can't just leave her here alone while I go to the restaurant to use their washroom. I'm going to leave soon, so will I see you at lunch?"

"I'll be there. If you're there fine, if not, that's fine too. Do what feels good for you. Take care of yourself first," I said.

Serge said, "You know, yesterday I thought I saw you. I went up to shake your hand, but when I got up close, it wasn't you."

I said, "There must be someone else in town that looks just like Kenny Rogers."

"Like Kenny Rogers, yes."

"Dennis, how you doin'?" bellowed Hippo.

"I'm good Hippo, how about you?"

"You know, I'm okay, I've been around. I found this lawn mower. It was just sitting there. It does mulching, side discharging or rear bagging. It runs. I started it, but it ran out of gas. I'm going to try to sell it."

I met Juan, who I haven't seen before. He was wearing a cowboy hat with plastic flowers around the brim. He said, "I have my name tattooed on my wrist in case I forget it. I'm 65 and my memory's not so good."

"I'm 65 as well," I said. "I have difficulty remembering names, so I may have to check your wrist the next time we meet."

"I go to a lot of Karaoke bars. I love to sing. I was in the Pro-Life parade yesterday. I don't have an opinion one way or the other, but I love to sing and dance. They had some great music." He moved on to talk to Joy. They'd met before.

Larry said to me, "I see you're having problems with your leg."

"Motorcycle accident," I said. "I had seven breaks in my right leg. I have a steel rod from my hip to my knee."

"Do you still ride?"

"No. Do you?"

"No. I've had a lot of problems, starting when I was nine months old. I've got a bad back. I had learning difficulties in school. I have some mental problems. Now, I'm alcoholic."

Joy came up to me and said, "Dennis, could you do a big, big favor for me. I know it's your lunch hour, but I owe Jacques $40 and he's watching me like a hawk. If I give you the money, could you buy me two bottles of Imperial Sherry from the liquor store? It's $7.49 a bottle."

"Sure, no problem."

When I returned, everyone was standing on the corner of the street. Joy motioned to me in the direction of the lawn. "Police!" Joy whispered, "Someone yelled 'six up' *(the police are nearby, so whatever you are doing that is illegal, you'd better hide it)* and everyone took off. Most because they were carrying either liquor, pot, pills or cigarettes smuggled from the U.S."

Most of the cigarettes come from the American side of the Akwesasne Mohawk Territory, the reserve straddling the borders of Quebec, Ontario and New York state. The cigarettes are removed from their packages and put in clear resealable plastic bags. Natives, or someone driving for them, will load the trunk of their car with illegal cigarettes for sale in other parts of the province or central Canada. Legal cigarettes would have a government seal on the packaging to prove that Canadian taxes had been paid, and they'd have a cancer warning.

Irene said to me, "The cops were just talking; they didn't take anyone away. When I was leaving, the woman cop said to me, 'Don't forget the bag with your beer.' Actually I'd hidden my beer, but I had cigarettes in my pack. Since I'm native, I'm allowed, but it looks suspicious having them in clear plastic bags. I'd just say, 'I bought them at the mall.' You can get anything at the mall. Right?" *(The mall is a meeting place where illegal substances, and services, aren't regulated by the chain stores or the law.)*

Joy, V and Chuck we're sitting together. V snuggled up to Joy. "Now you're being friendly." Joy reached around to pet him and V bit her arm. "Did you see that? He bit me. He bit one of my regulars yesterday."

Joy said to Chuck, "Why are you being so cheesie?"

"Oh, now you're going to talk to me. You haven't said more than five words to me since yesterday."

"So, why are you in a bad mood?" she asked.

"I've only had a six-pack of beer this entire week. I've got no pot, no money, nothing to drink."

"We've got pot."

"You mean, you've got pot," Chuck said.

"I mean, we've got pot and I'll buy you some beer later. Now, stop pouting. Do you want a sip from my bottle?"

"That goof, no thanks."

"It's just watered down; it tastes the same."

"I got a bottle coming."

"If you'd get your sorry ass out of bed in the morning, you could come down with me and make some money."

"I will tomorrow."

"I'll hold you to that. Come 4:30, I'm going to be flipping the lights on and off. I'll be yelling, 'Chuck, get the fuck up.' "

Two young women came by from the a social service agency. Joy said, "I hate those bitches, especially the blonde one. When I was sleeping behind the dumpsters with Big Jake, trying to bathe in the washroom of the restaurant, they said to me, 'We can't help you because you're not a man.' They helped Jake. They helped Irene, and they helped Loretta. I think it's because Irene is native and Loretta is Inuit. I don't have my status card that says that I'm Métis (*one of the recognized Aboriginal peoples in Canada*)."

Loretta came over. She is a small pleasant woman, always polite, always smiling even though she has no teeth. Joy said to her, "You talk to that bitch."

Loretta said, "Sheena? I have to, she's my worker."

Joy said, "That group is the biggest fucking organization in the country and they do nothing. That blonde one is the worst. You see? She stays away from me. She knows what she'll get." Joy bared her teeth, hissed and snarled at the woman. "Of course, if I hit her, I'd go straight to jail. She'd better keep her distance."

Loretta said to Joy, "I heard that you're getting your own place. Would you like a roommate?"

"That would be great. I would have asked you, but I thought you were still with your old man."

"No, I kicked him out. I said, 'Until we can go for six months without an argument, I don't want to live with you.' Thank you, thank you, thank you. I'm so looking forward to moving in with you."

I thought they were going to hug each other, jump up and down and scream, but that may have been seen to attract too much attention, especially with the police so near. They were parked on the curb to see if people came back.

Joy said, "It will be so nice for a change, to have a place that smells feminine, instead of one that's full of men's farts."

I said, "Oh, I forgot. Women don't fart!"

"Not as much as men do *(it's been scientifically proven that men and women fart the same amount)*, we don't pee on the toilet seat, or leave the seat up."

"Women rule!" I said.

"You got that right, mister!" said Loretta.

"Joy said, "I just know that we're going to get along great. There are none of these other women that I'd want to share with, and definitely none of the guys."

"My boyfriend won't even be sleeping over."

Joy said, "I don't care if he does. With Jake in prison, I can't see anyone staying over with me, except perhaps Outcast."

"Aren't you worried about him stealing from you?" I asked.

"I've nothing to steal, except my bed. I'll go to the Mission tomorrow to see if there are any listings."

"I'll go to the Shepherd," said Loretta. "Thank you. Thank you. Thank you!" She walked away.

Joy said, "You know, she reminds me of myself when I was with Jake. I was always saying, 'I'm sorry. I'm sorry. I'm sorry.' With Loretta it's, 'Thank you, thank you, thank you.' I'll have to get her to stop that; it's getting on my nerves."

I said, "I'm glad to see you happy, Joy. I'll see you Monday."

Up on the Lawn

14 May 2012

Serge, sitting alone on the curb, in the shade, said, "Everyone is up on the lawn. I'm not so good today. I have pains in my legs and in my hands. It feels good just to sit here and stretch my legs out. It's because I drink too much. What I drink *(rubbing alcohol diluted with water)* costs me $2.35 a bottle. That's all I can afford, but it's not good for me. I think I have arthritis in my hands."

He stretched his fingers to show me how stiff and swollen they were. "In the morning, I have to hold my hands under hot, running water for a while, just to get my fingers moving."

"Have you tried hot baths for your legs?" I asked.

"I don't have a bath tub. I'm staying at the Shepherd now, but I have to find a new place. They have me on the Wet Program. I don't know why. I don't like it. I used to be on the other side."

Serge continued, "There's too much noise. One guy there, he opens and closes the door all night long: open, close, open, close. The man in the bunk beside me, he speaks French, so that's good, but in the middle of the night, instead of going down the hall to the bathroom, he sits at the edge of his bed and shits on the floor, not once, but twice. That's no way to act, shitting on the floor like that. I'm going to move to the Salvation Army. I think it will be better there."

"Hey, Dennis," yelled Hippo. "I sold that lawnmower. I took it down near the Mission. A taxi driver stopped and asked me if I wanted to sell it. I said, 'Sure!' He gave me $10 for it.

"Today, I got kicked off the street. A cop gave me half of a sandwich. Five minutes later, another cop came along and told me to move away from there. I only made $1.72, plus the sandwich."

"Hi, Joy," I said, "have you had any luck finding a new place?"

"Loretta found a two bedroom apartment close to downtown. She walked by, it looked good from the outside. She may be phoning about it right now. There's also a friend of Chuck's that would rent me a room for $450 a month.

"I'm not feeling so well today. Yesterday I was drinking vodka and cranberry juice. It didn't agree with me. You couldn't buy me a bottle of sherry, could you?"

"I'm sorry, Joy, I don't have any cash with me. I can give you some bus tickets, but I don't have any Subway cards. They ran out and won't have any more until next month."

"I probably couldn't handle the sherry anyway. The thought of it makes me feel sick."

I asked Outcast, "Did you have a birthday on Friday?"

"No, it was Wolf, the one with Shaggy. We had a party at my place. Irene and Shark brought over some spaghetti sauce. We sat around playing dice. Wolf, Irene and Shark left early. I've been eating spaghetti since Friday. I've had so much it's coming out my ass, literally."

Silver said, "I bet that Joy doesn't remember the first time we met. I was panning in her old spot. Of course, I moved when she came along. That's only right."

"I remember," said Outcast. "Crash Test was on the other side of the street. He'd throw handfuls of pennies at her. One time she threw a pear. It splattered all over the wall, and all over Crash. The pigeons loved it; they were all over him pecking at pieces of pear. He said, 'You didn't have to throw it so hard.'

Silver started packing his bag to leave. "I'm concerned that the cops will come again and I'll lose all my beer. I've got more to lose than anybody

When he was out of earshot, Joy said, "That guy really annoys me. He talks even more than Chuck, and what he says doesn't make any sense." Fifteen minutes went by and Silver was still saying his goodbyes.

"Hey, Silver!" said Joy, "I thought you said you were leaving. Why don't you quit saying goodbye and just go away."

"In that case," said Silver, "I'm not leaving, so 'liar, liar pants on fire, kissed the boys and made them cry.' "

"Silver," I said, "I think you have your nursery rhymes mixed up."

"Yeah," he said, "I guess that was Georgie Porgie. Oh, well."

Joy said, "Get out of my face, Silver, or I'll kill you! Silver, I will kill you!"

"Okay, Joy, take it easy." Silver quietly left.

Silver Concerned About Cure

15 May 2012

"How are you feeling, Joy?" I asked.

"I'm a lot better than yesterday. I went home, lay down and drank a lot of water. I was able to sleep most of the afternoon, until Chuck came home at 4:30. This morning, I was able to keep my breakfast down."

"How is it going with you and Loretta, getting a place together?"

"She's going to phone them today and hopefully we'll be able to see it this afternoon. It's furnished, that worries me a bit. I don't want to be in a place with bedbugs. There are mattress covers that have a very fine weave that the bedbugs can't get through. A friend of mine has one, but you can still see the bugs crawling around underneath. It creeps me out.

"Some people have told me that I shouldn't move in with Loretta. They say she can get wild when she's drinking, but she's cut back quite a bit. I think we'll get along fine."

"If she does get wild, I'm sure you can handle her."

"No problem there."

"Have you heard anything more about the funeral for Butcher?" I asked.

"That was a mistake. I talked to a friend of his and he's doing fine. He just hasn't been downtown for a while. He was in hospital and is still very weak. He prefers to pan on the other side of town, since he's been robbed several times near here.

"You'd think they'd pick on someone with more money. Panhandlers just make enough to get by. Whenever I get my check at the end of the month, you won't see me on the street for a couple of days.

"Silver is down here almost every day. I asked him, 'What are you hoarding your money for? Are you that greedy?' He's not here today, though. There was someone else sitting in his spot this morning, but it wasn't very long before a gray-haired man chased him off. I don't know what that was about."

I said, "I saw Nick panning yesterday but the police made him move along. The same happened to Hippo and Jake."

"It's the same every summer."

"I talked to Serge yesterday. They have him on the Wet Program. He doesn't like it."

"On that program they give you a bit of homemade wine every hour, sometimes it's watered down. Serge is used to drinking rubbing alcohol and Listerine. He wouldn't like drinking wine. He doesn't panhandle. I don't know where he gets his money. He probably has a small pension. He's another one that won't be around much longer; another one to add to the list."

A man stopped and handed Joy a banana. She said to me, "Do you want this? Since my kidney failure, my doctor said I'm not allowed to eat bananas. They have too much potassium."

At noon I talked briefly with Serge. "Hi Serge, how did you sleep last night?"

"I slept at the Shepherd."

"Yesterday you mentioned that someone was opening and closing the door all night. Did that happen last again?"

"Yes, he did that for a while."

"How about the other man who shit on the floor? Did he do that again?"

"I don't know. I'm not sure. I changed beds, so I'm near the kitchen. I like it better there.

"I hear they give you wine every hour. Is that right? Do you like wine?"

"No, I don't like it. They give me cheap wine, and the beer they give me has no alcohol. It's awful."

"How is the pain in your hands and legs?"

"My hands are worse in the morning. If I try to move them before I've soaked them under hot running water, the pain goes right down to the bone. I have pains in my legs, and I can't walk fast, but apart from that I'm okay."

"Can you talk to the doctor? Maybe he can give you pills for your pain."

"I'll just wait. I'm going to move to the Salvation Army."

A group of people were standing in a circle on the lawn. As I approached, I heard Outcast giving advice to Silver, "For your blood test tomorrow, don't eat after six tonight, and drink only water."

"What do you mean, 'drink only water?' I can have juice and coffee in the morning, can't I?"

"No, Silver. Only water and lots of it. It'll make your veins stick out, so they'll have an easier time extracting your blood. They love to see addicts come in because they have such large veins."

"Here, Silver," said Joy, "Have a swig from my water bottle so you'll know in advance what it tastes like."

Silver said, "My doctor wants to prescribe some pills for my alcoholism. If they make me better, will I have my ODSP cut off?"

"Silver, you're too far gone," said Joy. "You're not going to get better."

"Outcast told me that they might cut off my ODSP if I get better. If that's the case, I don't want to get better."

"Silver," said Outcast, "If I said that, I was only joking. Get the doctor to prescribe as many pills as possible, and while you're at it, tell him that you have a bladder problem and you need a diaper allowance. Wet your pants right in his office if you have to."

Joy said, "You can let a juicy, wet fart that stains your underwear. Wear white, so the stain shows. It would have worked great yesterday when you split your pants."

Outcast turned to me and asked, "Dennis, how long have you been around this area?"

"I've worked around here for the past five years."

"You wouldn't remember it then. This whole area used to be covered with bushes. Now, they've cut them back. Shark and Irene lived here for nearly a year. They had a tarp stretched out to keep the rain off. We could all sit under there and keep dry. It wasn't even visible from the sidewalk.

"There was a rumor going around about a tent city being erected; part of *Occupy Toronto*. It was supposed to start last Saturday. The city tore up all the grass, like they did last year. It's not so pleasant camping in the mud. I haven't heard what's going to happen next."

He asked me, "So, how did you come across this group? You don't drink, you don't smoke. Did you just stop by one day and start up a conversation with someone?"

"It's not that I don't drink or smoke; I just don't do it during working hours. I've known Joy for about a year and a half. She invited me here in January, to meet some of her friends."

Joy said, "Dennis asked me if he could buy me breakfast. He does that most mornings, when I'm panning."

Wolf called me over, "Dennis, you're really looking dapper today."

"I'm wearing Second Chance from top to bottom." (*Second Chance is a used clothing store, similar to Goodwill or the Salvation Army Thrift Store.*)

"I don't care what you're wearing. I just wanted to say something nice to you. I just celebrated my 57th birthday. I wanted you to know that. I'm more miserable and grumpy than ever. I've been really nasty to Debbie. Half the people here I don't talk to at all. I just like to come down sometimes to have a few beers, talk to my friends.

I asked, "How is Shaggy doing under her trailer? I can't see her."

"She's got her head out, watching what's going on. Trying to decide who to bite next. I won't keep you, Dennis. I just wanted to shake your hand, and I'm not sure I can get up."

Silver was asking Joy, "What's Debbie's problem? She hasn't said more than three words since she's been here."

"She's got the same problem I've had all week; she's starting menopause. Since September, my period hasn't been regular. It's all over the place — four months off, one month on. It leaves me feeling miserable."

Rain on the Street

16 May 2012

A strange-looking man was seated directly across the street from Joy. He was holding a sign that neither of us could read.

Joy said, "I don't know what that guy is all about. Earlier he motioned me to move on, but that's not going to happen. I've been here too long and fought too hard for this spot to take shit from some newcomer who doesn't know how things work. I may have to go over and talk to him."

A light rain started. Joy said, "If it's just small drops, I don't mind. If it's those big ass drops, then I'm taking cover. There is an overhang, so depending on the wind, if I move back to the wall, I can stay dry."

I asked, "Do you have any news about getting an apartment with Loretta?"

"I haven't seen or talked to her since the other day at the park. I don't know what's going on with her."

"Are you feeling better today?"

"I feel a lot better. I've been asking a few women, regulars of mine, if they have any spare tampons because I started today. Apart from that I feel fine. Debbie and I were at

Outcast's place yesterday afternoon. He made a stir fry. It was a bit too sweet, but really good. Later on, at Chuck's place, I cooked spaghetti. Rocky was really wasted on something. He had spaghetti sauce all over his shirt, his face and his hands. I said to him, 'Rocky, go to the bathroom and clean yourself up.' Before he got up, he wiped his sauce covered hand across the wall. Chuck hauled him outside and told him to get lost and never come back.

"Later, after supper, Raven said, 'Okay, where's the beer?' Chuck said, 'We don't have any beer.' She started swearing, so I grabbed her by the hair and threw her out the front door. She was swearing all down the block saying, 'You fuckin' bitch this, you fuckin' bitch that.' I just closed the door and let her rant.

"Chuck told me, 'I'm glad you did that, because I couldn't have.'

"Chili was looking better after being straight for the last month. I said to her, 'I'll bet your mom wasn't too pleased to see all those track marks on your arm.' She said, 'No, she wasn't pleased at all.' Her family is taking her to visit relatives, and then back home, where her parents live. It's such a shame to see someone her age so messed up. She's only 21 years old.

"I told you earlier that I was feeling fine. A wave of nausea just came over me. I'm going to have to go." Joy stepped into the alley and threw up.

"I'm glad I just had water this morning; otherwise, it could have been messy. I think that came from eating so late at night.

"Ann is staying at Chester's place now. He really likes her, but with Ann comes her daughter Trudy and her son Larry. That's a lot of people to feed. Chester has a couple of pensions coming in. He does all right.

"If it's not raining at noon, I'll be up on the lawn with the guys. I'm not going under the bridge. It's like a wind tunnel there. Look out your window before you come, you'll be able to see if any of us are around."

Playing Risk

17 May 2012

Joy said to me, "I don't know why I have to pee so often. Hippo's across the street shrugging his shoulders, *Again!* It's girl stuff."

"Does it have to do with your kidneys?"

"Yes, but I'm okay as long as I keep peeing."

"You mentioned before that it was a dark color. Are you concerned about that?"

"No, it seems fine. I think I just needed to drink more water."

"I saw Alphonse and Maggie last night after work. I couldn't tell if she'd had an abortion or not, but it was good to see them so happy together. Alphonse seems like such a good man."

"Yes, he is. I don't know what it is about Inuit women. Inuk went out with another guy the night before Bearded Bruce went to prison. An hour and a half after he signed himself in, she came down and expected us to be friends with her. Maggie acts the same way."

Joy and I were discussing a local bar that we both had frequented. I said, "My friends and I would often meet there for beer and spaghetti."

Joy said, "The last time I was at that bar was with Big Jake. There was a woman there playing pool. She was wearing a low-cut blouse and every time she bent over to take a shot, her boobs nearly fell out on the table. I walked over to her and said, 'I'm going to ask you nicely to stop flashing my old man here. It's very rude.' People don't need to see that when they're eating. She kept doing it, so I picked up the cue ball and threw it at her; caught her right in the middle of her forehead. She was out cold. The bartender came over and said, 'Joy, this is probably a good time to leave.' I said, 'Cool, dude. We're on our way.'"

"I'm going to go over to talk to Hippo," I said, "He looks lonely."

"I told him to use that spot. That's where Crash used to pan. As long as he's in that alcove, they shouldn't be able to touch him."

"Hi Hippo, have you found any more lawnmowers?"

"No, I found that last one in the garbage. It was a Craftsman 650 with a 170 cc motor. All I had to do was add oil and gas and away she went."

"Have you heard anything more about your inheritance?"

"No, I signed the papers last August. That's eight months ago. I don't know why it's taking so long."

A woman wearing a gray suit came over to us and said, "I'm afraid I'm going to have to ask you to move. You're sitting in front of hotel property."

"Okay," we said and left.

Sitting on the curb at the park were about a dozen humans and Bear.

"Hi, Shakes, how are you doing?"

"I'm getting there, slowly but surely. Last night we were up until two in the morning playing *Risk*. I finally asked, 'Aren't you guys getting sleepy?' "

Hippo said, "We used to play that game, my mother, sister and me. My dad never wanted to play. He'd go out to the garage. Another game we used to play was *Clue*."

"It's nice to wake up in the morning," said Shakes. "If you don't, you know that something's wrong."

"We were worried about Luther yesterday," said Hippo. "He usually joins us, but he just sat on the curb and fell asleep. We thought he might be sick."

"He's back on the rubbing alcohol," said Deaf Donald.

I said, "He also drinks Listerine."

"Both of those really mess up your mind," said Hippo. "I've tried them once, but never again."

Donald said, "I've heard of people drinking Old Spice, Aqua Velva, Purell, shoe polish, melted and strained through bread. I've heard of people huffing Lysol, Clorox bleach and gasoline. They're all poisonous.

"I've been looking at the plants in the flower garden over there. One of them looks like marijuana. I know it isn't, but it sure looks like it. If you grow marijuana in the woods, it's best to pick a place where there are a lot of trails. People looking for it can get lost, and if someone surprises you, there are lots of escape routes."

Donald turned to Hippo. "Where do you live, Hippo?"

"I'm staying at the Salvation Army now, but I'm hoping to get a place of my own. Where do you live?"

"Now I'm living in Mississauga. I have to take the bus in for my methadone (*used to treat opiate dependency for drugs such as morphine, heroin and OxyContin*). It takes me from an hour to an hour and a half to get downtown."

I asked, "Why did you choose to live so far out?"

"My mother lives there. I have a bachelor apartment with a fireplace just a few blocks from her. The place where I used to live, there was too much crack around."

Methadone

18 May 2012

"My tooth is really bothering me," said Joy. I was eating sunflower seeds, with the shells on, and something got imbedded between my tooth and my gum. I've tried brushing, flossing, but it's below the gum line and anything I do just makes it hurt more. I had a microwave heating pack on it last night. It helped me get to sleep.

"I was on my way to the dentist this morning, then I realized that I didn't have my dental card. I went back to the house, but couldn't find it anywhere. I went to the dentist. They wouldn't see me without my card. I said, 'This is an emergency! Will you see me now?'

"She said, 'I'm sorry, we can't see you without your card.'

"I said, 'Can't you check my records. You must have my number on file.'

"She said, 'Only Joyce has access to the records and she's not here today.'

"I said, 'You mean I have to wait until after the long weekend to get this looked at? If I threw up blood all over your computer, would someone see me then?'

" 'I'm sorry, ma'am,' she said. I was so pissed off.

"Hippo's there across the street. I don't think he's doing very well. I saw him get a few drops *(people dropping change into his cap)*, but I'm going to have to give him some pointers. He sleeps at the Sally *(Salvation Army)*. They have access to showers, soap and razors, but his hair is so greasy that I'm sure he hasn't washed it in a week. He couldn't even get a comb through it this morning. It was disgusting.

"He's one of the few men who don't try to touch me. He knows it wouldn't get him anywhere. Even Weasel, dying of AIDS, kissed me on the cheek the other day. He did it just to bug me. He still has that open sore on his arm. He was letting Bear lick it. He said, 'It's okay, a dog's saliva is clean.' I said, 'But dude, think of what you're doing to the dog.' His answer was, 'We all die sometime.' He's wasting away to nothing. He doesn't have much time left.

"I'm really careful about who I share drinks with up there. Did I ever tell you how Little Jake got AIDS? He had a fight with his girlfriend. She may have been seeing someone else, I don't know. Anyway, he was drunk, they had a big argument and she threw him out in the snow. He crawled into the alley and fell asleep. Sometime in the night he rolled over onto some used fits *(hypodermic needles)*. They were contaminated with HIV.

"I'm not sure about the details of how Shark got AIDS. He was pretty messed up on crack, and he was into some anal shit. When I asked him about the AIDS, he said to me, 'That's what I get from fucking a pig in the ass without a condom.'

"I've got Hep C. I think I got it when I had my tattoos done in prison. I'm a carrier, but I'm not infectious. It'll kill me, but nobody else."

Hippo walked across the street. We shook hands. He said, "Joy, can I buy two cigarettes for a quarter?"

"No, but I'll give you one." Hippo threw a quarter into her hat.

"Well Hippo," said Joy, "it's 8:20 and that lady hasn't asked you to move."

"I don't think she's in today. The guy was out sweeping the sidewalk."

"You're in luck then." Hippo shrugged his shoulders and walked back across the street.

Blaine walked by and said, "Hi Joy, I'm short fifty cents. Can you help me out?"

"I'll give you a quarter. Now, you're only short twenty-five cents."

"Thanks Joy."

To the world in general Joy said, "Yes, a panhandler did give him money.

"I'm really losing it. I wanted my mom to come to Toronto before she died. I want my kids to come to Toronto. My oldest son has a job as a cast fitter. I don't know what that is, but he gets paid $27 an hour. I miss them.

"I've got to get away from Toothless Chuck. He was on my case about groceries. Yesterday, I bought two loaves of bread, some of those frozen hamburger patties and some other stuff. He bought sausages. Last night he told me he's invited Tony and Dora, Butcher and his girlfriend and a bunch of other people over for a barbecue. I can't afford to be feeding all those people.

"He tells me that I'm not paying my share. I said to him, 'Stop inviting so many people over.' I haven't talked to him since. I pushed V out of the way, so I could get out the door, and he knocked over Chuck's table. I just left it. It's his dog; he can clean up the mess.

"I don't know if I'll be visiting the guys at noon. Maybe I will, but I'm not sure. Most of those people are getting on my nerves. I see that Lucy-in-the-Sky is hanging around with Buck. That will stop once her old man, Daimon gets of jail in a few weeks. He's the one that robbed Shark of his change, then beat him up because he had no bills. Then Lucy went after Irene. You've seen how small Irene is. Big Jake and I were still together then.

"When Jake heard about it, he took the plastic handle off a bathroom plunger, sawed the bottom off it, then filled the hollow part with dimes. It must have been a couple of hundred dimes. He used duct tape to seal the sawed off end, then unwrapped a metal coat hanger and wound it around the duct tape. That made quite a jailhouse club. The next time he saw Daimon, he hit him three times with it. Daimon didn't get up.

"I've talked to Lucy recently; she's so excited about her old man getting out. I said to her, 'We've gone toe to toe together before, but if you ever try anything with Irene again I'm going to smash your skull to pieces, and you know I'll do it.'"

At noon, as I was walking to the park, I met Joy and her friend Butcher waiting near the bus stop. Joy introduced him to me as one of her best friends in the world. I remembered having met him during the winter, but he's shaved his beard and looks completely different.

Joy said, "I've had it! I snapped at Silver. I snapped at Hippo. I'm going home before I end up in jail. Chuck is panning, so I'll have the house all to myself until about 4:30. I'll see you on Tuesday."

Sitting in his usual place was Serge. "Hi Serge, are you still at the Shepherd or have you moved to the Salvation Army?"

He said, "I'm still at the Shepherd. I have to go there between 4:00 and 6:00 to sign the card that says I'll be staying another week."

"Has it been noisy? You mentioned that a man kept opening and closing the door. Is he still doing that?"

"Yes, he starts at six o'clock in the morning, opening and closing, opening and closing."

At the park, Hippo wasn't looking very well. He said, "I've been puking up blood. I've also been shitting blood. I've got ulcers, two of them."

"You should go to the hospital," said Donald.

"I can't. They won't take me. I don't have my health card. First I'd have to get my birth certificate, then my social insurance card, then I could apply for my health card."

"Why do you drink, then?" asked Donald.

"Welfare asks me the same question. I don't know why I drink. If I didn't drink, I wouldn't be me. If I didn't drink, I'd die."

"You should think of your mother and father. They love you, don't they?"

"They're my parents, of course they love me."

"You should quit drinking for them. Think of how they'd feel if you died."

"Everyone is going to die, but I hear you, man. Can I stay at your place this weekend? I'm feeling really rough. I couldn't take another night at the Sally right now."

"Sure, man. I have to go for my methadone treatment at 1:00, but I'll come back, and I'll bring some beer."

Wolf said to me, "I haven't been here for the past few days. I had my 57th birthday Friday. I had a forty ounce bottle of twelve-year-old scotch that I started at 5:30 Saturday morning. I finished it by 12:30 that night. I also had some sherry.

"The next morning I had the hangover from hell. I'm too old to do that sort of thing anymore. I was here drinking beer on Monday, but I haven't had anything else between then and now.

"I just wanted to tell you why I hadn't been around. When somebody hasn't been around for a while, the first thing people think is that they're dead. I came here today to tell everyone that I'm not dead."

Donald said to me, "I have to go to the Addiction Center for my methadone treatment at 1:00. When you go back to work, I'll walk with you."

As we were walking I asked, "Why are you having methadone treatment?"

"My father used to beat my mother when she was pregnant. I was born three months premature. I was deaf and had to have an operation removing nine feet of my intestines." He lifted his shirt to show me his scar.

"When I was older, I had a lot of pain. They prescribed OxyContin. I was on it for seven years. The methadone helps with the cravings. I also got into other drugs and became an alcoholic.

"I had been living with my mother, but because I was into drugs and alcohol so much, she put me on the street. I'm 35 years old. I shouldn't have been living with my mother. Now, I have my own apartment and have more control over the drugs and alcohol.

"By the way, can you spare some change?"

"I'm sorry, man. If I had it, I'd give it to you, but I didn't bring my wallet with me. I don't have anything with me at all, not even bus tickets."

"That's okay. I'll see you next week."

Wild Night at Bingo

22 May 2012

I heard someone say, "Here comes Dennis!"

Joy came up to me and said, "I've been asking everybody if they'd seen you. When you didn't come by this morning, I was so worried. I stayed on the street until 9:30 thinking that maybe you had missed your bus. Then I began to worry that, because it was a long weekend *(Victoria Day in Canada)*, you'd been on the highway and had a car accident."

I replied, "I got a ride to work, that's why you didn't see me. I'm sorry you worried."

"It's just that I've never known you to miss coming by in the morning."

"How was your weekend?" I asked.

"Fine, Chuck and I looked at an apartment for $700 a month — a one bedroom. If I had been by myself I would have taken it. Chuck is saying to everyone, 'I don't know what I'm going to do if Joy leaves.'"

"That's understandable," I said, "You pay half the rent, buy groceries and do most of the cleaning."

"Chuck gets a lot of money from other people who stay over, more than I pay him. I think he's afraid of being alone. So am I, for that matter. Sometimes my brain starts acting up and I'm not sure if I trust myself being on my own."

Irene had streaks of orange, green and blue on her arms, legs and face after a wild night of bingo. She said, "Shark wasn't even going to get on the bus with me this morning until I cleaned my face. I asked Wolf if he had a face cloth, but he didn't. I wiped it with some wet toilet paper, but I only managed to smear the smudges; now it looks like I've been in a fight."

Irene turned to me. "What time is it, Dennis? I have to see my doctor at 3:00. Shark's gone to get his prescription filled. I hope he's not late coming back."

"Do you have far to go?"

"No. It's in the same building where I worked for the accountants and lawyers. I always wave at them as I'm going by their office. One of my cancers is acting up. I've had cancer twice. I only have half a nipple on my right side."

Joy was sitting on her backpack, looking at her ankles. "I haven't shaved my legs in a while. Do I look concerned?"

"I'm native," said Irene, "I've got nothing to shave. I haven't had sex for six and a half years, so I don't even bother trimming."

"I'm half native," said Joy, "so I don't have much to worry about, just a bit of stubble. I don't have sex very often, but I still trim, just for personal hygiene and common decency."

I wasn't quite sure if Serge was awake, but I went over and sat beside him. He raised his head and shook my hand.

I asked, "How was your weekend, Serge?"

"It was okay. I've been sleeping behind the hotel. It's quiet, nobody is opening and closing the door, nobody is shitting on the floor. I was drinking outside with a friend of mine at 4:30 this morning. When the store opened at six, we went there for coffee."

"You must be tired," I said.

"No." Shortly after, he nodded off.

"Has anyone seen Hippo today?" I asked.

Joy said, "Yeah, he was by earlier. I sent him on a run. He came back and kept wanting to drink from my bottle, so I told him he'd better do some panning and get his own. He seemed fine. He wasn't puking blood, like he was Friday. He wanted to get drunk, so I guess his stomach wasn't bothering him.

"I haven't had a drink for two days, but today I'm going to get drunk. I wish I could drink beer. Since my kidney trouble, I can't even stand the smell of it, but at least it would make me belch. This sherry is sitting in my stomach like a rock."

"Would you like some vodka?" asked Irene.

"No, I wouldn't like some vodka; it would make me crazy.

"Wolf isn't here today because Weasel kicked in his door. He's at home guarding his stuff. That's really ignorant of Weasel. It's Wolf's place, not his. The man is kind enough to let him stay there, and that's the way he repays him. Weasel is really something else."

The rain started, slowly at first. We moved under the trees, then it started to pour. The trees were no protection at all. Little Jake and Jacques left to take cover under the overpass. Irene put up her umbrella. Joy put on Bearded Bruce's raincoat. "Bruce's in prison, he doesn't need this, but I do. He signed himself in. He got 180 days for two counts of trying to sell crack to an undercover cop. If it was me, I would have gotten years. Once he does his time and pays his fines, he'll be in the clear. That's better than trying to run."

Chester said, "I'm going to go home now."

"Do you need bus tickets?" asked Joy. "I wouldn't like to see you walking all the way home in this rain."

"Thanks, Joy, I'd appreciate that."

Serge had taken refuge in a glass bus shelter and was fast asleep.

There's Something About the Number Five

23 May 2012

"This morning has been slow, said Joy. "Yesterday, I made $19. So far today, I've only made $5 and I've been here since 6:00. Come on people!"

Chantal stopped by to talk with Joy. She squatted, put some change in Joy's cap, then put her hand on Joy's shoulder. "How are you doing, Joy?"

"I'm fine."

"Are you eating well?"

"Yes, I'm eating well."

"You mentioned that you were looking at a new apartment tomorrow. Is that still on?"

"Yeah, Chuck and I are going over tomorrow to have a look at it. It's a one bedroom for $700 a month. It's just down a block from the one we're in now."

"You take care, Joy."

When she left, Joy said to me. "She's really beautiful. That's the religious lady. Last fall when I was beaten by Big Jake, and I had the broken nose and broken ribs, she prayed with me. I felt a warm glow spreading through my body. For the first time in a week, I could take a full breath without chest pain. I'm not a religious person — well, I used to be a Catholic, but I haven't been to church for a long time. It really spooked me. I felt better all day.

"There's something about the number five. I have five boys. The marriage to my first husband lasted five years. Jake and I broke up after five years.

"I don't want to live with Chuck. He wants me to go over and see about the apartment, but I'm going to let him go by himself. I'll phone back later in the week, talk to the lady, and maybe take it myself. Toothless and I are always arguing. He feeds so many people, and I just can't afford that.

"Hippo found a bicycle, that's it over there." She pointed to a blue bike in the bicycle rack. "I told him it looks like one of those bait bicycles. The police put them out every so often. If you're caught riding one, you're charged with theft."

"Is it locked?" I asked.

"It has a lock on it, but the lock isn't fastened. It only looks like it's locked. I can just imagine Hippo riding that. One good thing about having a bicycle is that it will help him lose weight.

"I brought him some soap and some shampoo. He said at the Shepherd they only give them a tiny bit to last for a week. That's why his hair looks greasy. People sometimes drop off s hotel soap and shampoo for me. I don't know why. Do they think I'm dirty?"

Hippo walked across the street. "Hi Hippo," I said. "How are you feeling?"

"Not so good. I was out drinking with Andre and we got into some bad stuff. I don't want to talk about it."

Joy asked, "What were you drinking, Hippo? If you were with Andre, it could have been Listerine or rubby *(rubbing alcohol)*. Which was it?"

"Rubby."

"Hippo, you know that stuff will kill you."

"I'm going off to do some things on my own," said Hippo. Joy said, "I don't even want to think about what that is."

After Hippo left, Joy said, "I've sunk pretty low, but I've never drunk Listerine or rubbing alcohol. Now they sell Listerine without alcohol. I don't know where Serge gets his. I can't stand to be near him. He reeks of the stuff. Lately, he's been acting funny. All he seems do is sleep *(a side effect of drinking rubbing alcohol or alcohol based mouthwash)*."

"Yesterday," I said, "Irene was complaining about leg pain. Does that have to do with her cancer?"

"I don't know what the leg pain is about. Yesterday, because she was wearing capris, I noticed how skinny her legs are. She had breast cancer and cancer of the uterus. She also has cirrhosis of the liver. It's because of the uterine cancer that she doesn't have sex with Shark. It's too painful for her. He goes off somewhere and pays for it. She's cool with that. Shark and Irene have been together eleven years. I think they had sex once."

"You mentioned that you lost a lot of weight. How did you do that?"

"When I came back from Winnipeg, I weighed about 365 pounds. My doctor told me it was unhealthy to be carrying that much weight, so I decided to eat only on Sundays. I wouldn't eat anything during the week. I drank lots of water. On Sunday, I'd go to the Mission and pig out all day until I was stuffed."

I noticed Clint, a man I work with, approaching. I said to Joy that Clint was going to Disneyland.

"Do you know what I love from Disneyland? It's the soap that's shaped like a urinal puck. On one side there is a picture of Mickey Mouse. They have them in all the rooms. I love the smell and it's so good for my skin."

I called Clint over and introduced him to Joy. I said, "Clint, when you go to Disneyland, will you bring Joy some of the soap that is in the hotel rooms?"

"Why?" asked Clint.

Joy replied, "It's not because I'm dirty; it's just that I love the smell of that soap. So, will you bring me some?"

"Okay."

I said, "Bye, Clint. I'll see you at work."

At the park, Wolf called me over, "I want to show you my Tilley hat. It's considered the Rolls Royce of hats. A friend gave it to me. Can you read without your glasses? I want you to read what's printed inside the hat."

"It says that it floats, it's waterproof, and it's made for persnickety customers. It also gives washing instructions. There's a four page owner's manual in the secret pocket, inside the crown of the hat."

"What does persnickety mean?"

"Picky," I said.

"Isn't that the darndest thing?"

Joy and Butcher were talking about V. I asked, "How long did you have to look after V this morning?"

"Chuck came back after about half an hour. He has him now. He's panning. I don't like that dog, but he respects me. If he bites, I snap my fingers on his nose and he'll obey. Chuck kicks him."

Butcher said, "I don't like the way Chuck treats V. He jerked the dog right off his feet for not obeying some command. If a man treats a dog that way, he's sure to beat a woman."

Joy said, "I can say one thing in Chuck's defense. He's never hit me and I'm not aware of him hitting any other woman. Trudy went out with him before, I'll ask her.

"Trudy, when you were going out with Chuck, did he ever hit you?"

Trudy said, "No, Chuck never hit me. Is Butcher starting a rumor that Chuck hit me? Don't believe a word he says. He's the one that started the rumor about Nick being dead."

"Okay," said Butcher, "This needs an explanation. Trudy has been going on about this for ten years. I don't know why she holds on to it. Why can't she move on? I have!

"She'd been going out with Nick for about three years. I'd known him for forty years. We grew up together. I hadn't seen him around for a while and my friend, Steve, said to me, 'Did you hear about Nick? The funeral is on Tuesday in Oshawa.'

"I'm not good at funerals. I went to the service, but at the wake, I didn't go near the body. Why would I? My own daughter died and I still haven't visited the grave site. I'd rather remember the good times we had together.

"Back to the wake. I expressed my condolences to Nick's parents and family, then I left. Later on someone asked me if I'd heard from Nick and I said, 'He died. I attended his funeral.' This person said, 'Nick didn't die, he was arrested and is serving two years. It was his brother Roger who died.' I didn't know.

"Getting back to Trudy, it was Steve who told her that Nick had died, not me."

As I was leaving I stopped to talk to Shark and Irene. Shark said, "My friend Wayne phoned me. He wants us to come to New Brunswick to help him finish a log cabin he's building. The trees he cut are from his own property. The logs are stacked and have been drying since last year. They'll have to be peeled, then he'll start building. He wants us to come up to help with the chinking, shellacking, and all the finishing stuff. It'll be a paid vacation. I'm thinking of going."

"I'm going for sure," said Irene, "whether you come or not."

New Shoes for Shakes

24 May 2012

"Hi Dennis" said Jake. Joy told me she wouldn't be here this morning, so I could use her spot. She'll be down later. There was a woman who passed here earlier. She asked me, 'Don't I usually see you on the bridge?'

"I said, 'Yeah, I'm there most days.'

"She said 'I'm the one who phoned 911 when you were passed out on the grass.'

"I said, 'Thank you.' That was the time they took me to the hospital. She asked if she could buy me breakfast. I said, 'No, but a coffee would be nice.' Alcoholics don't usually drink in the morning."

"How are you feeling?"

"I'm not feeling too good. I should have my meds. I don't have a health card. Either the police have my cards or the hospital has them. I'm not sure which. Three times the cops have taken my identification and not given it back.

"I got kicked out of my place, so I'm back on the street again. I was staying at an apartment in Cabbagetown. It was mostly crusty old drunks. I know you're 65, but these guys are really old -- You know, I was talking to Shakes yesterday. I found out that he's only 46. That's only five years older than me. I couldn't believe it."

"I can't believe it either. I was talking to him the other day and he said, 'It's nice waking up in the morning. If I don't, I know something's wrong,'"

Jake said, "Anyway, I got a noise complaint my first day there. Since then I could just feel that they didn't like me. You know that feeling, when you just don't fit in? As I was walking past the super's office he called me in. He said to me, 'We've had complaints' — there was only the one — 'and we'd like you to move out. If you leave now I'll give you back half your month's rent.'

"I said to him, 'Can I have a day?'

"He said, 'Sure.' He had a forty ounce bottle of vodka and a twenty-six of Grand Marnier on the top of his desk. He always has them there."

I said, "Grand Marnier and vodka would be nice. The Grand Marnier by itself would be too sweet."

Little Jake continued, "When I was a chef, I used it for flambés. You know, I'd throw some in the frying pan and it'd catch fire. I worked as a chef for quite a while."

"I've used sherry for cooking. I've made sherried crepes. My kids loved them," I said.

"I had a good job, as a waiter," said Jake, "in a really high-class, snooty restaurant. You know — white tuxedo shirt, black pants, a vest. I was good-looking then. Still had all my teeth. I was only 22 at the time. One night, it was really slow. Only one table was filled. I was there every time they needed a cigarette lit. Every time a plate was empty, I took it away. Water glasses were always filled. I really did my job to perfection. They left me a tip of a 150 bucks. Can you believe that? I was in big money back then.

"Anyway, back to Cabbagetown, where I was staying. I thought about it for a while and said, 'Fuck it. I don't want to stay where I'm not wanted.' I went down to the super's office and said to him, 'Give me my money. I'll be gone in an hour.' I left a lot of stuff there, my dream catchers, my wolf pictures, the food in my kitchen.

"So, I'm out on the street now. I spent last night sleeping by the heater. I didn't have a sleeping bag, just the clothes I'm wearing now. Somehow, I scraped my arm. I don't know how that happened. Wolf and Shaggy were there as well. The first thing Wolf said to me was, 'Jake, am I ever glad to see you. Now, I can get some sleep.' You know, he acts all tough, but he's really a pussy cat."

"Was Shaggy barking?"

"No, she was tired, just wanted to sleep. She's over ten years old. She mostly barks when there are other dogs, or skateboarders around. Bear barks at Brinks trucks. They have a distinctive horn that goes, *beep, beep*. Weasel used to know one of the drivers. He'd beep his horn, open the door and throw a cookie to Bear. Every time the dog hears that horn, she starts to bark. She thinks she's going to get a cookie. When she sees a hot air balloon, she goes wild. I don't know what that's about."

"I heard that Weasel kicked Wolf's door in. He was at home guarding his stuff until the door was repaired. I wonder if anything else happened?"

"The night before last, I stayed at Weasel's place. He thinks I'm going to stay there for a while, but I wouldn't stay in a mess like that. I've lived with him before."

"Has he got his window fixed? I heard that he had a broken basement window for most of the winter."

Jake said, "Yeah, they fixed it. Do you know how that happened? He cheated some guy on a drug deal. The guy came back and threw a brick through his window."

"Tell me about your wolf pictures."

"When I was on my hiatus — when I stayed sober for a month at my parent's place — I took up painting again. I painted a picture of a wolf on black velvet. It was about two by three feet. After I left, my parents had it framed. It's hanging on their wall now. I've never actually seen it framed. So, what I have is a photograph of my painting."

"You went for a reunion there, didn't you?"

"Yeah, last summer. It was my grandparent's 60th wedding anniversary. I saw my brother for the first time in thirteen years. He's living in Winnipeg. Works as a letter carrier with the Post Office. He's also a licensed mechanic. His wife is a teacher. Between them they bring in a lot of money.

"I should get back there. I've hitchhiked there hundreds of times, but now that they've made it four lanes, and it's an expressway, the cops are always patrolling. You know the expression, 'There's never a cop around when you need one?' Well, there's always a cop around when I'm hitching."

Chester came by looking for cigarette butts on the sidewalk. Jake said to him, "I've got one here. It's only half smoked." Shortly after, Serge came by looking for butts. "Sorry Serge, Chester beat you to it. He's already collected them all."

At the park Shark came over to me and said, "Do you see Shakes' new shoes? They're my old ones. Shakes, show Dennis your new shoes!"

I said, "They look great, Shakes — a lot better than the ones you were wearing yesterday with the red duct tape on the toe."

I walked over to Donald and asked, "Did you take good care of Hippo on the weekend?"

"He didn't come," said Donald, "We were both drunk. We took the bus. We got off at a stop right near my place. I turned around and he was gone. I was really upset."

Hippo just shrugged his shoulders.

I said to Hippo, "You haven't been drinking bad stuff with Andre, have you?"

"No, I'm sticking to beer for now."

Donald said, "I told Hippo that he is invited to come over to my place this coming weekend. I'm going to barbecue steaks. You're going to come, aren't you, Hippo?"

"I'll be there."

Donald said, "Trudy told me that she had seen my girlfriend, and that she's alright. I'm so relieved. She also said that she still loves me. If she loves me, why doesn't she phone me or visit me? Does she think I'll be angry? She left me for three weeks, but I forgive her. Does she think I'm going to hit her? I'm not a woman beater. I hate men who do that. That's the reason I'm deaf and have this scar." He lifted his tee-shirt to expose the scar crossing his stomach. "It was because my mother was beaten that I was born three and a half months premature. I weighed just over four pounds. My aunt could hold me in one hand. My mother was fifteen years old when she was pregnant. Several days before I was born she had her sixteenth birthday.

"She's 51 now, is very attractive and very smart. She works in the Library Building. I'm going to meet her at one o'clock. When people see us together, they think that she is my twin sister."

Donald asked me, "Do you read the Catholic Bible?"

I said, "No, I'm not very familiar with it. I read a lot about Buddhism."

"It doesn't matter what religion we are, whether we're Catholic, Anglican, Jehovah's Witness or Baptist. We all believe in the same God, or a higher power. We're all the same. Within us all of us is good and bad. We just have to choose the good."

I said, "There is an American Indian legend about a grandfather giving advice to his grandson. The grandfather said, 'I have two wolves fighting in my heart. One wolf is the vengeful, angry, violent one. The other is the loving, compassionate one.' When his grandson asked which wolf will win, the grandfather answered, 'The one I feed.' "

"That is very wise," Donald said. "I was in prison for sixteen months, and I had a lot of time to read the Bible. I learned that to understand it, you have to read the end first, then the middle, then the beginning. That way it makes more sense. There are certain things in the Bible that I don't believe. I don't believe that hell is a place with fire, brimstone and red devils with pitch forks. I believe that hell is right here on earth. Wars, famine, sickness; that's hell. I try to live a good life so that on Judgment Day, I'll go up there." He pointed to the sky. "Every minute people die and people are born. I believe that when we die, we go into another body. Not right away, but eventually. When you look up to the stars, it goes on forever. Maybe, we go to another planet. Who knows?"

Hippo

25 May 2012

As Joy and I were sitting on the sidewalk, Chantal stopped by. She asked Joy, "Did you have a look at the apartment you were telling me about?"

"Yes, Chuck went over. He said it's beautiful. It's on the second floor. It's furnished, utilities are included. We just have to pay for cable. There's a deck in front and a deck outside my bedroom. Chuck is going to sleep in the living room. It's $700 a month."

"What's the location?"

"It's near the market, just a few blocks from where we're living now."

"It sounds ideal."

"It is. Chuck has already said we'll take it. The owner has to speak to his partner before he can confirm. If everything goes okay, I'll move in right away. Chuck's check goes directly to our present landlord, so he'll have to have that transferred, then he can move in.

"So, Chantal, do you have any big plans for the weekend?"

She answered, "I'm running. Saturday is the big 10k Race. If you want, you could meet me at the finish line. I could use some cheering and support. Later, we could go for a coffee or something."

"Sounds great," Joy said.

"I have to be at work soon, so maybe I'll see you Saturday."

We both said goodbye to Chantal. "She's such a nice lady," said Joy.

"If I'd seen that place on my own, I would have taken it for myself. Chuck is afraid of living alone, and I've been feeling really hyper lately. I didn't see the guys yesterday because some of them are getting on my nerves. I thought if I went there, I'd get in a fight, then go to jail. I just wanted to relax. I've had these weird feelings lately that I want to cut myself."

I asked, "When I arrived Wednesday noon, you were arguing with someone. What was that about?"

"That was low life, Gerry, the wife beater, down in the park. He usually drinks Purell, but he had a bottle of sherry right out in the open. The security guard came along. Gerry told him that his bottle was sealed — it was half empty. The guard poured the sherry out on the grass. I was just standing there, at the railing. Gerry said to me, 'Fuck off Joy! If you didn't have all those guys around, I'd come up there and beat the shit out of you.'

"That made me mad. I said, 'I don't need any help to cut a woman beater like you down to size. I fight a lot better than the women you've taken on. I'd have you on your knees whimpering like a puppy.' I tried to run down the hill, but Shark and Buck held me back. I've had lots of practice fighting with Big Jake. I may not have won the fights, but I left him hurting.

"When Gerry was in prison, they kept him in PC (*protective custody*) along with the pedophiles, diddlers, woman beaters and other sex offenders. I don't think Jake would be in PC. He's six foot four and can take care of himself, but it depends on where they send him. Last I heard he was in transition at Millhaven. In some prisons there are inmates three times the size of Jake.

"I haven't been sleeping well lately, with V slobbering and licking himself all night. Last night I got out of bed to go to the bathroom and he bit my ankle. It wasn't as if I pushed him out of the way, like I usually do; I was walking around him. I grabbed him by the head and chomped down on his ears. He whimpered and went back to his corner."

177

"Have you seen Hippo?" I asked. "I'm worried about him." "He was across the street earlier until the lady made him move. He and Ian slept in the bank last night. He was here before six. I said to him, 'What happened? Did you shit your pants?' "

"Is he drinking rubbing alcohol?" I asked.

"Last night they both drank two bottles of sherry before they passed out. I told him, 'That shit is hard on your system. Why don't you go back to beer, or at least water the wine down like I do, or add apple juice, or something.' "

I showed Joy the poem that I had written about Hippo. "What do you think? I'm wondering if he'll be offended."

Joy took the poem and read it.

My name is Hippo,
I'm an alcoholic.
Joy was the first
to call me Hippo.
My face swells
when I drink beer.
I guess, I look
like a Hippo.

Why do I drink?
Welfare asks me that
all the time –
I'm also homeless –
I don't know why I drink.
I have bleeding ulcers;
I shit and puke blood.

I drink because
that's who I am.
If I didn't drink
I wouldn't be me.
If I didn't drink

I'd die...

"No, it's fine. I'm surprised you wrote 'shit' and 'puke.' I've just never heard you talk that way. Hippo will be fine with it; after all it's what he said to all of us. How could he be offended?"

Hippo is a friend. Now, he has no health coverage and can't see a doctor or a hospital about his bleeding ulcers. I've provided him with application forms to obtain his Birth Certificate, Social Insurance card and Health card. Next year, I hope to write a poem about him receiving medical help, finding a place of his own (instead of sleeping under a bridge) and having some control over his drinking. I'm not trying to control his life, or give him my opinion of what I think he should do. I'm trying to enable him to have more control of his life, the way he wants to live it.

At noon I saw Little Nick sitting on the sidewalk beside the church, panning. A few weeks ago Nick had insulin shock and had to be rushed to hospital.

"Hi Nick, you had us all pretty worried a while back when they took you to hospital. How are you feeling now?"

"I'm okay now. I have some fruit and sandwiches with me. Whenever I feel weak, I eat something. A man at church gave me some sugar pills. I always check my insulin level. When they took me to hospital, it was over three times above my normal. It felt like I had drunk a quart of whiskey. My vision was blurred, heart was pounding, head felt like it was splitting. Everything was spinning. I was sweating. I didn't know where I was. It felt like my brain was boiling.

"My doctor gave me some special medication, but it makes me feel sick. I have an MRI scheduled for next week so they can see what's going on. If it doesn't show any improvement, I'm going off these pills.

"I try my best to get along with people, but if someone gets in my face and really pushes my buttons, I lose it. My mind goes blank. It happened a while ago. I was down behind the Mission and this guy just kept coming at me and at me. I grabbed him by the neck. I squeezed so hard that my hand broke. If someone hadn't pulled me off, I would have killed him. I wasn't going to attend church on Sunday because I felt so bad, but my friend talked me into it. He said it would help me to feel better, and it did.

"My Bible has all the important passages highlighted. I know it says, 'Thou shalt not beat up your neighbor', and 'Thou shalt not kill.' I asked the church for forgiveness, and I asked forgiveness from the man I fought. There were a few tense days. Whenever I saw him, I'd wonder, 'Is he going to come at me or not?' He lives in the same rooming house as me and there are always confrontations among the residents. I have the pain in my hand to remind me to control my temper.

"I try my best to help people. Each morning at about 4:00, I make about ten sandwiches. I go past the Mission, through the park, under the bridge, anywhere I think there may be homeless people. If I find someone who is hungry, I give them a sandwich. The other day, under the bridge, I didn't see anybody at first, but out from somewhere crawled a little old lady.

"I talk to people about helping the homeless, sometimes they'll say, 'They can always go to the Mission, or the Salvation Army, or the Shepherd.' I explain to them that some people, because of mental conditions, like agoraphobia, or because of anti-social personality disorders, or alcoholism — where people do inappropriate things when they're drunk — there is no place to eat, no place to sleep, no place to be safe. It's our duty to help them, because they can't help themselves.

"I was in the store the other day. An elderly woman was trying to buy a coffee with a gift card. I guess there wasn't enough money on the card. She kept saying to them, 'Try it again. Try it again.' It was humiliating for her. I went up to the woman and said, 'Try my card.' It was one that someone had given me. She got her coffee. Later on, she was walking down the street and saw me panning. She came over to me and said, 'I can't believe that a man who begs for money bought me a coffee.' I said to her, 'Ma'am, we all have our hard times. If we can help each other, it makes life a lot easier. That card was a gift to me, now it's my gift to you. If you like, you can buy someone else a coffee when they need it.'

"The other day I was talking to a man. He'd slept on a park bench, so I knew he didn't have any money. I offered to buy him a sandwich. We went to a restaurant. He said, 'I'd really like a beer with that sandwich.' I said, 'I'm sorry, I'll buy you a sandwich, but I won't buy you a beer. I don't think the Lord intended that I buy beer for people.'

"I was at a 24 hour McDonald's the other night. There is a gay club nearby. When it was near closing time for the club, a lot of people started filtering over to McDonald's. I thought it strange at first. I saw women making out with women, and men making out with men, but I got talking to some of them and they were really nice. One of them gave me this rainbow flag that I sewed to my backpack. I'm not like that, you understand, but as long as nobody touches me, whatever they do is fine.' "

I wandered to the park where there was a congregation of about a dozen people and two dogs, Shaggy and Dillinger.

Irene called me over. "I want to tell you something," she said. "Shark has been staying over at my place for the last week, but they are going to fumigate today, so we had to pack everything away, wash the walls, cover things with plastic, make the place ready for the fumigators. It was a big job. Then we went to Shark's place in Chinatown. He'd left one of the windows and the screen open. There was a pigeon in his apartment. It took forever to get the pigeon to leave. I looked under his futon — he has a really nice futon — there was a nest with two eggs in it."

Irene waved Shark over. "Shark, I was just telling Dennis about the pigeons."

Shark interjected, "There must have been two birds coming in and out because they'd built a very intricate nest of twigs. They must have been at it for most of the week."

"It just freaked me out," said Irene. There was bird dirt everywhere, and I'm really fussy about germs; I'm taking antibiotics. I hardly slept at all."

"Eventually," said Shark, "we're going to move all my stuff over to Irene's. I've got two wide-screen TVs, a sound system. They're just going to waste, because I'm never home."

I walked over to Hippo. "How are you feeling?"

"A lot better than this morning. Ian and I slept at the bank until they kicked us out. I still got a bottle of wine we'd been sharing. He knows where I drink. If he doesn't come soon, there won't be anything left. Oh, well."

Shaggy Goes to the Spa

28 May 2012

As I crossed the street this morning I met Metro. "Good morning, Dennis, or is it Gordon today?"

"I'm anyone I want to be." I laughed.

"As long as you're not late for dinner. Right?"

"That's right, Metro. Have a good day."

"You too, Dennis."

Joy seemed to be in good spirits. In the distance I could see Little Jake's green cap and Silver's black cap. They were both panning across the street in the next block.

Chantal stopped by. "Good morning Joy, Dennis."

"Hi Chantal," said Joy. "How did the race go on Saturday?"

"It went. I finished, but it was hard. Did you go?"

"Yes, I was in the crowd waving, but there were too many people."

"How did it go with the apartment you were looking at?"

"I phoned the guy. It sounded as if he had his hand over the mouthpiece of the receiver, and I could hear giggling in the background. I asked, 'Did you speak to your partner? When can we come over and sign the papers?' He said, 'I talked to him, but because it's furnished, we decided to up the rent to $1775 a month.' I said, 'Your manner is very unprofessional. It's no wonder the place has been vacant for so long.' Then I hung up.

"I'm not concerned, there are lots of other places."

Chantal said, "If you need to move, and want a place to store food or other things for a while, we have lots of room. I'm free after work if you want to join me for coffee. I could meet you here."

"Sounds great, I'll see you then."

We waved. I said to Joy, "I'm sorry that the apartment didn't work out for you. Are you okay staying where you are for a while?"

"Yeah, there's no rush. I'd like to get away from Chuck though. He didn't take V out very often on the weekend, so he just growled at me for most of the time. I didn't sleep very well.

"Chuck was muttering on about something this morning. He looked at me expecting some sort of response. I just said, 'Mutter away, don't mind me.'

"He took V with him when he went panning this morning. Hopefully, the dog will be tired out when they get home.

"Nicholas and his girlfriend were over for a barbecue on Saturday. V kept jumping on Nick, who just pushed him down. Chuck said, 'Knee him in the chest, that's what I do.' Nick said, 'I'm not going to do that. You can't treat a dog that way.' If Chuck treats V like that on the street, someone may phone the SPCA. He could be charged with cruelty and V will be taken away. That may be the best thing for everybody. I hope that happens. Chuck doesn't have the energy or the patience to care for a dog.

"I used to have a red King Doberman. He was a great dog. I had to leave him behind in Montreal. I miss my family. You know, I didn't even hear about my mother's death until my uncle breezed into town three months later. He said, 'Don't worry Joy, everything has been taken care of.'

"'That's not the point,' I said. 'I didn't even know that she was sick. I would have liked to say goodbye to her. She may have died not knowing that I loved her.' "

"Joy," I said, "she knew that you loved her. You bought her a house."

"I know. Here I go crying again."

I said, "I noticed that Anne and Chester haven't been together lately. Are they not seeing each other anymore?"

"As soon as Chester's money was gone, so was Anne. They're all like that. Now Anne is hanging around Nick."

I said, "I talked with Nick on Friday. Did you know that he gets up at 4:00 am, makes sandwiches and takes them to homeless people?"

"Yes, I knew that. Nick's a sweetheart. I hope Anne doesn't take advantage of him. He's become religious lately. I think he's trying to atone for past sins. He's going to the doctor today to have a cast put on his hand.

"Outcast and Debbie are back together again. She has a regular freezer order coming every month. He'll love that. He can eat any time he wants."

"Does he work?" I asked.

"He used to have a job at the Salvation Army, washing resident's clothes. It was Debbie that got him the job. Then they had that big strike and staff was cut back. He was the last hired, so he was the first to go. Debbie still has her job. Outcast is such a leech."

I changed the subject, "So, what do you think will happen when Big Jake gets out?"

Joy said, "There's a restraining order saying that he can't come within 1500 feet of me, but that's never stopped him before. We have the same friends, so we're bound to come in contact with each other. I'm not worried; my friends will protect me."

"I get the feeling that, eventually, you want to get back with him. If that's what you want, that's what I want for you, but you said, 'Next time, he's going to kill me.' Perhaps, you should keep your meetings public, where you have witnesses."

"I don't want to get into a relationship with anybody. I still love Jake. Maybe one day we can be friends. We'll have to see what happens."

Little Jake came over, "Joy, I'm going to the liquor store. Do you want anything?"

"I've only made eight bucks this morning. Oh well, here's eight, get me a bottle of Imperial Sherry."

At the park Wolf said to me, "I've got something to tell you. There was no point in telling Little Jake. Sometimes, I don't want to talk to you either. Sometimes, I'd just as soon you'd chill somewhere else, but that's beside the point. The point is, and I thought you'd find this interesting, I read two books on the weekend. One's called *Daniel X: Alien Hunters*. According to the book there are aliens all around us. I'm not usually into that kind of stuff. I'm more for detective and espionage stories. The other was a Spencer novel. Do you like the Spencer stories?"

"Yes, I've read a lot of them. I especially like the ones with Hawk, his sidekick."

"Yeah, those are the ones. I've got the last book that Robert B. Parker wrote before he died. It's called, *Chasing the Bear*. It's in hardcover, with large print; I like those, easier on the eyes. I'll lend it to you if you want. A friend gave it to me, but I'll want it back. They're both easy reads. I read one on Saturday, the other, Sunday.

"The reason I was reading is because they cut off my cable. I've got no phone, no TV. I wouldn't have a computer either, but I'm not computer literate, so that doesn't matter. I've always been about $200 behind in my bill, but they've let it slide. This time I ran it up too high and they cut me off.

"I think I'm going to sign up with someone different; not under my real name, of course. I've bundled up all my old equipment. I don't want the new service to suspect that the old service cut me off.

"On Thursday I get my check. That's the day I have Shaggy booked to go to the spa. That's another reason I didn't pay my cable bill. It costs about $100 for what they call a full groom. That includes clipping, teeth brushing, ear cleaning and nail cutting. Some people don't understand why I spend all that money on a dog, but she's like my child. She sleeps under my bed or under my futon; wherever I am, that's where she sleeps.

Trudy came to where Wolf and I were sitting, "Wolf, can I buy a smoke from you for a quarter?"

"Sure," he said, as he pulled out a clear plastic bag filled with cigarettes. He handed her a cigarette, she handed him a quarter and left.

"Did you see that? I buy these cigarettes for ten cents and sell them for twenty-five. I make one hundred and fifty percent profit. Not bad, eh?"

I nodded and Wolf continued.

"What do you think of this Quebec student strike and the riots? Now Toronto students are going to be joining them. I guess they feel they have to because of their student union. What have they got to complain about? They already have the lowest tuition in Canada, and Canada has the lowest tuition in the world. I think they should all be shot. That's the German in me coming out.

"I can tell you're about to say something, but if it's in defense of those students, I don't want to go there."

I said, "What I was going to say is that Iceland has free tuition for universities. My grandparents came from Iceland in 1900."

"Okay, I knew I was wrong there. So you're second generation Canadian. You're descended from Vikings. Right on! All that raping, pillaging and stuff. They were good fighters, and they controlled a lot of the world at one time.

"I'm first generation Canadian. My parents came from Germany. My mother always said I come from solid German stock. When my dad was nineteen, do you know what he was doing? He was carrying a rifle in the German Army during World War Two. He was shot four times. Then they were kicked out of their own country.

"When I was nineteen I was just trying to get laid."

Shark is Robbed

29 May 2012

This morning, Silver was the only panhandler I saw on the street. I asked him if others had been by earlier. He said, "Joy was here, but she packed up and left."

I said, "I know that Joy had a court appearance this morning. It was for the breach she was given while in hospital with kidney failure. Her lawyer expects that the breach will be thrown out."

Silver said, "Hippo and Jake came by. I don't know where they went. Outcast came by. He doesn't like me calling him that. Joy gave him that name. He paid me the five bucks that he owed me, and gave me another five as interest. He'll probably be at the park at noon."

"Jacques won't be pleased to see him. He said so yesterday."

"Well, look what he did to Jacques. I don't blame him."

"Lucy-in-the-Sky's boyfriend, Daimon, is out of jail now."

I said, "I heard that Daimon robbed Shark of his change, then beat him up because he had no bills. Then Lucy beat up Irene. Joy told her if she so much as touches Irene again, she's going to get her skull smashed."

"Joy has a temper, all right. That's the native in her."

I asked, "So, how long have you been panhandling. Do you have your own place?"

"I stay at a rooming house. Rent is $450 a month. I guess I've been panhandling for about six years.

"Way back, I was in a group home, then reform school, then I was sent to another group home, then jail, jail again, and again, and again. I didn't mind the federal prisons like Millhaven. I had my own cell and even had a curtain that blocked part of the light. As long as the guard could see me when he did his rounds, there was no problem.

"In the provincial jails: Joyceville, Kingston and Collins Bay, I had to share a cell. I guess Kingston was the best. I learned to mind my own business. If I heard a scream, or the sound of someone getting beaten up, I'd just move on, go back to my cell and watch my soap opera.

"One time this guy was getting a lot of hamburger, and he didn't even work in the kitchen, a short stocky guy. He must have been ratting on someone. I was walking past the exercise yard and saw someone beating this guy. The guy who was beating on him signaled for me to move on, so that's what I did. Anyway, I'm no fighter.

"If someone has a lot of something, like hamburger, they're expected to share. It's only right. Same as we do here.

"When I worked in the kitchen, I used to smuggle subs in my underwear. I'd also bring a sub and an apple juice to the guard. He would pat me down when I left the kitchen, but I was never caught with food."

The situation at the park was awkward. There were two groups of people. Outcast, Hippo and Shakes were sitting on the curb by the sidewalk. Jacques, Silver and I sat on the opposite curb facing them.

Outcast said, "I don't mind being blamed for something I did, but I can't stand being blamed for what I didn't do. I was at Jacques' place — he'd been sleeping — I was sorting through his DVDs looking for one to watch. I wasn't stealing anything. I don't even own a DVD player. Why would I steal DVDs? He's been spreading rumors that I stole from him and it's a lie. I could tell about him fondling women who had passed out at his place."

Silver said, "I saw Joy wandering off with Chester. I'll bet she's after his money."

Shakes said, "Daimon is out of jail. I was there when he robbed and beat up Shark and Lucy beat up Irene. I stood up for Shark. I said, 'If you fight Shark, you're going to have to fight me too.' He said, 'I got no beef with you Shakes. Shark owes me something and he won't pay up.' I said, 'It's you that owes Shark, not the other way around.' "

I said to Hippo, "How have you been feeling?"

"Okay."

"So you haven't been throwing up blood or having stomach pains?"

"No, I'm feeling fine."

"I was talking to Silver earlier about how to get a health card, so you could see a doctor."

"I got all the papers here in my pack. First I have to get my birth certificate. Because I'm adopted I need information about my real parents. I don't know where to get that. Then, I can get my social insurance number, then my health card."

I said, "I can research the internet and see if there are forms that can be downloaded. I'll let you know tomorrow."

Silver gave Hippo some advice on the different agencies that could help.

He then said, "Hippo and I had quite a time in the Market yesterday. We were at a loading dock, in the alley across from the Oven. We turned around and saw a ghost police car with two cops in it. We went the opposite way and found another loading dock. This one smelled bad because it was near the garbage.

"I said, 'This is stupid. Let's go to my place. We can drink our beer, order some pizza and watch television."

Outcast walked up to Jacques and said, "I don't want you spreading any more lies about me stealing from you. You know they aren't true."

Jacques sat there — that's as far as it went.

Ride to Remember

31 May 2012

Yesterday, was check day for all the people on government assistance. Today, a motorcycle parade, RIDE to REMEMBER 'say never again,' is in progress. Motorcycle clubs from around the world are riding from Toronto in remembrance of veterans and to say 'never again' to the Holocaust.

Some Jewish and Christian bike clubs have made the trip from as far as the UK and Australia to remember those lost in the Holocaust and to support Israel.

Anastasia, white-haired, probably in her sixties, was jumping up and down. "There's one with ape hangers, one with a side car, some BMWs, a few Indians, on the trailer is a 1939 Knucklehead Bobber. I've ridden one of those."

Little Jake said, "This is Harley heaven, man. Listen to that rumble. There must be hundreds of them."

"Settle down you two," said Andre, wearing a women's hot pink, peaked cap. You're going to have an orgasm."

I talked first to Irene. I knew that she had been to the doctor, so I asked how she was feeling. "Not so good. I'm on antibiotics, but they gave me the wrong kind. I'm menopausal, borderline diabetic, I have cirrhosis, Hep. C, cancer.

"From the head up I'm okay, the rest of me is falling apart. Yesterday, I didn't even get out of bed. I needed a beer to get me feeling level. Shark is in better shape with AIDS than I am. He'll far outlive me."

Shark said, "You're going through alcohol withdrawal. That's the way I feel when I haven't had my morphine. I take medication for AIDS, but I only take two tablets a day. Some people take about nine pills, and they have to be at different times during the day. I've been this way for about seven years."

Irene said, "We're looking for another apartment, a two bedroom. We can afford it, and it doesn't make sense us each having our own places. We're either at one or the other. I want something closer to downtown. I can't take the long bus rides from where I am now."

"How about a place near where Joy is?" I asked.

"Near the Market? No, I know too many people there. Maybe in Cabbagetown, but I know too many people everywhere.

"I'm giving my two months' notice where I am, so we have quite a while to look for a place. I want to make sure it's in a nice neighborhood."

"That's important," I said.

Little Jake came up to me, "Do you see how everyone is broken up into little cliques today? Shark, Irene and Outcast have moved away because they think this is the place where the police will come first."

Silver said, "I'm not sitting with those women; they're the ones that took Chester's money. They got him drunk and then went through his pockets. He had an $8,000 inheritance that they went through in a month. Now that he's run out of money, they won't have anything to do with him."

Loretta was holding on to Shakes. She asked me, "Can you give me a hand?"

"What's he trying to do? Get up or sit down?"

"He says it's slow motion."

I held Shakes' hand, and he gradually lowered himself to a sitting position.

I asked him, "How did you get the cut on the bridge of your nose, Shakes?"

"I was jumped by two guys last night. I'll remember their faces. They even wanted to press charges against me. It was them that started it.

"I've lost something. Can you help me? I'm looking for two brown envelopes." He pointed to a plastic grocery bag. "Whenever I go to the bank, I put my money in a brown banking envelope."

"I'll have a look, Shakes. You've got lots of brown paper napkins, packs of pepper, plastic knives and forks, a muffin, your bottle of wine. Here's one brown envelope. I can't find a second one. I'll put your bag near the fence."

Loretta said to me, "Did you hear my good news?"

"No," I said, "what's your good news?"

"I'm going to be moving. I have permission from my probation officer. I came here today to collect my clothes from all my friends. Tomorrow, I move. My roommate is going to be a woman I've lived with before. She's six months pregnant. We're getting a two bedroom apartment."

"Congratulations!" I said, "You must be excited."

"Yes, I am. Have you seen Joy today?"

"No, she wasn't in her usual spot, but I wasn't expecting her. She usually stays away for a few days after she gets her check. She likes to be on her own for a while, where it's quiet."

"There's nothing wrong with that. That's the way you get to know yourself."

"I agree. It's a good idea. I enjoy doing that as well."

I walked over to where Hippo was standing alone. I shook his hand, and he winced.

"Did you break your hand?" I asked.

"Yes."

"Shouldn't it be in a cast like Nick's?"

"No, they said it wouldn't help."

"I see that you have stitches above your eyebrow."

"Yeah, they stitched it on the inside then on the outside. I can't wait to get my hands on the guy who did this to me. He was a crack head.

"I also got barred from the Sally again. I was eating my dinner when a guy came and said, 'You can't eat here. You've already eaten.' I said, 'Okay, you eat it then!' I tossed it into the bubble *(the information desk)*.

"I really liked the poem you wrote. I made copies and gave them to all my friends. Some people think I'm kinda slow, but here I am."

"I love you, man," and I gave him a hug.

Hippo said, "I don't want to cry, but I feel it coming. Someone still loves us."

"Take care, Hippo. I'll see you tomorrow."

As I was leaving, a man came up to me. I shook his hand and said, "Hi, my name is Dennis."

"Yeah, we've met before. I shaved off my beard."

"I haven't seen you for a couple of months."

"Yeah, I've been away. I bought beer for the guys. Would you like a beer?"

"Thanks, but I have to get back to work."

"Do you need any money?" he asked.

I said, "No, I'm good, but thanks anyway."

"You've always treated me like gold, man. I appreciate it." He gave me a hug, and I returned to work.

June 2012

The Usual Suspects

"Hi Hippo." I shook his broken hand very gently.

"My head hurts."

"How is your hand?"

"It hurts too. Little Jake and I slept at the heater last night, not together, just in the same place. The streets aren't safe anymore."

"Hi Jake, How are you?"

"I'm drunk. Hippo and I started early."

"I guess that's a good thing."

Shakes was sitting on the lawn and was having trouble getting up. "I'll use this wine bottle and this container as a crutch to help me up." He made it half way then tumbled over.

Jacques stood up and took Shakes' arm to help him to his feet. Shakes said, "Did you know that Rocky got jumped last night. It was the same guys that jumped me. He's in about the same shape as I am."

"Do you know why they jumped Rocky?"

"Because they're assholes," said Jacques.

I turned to Donald. "Hi, how are you?"

"I have my methadone treatment at 1:00. Everybody hates me. I don't know why. They make fun of me."

I said, "I've never heard anybody say anything against you."

"I appreciate you being my friend."

I greeted Shark. "Hi Shark, how is Irene feeling today?"

"She's with Anastasia. They're drunk to the tits. They bought a case of Maximum Ice. It's 7.1% alcohol. I bought myself a twenty-six ounce bottle of watermelon vodka. It's 37% alcohol. I thought I should get something to catch up. You don't need any mix with it. Have a swig."

I took a swig. "That's smooth. I've never tasted that before."

"I had to kick Irene out at 11:00 last night. She was drunk. When she gets like that, her mind goes on retard. She'll have about five conversations going and she keeps repeating them. I guess she forgets that she's said the same thing five minutes before.

"We're planning to get an apartment together. The problem is she wants to go through the Salvation Army. I want to get something through my landlord. He has a bunch of buildings. If we get these workers involved, one group doesn't talk the same language as the other group. I've been in the Welfare system for twenty years. I know what to say to them so they'll understand it, and I'll get what I want.

"Maybe it would be better if Irene and Joy got an apartment together. The only problem is that Irene drinks more than Joy. Joy has her drinking fairly well under control.

"Anastasia wants us to go with her to her mother's house. It's on Georgian Bay, so there would be boating, swimming, fishing. The water isn't very deep, but you can still catch bass. The only problem is that Anastasia is a bit nuts. You must have noticed that yesterday.

"I have to be back every week to see my doctor and pick up my meds."

I asked, "How old is Anastasia, and how old is her mother?"

"I guess Anastasia is about 61, her mother is in her nineties," Shark answered.

He continued, "The problem would be getting back and forth. I guess we could arrange something with the bus. It's a long trip. Something to keep in mind though."

Chester and Outcast were going over Chester's bank statement. Outcast said, "We were playing cards last night and then I left. What's the last thing you remember buying?"

"I bought beer at the store."

"Okay, that's listed here. Then, there's a purchase in Scarborough. Did you go to Scarborough?"

"No."

"There's also a purchase at the gas station. You don't drive a car, so that's not you. There are withdrawals of two hundred, three hundred. These are since you lost your card. Do you remember giving your card to anyone?"

"No."

Silver said, "Look at Donald, he's never going to make his methadone appointment. I've been drinking since 4:30 this morning and I can stagger straighter than that. I get up at 4:30, have a shower — yes, I drink beer in the shower. It's okay as long as I don't fall and hurt myself."

"Hello Wolf," I said.

He said, "Have a look at my dog."

"Is that a different dog? That doesn't look like Shaggy."

"That's Shaggy. They clipped her, did all kinds of stuff to her. I brought her blanket and her bed so she'll get acclimatized. Is she breathing?"

"Yes, I can see her chest going up and down."

"I was just joking. I guess I haven't known you that long. You haven't seen Shaggy when she's been clipped? I have her done once a year."

"No, I only met you in January, so it's been about five months."

Donald didn't make his methadone treatment. He was too drunk to walk. Even if he had made it there, they wouldn't have taken him in his condition.

A Brand New Start

4 June 2012

This morning the rain continued for the third day. The showers were light and intermittent, as opposed to the downpour we experienced throughout the night.

Metro greeted me as I got off the bus. "Good morning, Dennis, or is it Gordon today?"

"Good morning, Metro, did you manage to stay out of trouble this weekend?"

"Yes, actually I did. I haven't seen Joy. I don't know if she's in her spot. I have something I want her to do for me."

"I'll tell her when I see her, Metro."

"You have a good day," he said.

"You too, Metro."

The sidewalk was free of panhandlers, except for Hippo.

"Good morning, Dennis."

"Hi Hippo, how does your head feel?"

"It's still sore. I get my stitches out in a couple of days. I haven't seen anyone this morning, no Joy, no Little Jake, no Silver."

"It's 8:10, how long do you think you've got until the lady from the hotel asks you to move?"

"I don't know, maybe ten minutes. I found a new place to sleep. It's down a flight of stairs near where we meet in the park. It's dry and nobody bothered us. There even seems to be a bit of heat down there."

"Was Shakes down there with you?" I asked.

"No, I haven't seen him for a few days."

"He's always told me that when he's tired, he lays down and goes to sleep, no matter where he is."

Hippo nodded. "Yeah, that's Shakes."

"Did you know that he's only 46? He's only five years older than Little Jake."

"Yeah, he looks a lot older."

"I guess it's partly because he used to be a boxer. That's not too good for the face," I said.

"I know, just look at me."

I asked, "How old are you?"

"36 — my birthday is March 24th, 1976."

"My son is two years older than you. He'll be 38 in June," I said. "Are you planning to visit your folks anytime soon? I guess by hitchhiking it would only take you about an hour."

"If that — it all depends on who's driving. I haven't made any plans to go there, but we always keep in touch by phone."

"That's great," I said. "I was thinking, you would probably be eligible for ODSP."

Hippo said, "I guess so. It's a lot of paperwork though."

I said, "You'd get more money, wouldn't you? Shark could show you how to go about it. He could even get you a diaper allowance."

Hippo laughed, "Yeah, he probably could. He gets about $1500 a month."

"How is your hand?"

"It's okay." He spread his fingers to see how much pain it caused.

I asked, "Did you work on the weekend?"

"I tried, but there was nobody around, especially with the rain. It's just as bad this morning. All I've made so far is two bucks."

A lady in a suit came up to us, "I'm from the hotel. I'm afraid you're going to have to move."

"Okay, thanks," we said.

At noon I met Serge sitting alone in the glassed-in bus shelter. "How are you, Serge?"

"I'm okay."

"Are you staying at the Shepherd now?"

"No, I don't stay there anymore. I slept in the park, just over there."

Further up the sidewalk I met Rocky. He said, "I'd shake your hand, but I just puked in the bushes and got some on my hands. I'm sorry. I was in hospital last night."

"Did you get jumped again? I heard that you and Shakes were jumped by the same guys. You don't look as bad as he does. Was it four guys that jumped you?"

"It was five kids that jumped me. If I'd fought back, I'd be back in jail. I didn't think it was worth it. They stole my cap. I was in hospital for alcohol poisoning."

"Was there anything they could do for you?"

"Not really."

Hippo said, "I got my papers sent in for assisted housing. I don't know how long it'll take, maybe a year, but it's done."

"That's great, Hippo,"

"Silver," I asked, "wouldn't Hippo qualify for ODSP?"

"Yeah, he should qualify. It's good to have a doctor to back you up. I had a letter from my doctor and my psychiatrist. Hippo's like me, he drags his feet with the paperwork. I'd like to get out of the place I'm in, as well. I just haven't applied." He turned to Hippo.

"Hippo, it's best if you go there. They'll fill out the papers for you. You just have to answer their questions."

"I got my worker filling out the forms for me. I'm just waiting for all my cards," said Hippo.

"Silver," I asked, "you don't like where you're staying? I thought that would be a great place to stay."

"There are a lot of crack heads drifting in. It's not the same as it was a few years back."

"I didn't see you this morning. Did you work on the weekend?"

"I opened up the office and worked Saturday and Sunday. I started at 8:30, Saturday, at one church. Later, I moved further down to another church. I have a lot of regulars there. I've been panning there for about four years. On Sunday, I went to the big church. Each day I made about $60.

"You did well," I said.

"Sorry for the cigarette smoke drifting into your face. I wish I could quit. It was my girlfriend who got me started again. She'd say, 'Just have a little puff.' Pretty soon I was hooked again. When I was inside, I didn't smoke. I couldn't afford it. I could buy pot for less than I could buy cigarettes, and I prefer pot."

Seated on the grass was another group including Wolf and a freshly clipped Shaggy. Standing at the rail were Donald, and Big Titties Rosie.

Shaggy was barking through the railing at some squirrels down below. It was a futile effort, but she seemed to be enjoying herself.

I went over and talked to Donald. "Hi, it's good to see you. Do you have your methadone treatment today?"

"Yes, I'm supposed to go every day, but I was too drunk on Friday. I kept falling down. I fell once on my tail bone, now every time I cough it hurts. I also lost my hearing aid. I'm going to ODSP this afternoon to see if I can get another one. I'm only allowed one every three years. My mom is really mad; if they won't give me one, she'll have to buy me a new one. It costs $2000. It's a good thing I learned to read lips."

"Hi Irene, "I said, "how are you feeling?"

"Not good, I ache all over. I've put in two months' notice at my apartment building. They're saying I signed a lease. I don't remember signing a lease. I'm moving anyway. What are they going to do – put me in arrears? I'll just put them on the list of all the other people I have no intention of paying."

"Irene found us a place," said Shark. "It's a two bedroom, all-inclusive. You'll never guess where it is. Right in front of the Mission where I know everybody. There would be a constant line up my door. I walked past the place. From the outside it looks good, but the location won't work. We don't need anything all-inclusive. I don't mind paying heat and hydro."

"I can pay for cable," said Irene, "I have a satellite dish."

Shark said, "I have two wide-screen TV's a sound system. We both have futons. Between us we've got plenty of furniture."

I said, "You want to live near the park, don't you, Irene?"

"That's my preference. I want to be able to walk to my doctor, walk here. If there's an emergency – I don't know. I don't like that long bus ride from where I am now. If you're walking back to work, I'll walk with you. I have to go to the bathroom."

Before I left, Shakes asked, "Dennis, can you spare me cash for a bottle?"

"Sorry Shakes, I don't have any cash with me. I didn't even bring my wallet. If I had it, you know I'd give it to you."

"I know you'd give it to me, Dennis; you have before."

Irene said, "I can't believe that Shark still wants to marry me, but he does. We've been together four years now."

"It makes a lot of sense to share expenses."

"We both want to get out of the places we're in now. We have the money. It'll be a brand new start."

"It sounds great. Perhaps, I'll see you tomorrow."

"Thanks for walking with me."

"It was my pleasure."

Daimon Released from Prison

5 June 2012

As I was approaching the corner, I saw Irene and Big Titties Rosie waiting for the 'walk' light.

"Hi Irene, Rosie, are you leaving?"

"We're just going to the restaurant to use the ladies' room; we'll be back."

"I'll see you then."

This afternoon at the park, Buddy had passed out on the lawn. I have often seen him panhandling on Queen, playing his harmonica. The police were expected, so people spread out into small groups, hiding any open liquor bottles. Large groups are illegal without a permit

I first sat between Shakes and Andre who was wearing a light blue cap with a 'Psssst' badge on it. He had taken off his tee shirt and spread it on the ground. On it was an imitation of the Warner Brother's movie logo and the words, 'If you see da cops, warn a brother.' He was feeling better than yesterday. His throat infection is healing.

He said, "A cop car just pulled up, the paramedics are following them. Just wait and see, after they take Buddy away, they'll come up to check on us. They'll say, 'How's everybody doing?' We'll say, 'Just fine officer, enjoying the nice weather.'"

Gene said, "Andre and I were throwing a hardball around. I was pitching to him. I used to be pretty fast in my younger days. I'd throw at around eighty, ninety miles an hour sometimes. I'm down to about seventy now. I asked Andre if he was ready, he said, 'Let 'er rip.' Twice I caught him right in the center of the chest."

Andre said, "When I was younger, both of my uncles used to pitch to me. They were fast. I used to catch the ball ninety-eight per cent of the time. I had really quick reflexes but not anymore. I remember my uncle throwing a bit wide one time. The ball missed my glove and went right through the backboard, left a neat circular hole."

Shakes, who was laying on the lawn, said, "Dennis, do you remember me?"

"Of course I do, Shakes. I'd recognize that hat anywhere." I shook his hand. He pulled me to the ground.

I moved on to the second group to say hello to Joy and Hippo. I was surprised to see Shark sitting next to Daimon since, before he went to prison, Daimon robbed Shark of his change, then beat him for not having any bills. I guess they settled their differences. Shark is skinny and is certainly not a fighter.

As I was approaching, I heard Joy saying to Shark, "I don't like you either, and I don't punch like a girl, so watch what you say."

Shark said, "You always pick fights with men because you know they won't hit you back."

I interrupted them. "Hi Joy," I said, "How've you been?"

"I've been keeping pretty quiet, staying at home and off the booze for the past few days. I've been cleaning the house, doing laundry, watching TV, resting. I've got marks on my arm where V has been biting me. I hate that dog."

"Hi Dennis," said Shark. "Irene and I had a tiff. I can't remember what we were arguing about, but I kept laughing at her. She hit me with her fist upside my head. I said, 'Irene, don't do that.' She hit me on the other side. I said, 'Irene, if you do that again, I'll hit you back.' Then she hit me in the nose. I just kept gaming on my PlayStation."

Joy said, "She's small and skinny, but with those knuckles she can pack quite a punch. Where is she now?"

"She took the bus home to get her health card, then she was going to the drug store to have her prescription filled, then she was going somewhere else. I wasn't paying too much attention."

"That's what I used to do with Big Jake," said Joy. "When he'd hit me, I'd just laugh and say, 'Is that all you got, big boy?' That would really make him mad. He's six-foot four. I didn't win many fights, but I hurt him.

"That's Rodent over there, Jake's so-called friend. He had to come and rub my nose in the fact that he's been in contact with Jake. He said he's sending him a TV at Millhaven. There's something strange about that. The last time Rodent was here he was flashing a lot of cash and giving money to all the men. Do you think he gave me any? No! If he was interested in women at all, you'd think he would have given me something.

Do you think he's ever shown any interest in me, since Jake has been in prison? No! He's a cock slinger *(male prostitute)*.

"Rodent bragged that he had been in prison for 25 years and he was affiliated with the gangs. I've had some experience with that in the past. If he was affiliated, and went around talking about it — like he has been — he'd be dead meat."

Daimon said, "Was he saying he was with HA *(Hell's Angels)*?"

"That's what he was saying," said Joy.

Daimon, who has distinctive prison pallor and crude tattoos covering both hands and arms, laughed and said, "There are lots of prison stories. Some of them are even true, but not many."

Joy said, "Daimon, what's that you've got on your face? Were you in a fight? It looks like you did a face plant."

"If I'd been in a fight, it would have been the other guy who would've done the face plant."

Lucy said, "I wondered how long it would take Joy to ask about that. Didn't I, Daimon?"

"It's an infection," said Daimon. "I must have picked it up from a guy in prison. He had sores like this on his thigh and his stomach. I didn't go near him, but I must have touched something he had touched. I went to the doctor. He gave me antibiotics and some cream to put on the sores."

Joy said, "It looks like impetigo. My sister got that when she was young. That's what comes of sitting on park benches wearing only a bathing suit."

"Impetigo, that's what the doctor said. I couldn't remember the name, but that's what it is. It hurts, and being near my mouth, it's always breaking open."

"Chester!" said Joy, "Where are you going? Just because Rodent is going over there, that doesn't mean you have to. These guys follow him around hoping he'll give them something, money, cigarettes..."

I said to Joy, "Did you hear that Rocky got jumped the other day?"

"I've seen him fight. He blacks out and goes wild, just like me. I fought with my sister once. I injured her neck, shoulder and back. That was before they charged people for things like that. I can imagine that Rocky did some damage to the other guy."

I said, "It was five kids who jumped him. Shakes thinks it was the same gang that jumped him. Rocky didn't fight them because he would have gone back to jail. They stole his cap."

"How are you feeling, Rocky?" I asked. "Any better than yesterday?"

"Not really. I've got a pain in my liver."

"What does the pain feel like? Is it a sharp pain or a dull ache like a bruise?"

"It feels like I have to shit, but nothing comes out. When I was in hospital, I asked them to check my heart and kidneys. I had surgery on my heart and had a hole fixed in my kidney when I was four days old.

"I was born near Greenland. My parents never wanted a boy. I have seven sisters. My youngest sister wants to come down here, but I told her not to. She's just sixteen. They all live up north."

"Toronto can be a tough place to live."

"I find it good where I am. I'm near the hospital. My father sometimes comes to the city, but he never wants to see me."

I said good-bye to the group. It was nearly time for me to go back to work.

Joy said, "I'll see you tomorrow. I won't be panning; I have to buy some groceries. I have Hamburger Helper at home, but Chuck wants to have a barbecue."

"Chester," I said. "I heard you were hit by a bus last Wednesday. How are you feeling?"

"It happened at the corner. I'm in a lot of pain, but I keep it to myself."

Panhandlers Feeding Panhandlers

6 June 2012

As I was walking along the street, I was approached by Stan. "Hi, brother," he said, "do you think you could help me out. I've been panning, but I've only made a dollar so far. I collected some beer cans, but had to walk across the bridge to get a refund on them. I've been walking all morning. I'm beat."

"Sure, I can help you, Stan."

"I really appreciate that. I've got to get back in shape. I have to start eating properly. I should be drinking more milk, eating more meat and eggs. I also need to go to a detox center to get help. I'm having trouble with my liver and I've been puking blood."

"Rocky and Hippo are having the same problem," I said.

"I know. Thanks again, brother."

When I got to the park I first talked to Rocky. "How are you feeling today?"

"I'm feeling a little better."

"You mentioned yesterday that you had an operation on your heart when you were four days old. Tell me about that."

"They had me taken to the Children's Hospital in Montreal. A valve in my heart had to be replaced. Two days later they operated on my kidney to fix a hole. I wasn't expected to survive the operations. I stayed in hospital for five years. They'll have to operate on my heart again soon to put in a larger valve."

"You mentioned that your mother and father didn't want a son. How did that affect you?"

"I didn't have a name for the first four days. It was my grandmother who gave me my name and raised me. They say that most of a child's development happens in the first five years. I didn't have that. I think that's what made me the way I am. I had my first cigarette when I was four years old. I started drinking when I was six. You may have noticed that I don't

206

talk much to people, I just hang around at the edge of the group and watch."

"I can understand that. I was in a similar situation when I was eighteen months old. It completely changed my personality."

Chester came over. I asked, "How are you feeling today, Chester?"

"I still have a lot of pain in my lower right leg. My toes started to turn black, but that's going away now."

I said, "So the bus must have hit you on the right side."

"I don't know. I don't remember."

"Take care, Chester."

I asked Joy, "Have you had any success finding an apartment."

She said, "No, Toothless is checking out a new place, you'd recognize the street."

"The street where Daniel, you and I lived?"

"Yeah, I lived in the pink house."

"I remember the pink house. I walked past it on my way to the shopping center."

"It's still pink," she said.

I wandered over to the railing where Gaston was standing by himself. "Hi Gaston, are you enjoying the warm weather?"

"Yes, it's nice to see the sunshine after so much rain. I come here to get reacquainted with my friends. I'll be going home soon to spend time in my garden. It's small, but I have cabbages, carrots, lettuce, and tomatoes. In the house, I raise my own herbs. I get milk in glass bottles from a farmer, just like in the old days. He puts some aside for me. The cream rises to the top. I love that, I can make my own whipping cream."

"I live within walking distance of here. I have my own house, I take courses at the university, teach courses at the university and at the HIV drop-in center. I also teach at another drop-in program, that's the place where they deal with people who have mental conditions.

"My main interest is psychology. We must first understand ourselves in order to understand others. We must understand our whole bodily system, how we are affected by nutrition, stress. Stress is a big concern. If we are stressed, it affects our digestion, our thinking process, our internal organs and our ability to heal.

"I also teach courses on HIV. Cleanliness is very important at every step. The first place people touch is the doorbell. I disinfect it after each person enters, the same with the door knobs. I've opened drop-in centers here in and Ottawa."

"That's fascinating, Gaston. Do you have a website? How can I register for your courses?" I said.

"It's listed under the AIDS Committee of Toronto."

"I'll check that out, Gaston. It was a pleasure meeting you."

I said good-bye to the congregation, including Nick, whose hand was in a cast up to his elbow.

"How is your hand, Nick? It must be feeling better having the cast on."

Trudy said, "He was supposed to have an operation, but he declined it."

"Did they want to operate on your hand?"

"No, on my liver. My friend died yesterday of the same thing. I decided to leave it in God's hands."

I said, "I'm sorry to hear that, Nick. I truly am. How are you feeling about your situation?"

"I don't know."

"We're all the same, Nick. None of us knows how long we have to live. It could be years, months, weeks or days. We're never sure. All we can do is take it one day at a time, one hour at a time, one minute at a time. I know you do a lot to help people. Just keep on doing what you're doing. Supplying sandwiches to the homeless is very important. We're here to help. That's all any of us can do."

"Yes, I panhandle to give to those who have less than I do."

"Take care, Nick. God bless you."

War Memorial

7 June 2012

Hippo and Andre were sitting on the lawn arguing over forty-five cents. They were short that amount to go to the liquor store. Hippo threw a nickel at Andre. Andre threw a quarter at Hippo.

Andre said to Hippo, "Do you want me to get up? Do you want me to get up?"

"No," said Hippo, "I don't want you to get up. Let's be reasonable about this."

I stopped to talk to Wolf who said, "If you wonder why I'm sitting with these wild men, it's because that other group over there is too near the war memorial. That's the first place the cops are going to stop. It makes sense, if someone has lost a friend or family member to the war, the last thing they want to see is a bunch of people standing around drinking beer. It's not respectful. There used to be two benches there, but they took them out. That was the reason. Since then, they've taken two more benches out. They're making a statement. Do you see what I mean?"

I wandered over to the other group. Joy was talking about an incident that happened yesterday.

"Sky punched Irene in the face and broke her nose. Then Daimon grabbed Shark and took his cell phone. He gave it back later. I said to Lucy today, 'I don't appreciate what you did to my friend. Shark was good to you; he sold you drugs at half the price he could have charged. Is this is the way you repay him? That's not the way that friends treat friends. Does Daimon want to go back to jail so soon? Anyone walking by, seeing someone putting the boots to someone on the ground, could have called the cops.'

"That's what happens when you're dealing with addicts. They don't think reasonably, they just think of their next fix," Joy said.

Andre said, "Jake has passed out on the bridge. The cops and the paramedics are sure to be here soon. Speaking of cops, there are four of them on bicycles talking to Hippo. One of them is riding in this direction. Dump your liquor!"

As he rode by, the officer on bicycle said, "Hi, Andre!"

Joy poured the contents of her plastic bottle on the lawn. "That should kill the grass," she said. Outcast kicked over the can of beer that he had placed on the bottom rung of the railing. Andre started staggering to where the action was.

Joy said, "They probably won't do anything to Jake because he has AIDS. He usually has a cut on his lip or something. They won't want to go near him.

"Earlier they talked to me. I said, 'Anything you want to know is on my dossier. Just look me up.' 'Dossier?' he said, 'That's a pretty big word for you.' 'Look dude,' I said, 'I've been in the system for as long as I can remember. If there's one thing I know, it's the system. You'll find that I'm red flagged for violence and there's a green C beside my name for Hep. C. Anything else you want to know is in there.' "

"Andre," said Outcast, "stay here, you're drunk. If you go over there you're going to be charged! Stupid bastard!"

Joy said, "That cop rode right by. I wouldn't have needed to dump my bottle."

"That's the third can of beer I've kicked," said Outcast. "That tells you how many times they've been here this morning. They've been coming every hour."

"Dennis, I think you may have been lucky for us. You look respectable. They'd treat you decent. You should have seen the bicycle cop that was here yesterday. A red-headed guy with big muscles. I wish I'd had a video phone. He stood there, in front of the women, scratching his balls. He was really disgusting. He said, 'They don't make condoms big enough to fit me,' and 'I'm so big that I'm cramped by this bicycle seat.' If I could have recorded that, I'd have been on the phone right away to the police. I'd say, 'This is how one of your officers talks to the public.' They think that because we're alcoholics they don't have to treat us like humans."

"Dennis is always lucky for me," said Joy. "Every time he stops by, I get two or three drops."

Outcast said, "The Chief of Police was on TV the other night. He said they're going to crack down on drugs in the Market. I guess that means here too. It's because of the tourists. He said so. They don't want tourists looking at people like us, hanging around drinking beer."

"I'll have to mix another drink," said Joy as she reached into her backpack for her sherry and water bottles. "Are there any female cops over there? If there aren't, they won't be able to check my bag. I hope there aren't because I'm carrying pot."

Outcast said, "I think Hippo has outstanding warrants against him, but that's in British Columbia."

Hippo came walking up, "They charged me with pissing against the wall. I got a $35 fine. I couldn't have held it any longer anyway."

"May I see your ticket?" I asked. "I'm just curious to see what they wrote."

"I threw it away. It didn't have my real name on it anyway."

"And even if it did, you wouldn't pay it, would you?" I asked.

"No, but maybe I should have given it to Jacques. He could have taped it on his wall with all the liquor violations, and Joy's ticket for jumping the bus."

Hippo walked over to Outcast, "Can I have forty-five cents? Rocky is going for a run."

"Will they let him in?" asked Outcast. "Is he sober enough?"

"Well, he's more sober than I am. I'm hammered," Hippo said.

Joy reached into her bra and pulled out a change purse. She gave some money to Hippo, "Buy me a bottle too, will you?"

"Joy, I knew you stuffed your bra," laughed Outcast.

"Earlier, Daimon saw me put money in my backpack and he kept eyeing it. I figured this way he'd have to come through me to get it."

"Hi Shark," I said, "I'm sorry to hear about what happened to Irene. Joy said her nose is broken."

"It's not broken. It was just bleeding. She'd be here but she's mad at me for not stepping in when Lucy punched her, but I couldn't. First, I was in the middle of a drug deal with Daimon. Second, he said, 'Stay out of it!' He grabbed my arm and held me down. See the bruises?

"I wouldn't say this to Irene, but she had it coming. I've told you before that when she's drunk, her mind goes on retard. She just keeps repeating the same thing over and over. She was saying, 'That person has sucked Sharks' cock, that person has sucked Shark's cock, and on, and on, and on ...' I said, 'Irene, this may be of some concern to you, but it isn't to anybody else. Now, shut the fuck up!' That's when Lucy popped her.

"She won't be mad at me for long. I talked to my landlord and I have a two bedroom apartment arranged."

"Where is it?" I asked.

"I don't know, he has buildings all over the city, we can take our pick. I told him that I'd pay him the last month's rent now and the first month's rent August first when we move in. He's willing to give me the last month in my present apartment for free. Not a bad deal, eh? I'll have a room to myself, so when Irene gets mad at me, I can go there and play my games."

Little Jake Gets Charged

"Hi, Serge, how's everything today?" He mumbled something that I couldn't quite make out. "Did you say, 'not bad?' " I asked.

"Not yet," he replied and chuckled.

"Take care, Serge, I'll see you on my way back."

"The others are all up there," he pointed up the hill.

Sitting on the lawn were a dozen of the regulars. Lying on the grass, sound asleep, was Shakes.

Joy came over and said, "I wasn't panning today because Chuck and I had a big fight. Chili has been staying with us. This morning before she left for school, she took some pills and drank half a twenty-six ounce bottle of Bacardi. We got into an argument and Chuck took her side. She isn't the one paying half of the bills; I am.

"I packed all my stuff into my bag and set it by the door. Anyway, Chuck got mad and threw my bag across the room. I said to him, 'I've got breakable stuff in there. If anything is broken, you're in big trouble.' I checked and everything was okay.

"He phoned me later and asked, 'Are we through?' I said, 'You're the one who hasn't been talking.' So, I don't know what's happening. I just know that he's there, and I can't have the place to myself like I do some afternoons. I could really use some peace and quiet right now."

I asked, "How is it going with getting your medical card?"

"I don't know. I'm going through the system, so however long it takes. I really need my meds. I'm psychotic, schizophrenic and I have all these voices going around in my mind. I can never get a good night's sleep."

I sat down between Ian and Andre who said, "Don't sit on the grass; it will stain your clothes. Sit on my jacket. It's dirty anyway."

"Thanks, Andre."

Silver said, "Dennis, are you sitting on the grass? Here's a newspaper. It's free."

"He's not sitting on the grass. He's sitting on my jacket," said Andre.

"Oh," said Silver, "I didn't see it. I guess you don't need this then."

"Thanks, anyway, Silver," I said.

"Andre," I asked, "How did everything go yesterday after I left?"

"I went to check on Jake. There were two bicycle cops talking to him. One was a big muscular guy with tattoos on his arms. Jake kept mouthing off to them. He was charged, and the cop gave me a carton of smokes."

"He gave you a carton of smokes?"

"Yeah, then I got up to leave and he said, 'You don't have to go if you don't want to, but this guy,' he pointed to Jake, 'has to move on. You stayed quiet when we asked you to, so we've got no problem with you.' "

Rocky was throwing up blood in the bushes. Joy said, "Rocky, stop drinking and eat something. I know you haven't been eating. Here's a bagel for you; you need something in your gut." He ate the bagel.

"This is the first thing I've eaten in five days," he said to me.

Ian said, "You know, I inherited a $27,000 commercial fishing boat. I don't own it any more. I kick myself for that. My sons will inherit it when they turn eighteen. It's working now. It brings in about $700,000 a year. I don't see any of that.

"Marlena wants me to quit drinking, but I explained to her. 'I can't just quit like that. It takes time and I need some help, but I'm working on it.' "

"You seem to be doing well, Ian," I said. "You seem to be sober now. Even at Alcoholics Anonymous they stress one day at a time. You'll get there if that's what you want."

Ian said, "Marlena and I were sitting on the sidewalk yesterday. I had just opened a beer when a cop stopped at the curb. I said to him, 'Officer, this is my first drink of the day. Can I please have another swallow before I pour it out?' He said, 'You lift that beer and I'll kick your teeth in.' I said, 'Okay, if you're going to give me a ticket, go ahead. If you want to go *(fight)*, we can go. It's fine with me. You put your gun down, and we can go right now.' He just gave me the ticket, but I'm going to see my lawyer. He threatened me and Marlena is my witness. I've got a good lawyer. I don't know why the cop couldn't have been polite. We weren't causing any trouble. He could have said, 'Excuse me sir, would you mind pouring out that beer? It's against the law to drink in public.'

"Another cop said to me, 'Ian, if you shave off that beard and moustache, we won't charge you next time.' I said, 'What do you mean? Do you mean that I can walk past you, drinking a beer, and you won't give me a ticket?' He said, 'Yes, that's what I mean.'"

Andre said, "The other night, well, I guess it was 4:30 in the morning, Shakes and I were wandering around. We went to the bank. Ian, Marlena and Hippo were asleep on the floor. Ian was closest so I said, 'Ian.' There was no answer, so I said it a little louder, 'Ian.' I kicked his pack sack under his head, no response. I kicked a little harder, still no response.

"Shakes said, 'Ian, you want a drink?' and his hand shot up. 'What do you think? Of course, I want a drink.' Hippo just said, 'Fuck off, I want to sleep.'"

Chicken Man

11 June 2012

"How are you doing, Serge?"

"Not bad. I'm just drinking my lunch. The others are up top." He was sipping from an innocent looking clear plastic water bottle that also contained rubbing alcohol.

"I'll see you later, Serge."

"See you."

Loretta said, "I'm sad today. It's my birthday, I had to appear in court on an assault charge, and I met my ex. We had a big fight right in the courthouse. They think I may get jail time. I hope not."

"Hey," said Silver, "my birthday is coming up this month. What kind of present are you going to buy me, Outcast?"

"How be I give you a kick in the ass? My birthday was in January. What did you give me?"

"Well, could I have a smoke?"

"I'll throw it over the railing. Will you get it?"

"Sure I'll get it."

"How be I throw you over the railing?"

"How old will you be, Silver?" I asked.

"On the 23rd, I'll be 52. Outcast is a couple of months older than I am."

"How old are you, Chester?" I asked.

Chester replied, "I'm 64."

I asked him, "How are you feeling? Are your toes still black from being run over by the bus?"

"Yes, they're still black, but they're getting better. I'm still in a lot of pain. I usually don't take pills. The only thing I take is Demerol. My doctor gives it to me for migraines. They get very bad. I get them about once a month."

Loretta asked Silver, "Have you seen Joy today?" "She was here yesterday. Maybe she panned large and doesn't need to

216

come out today. I'm just staying around until the pigs come. Then I'm taking off. I hid my backpack with my beer in it, so if they come, all I can lose is this can on the railing."

"Friday, they were here nearly every hour," said Outcast. "I kicked over three cans."

Loretta said, "I left my beer on the railing, right where it was. They didn't say anything."

"Debbie's computer crashed today," said Outcast. I had some savings put away, so I bought her this laptop. It was regularly $400; I got it for $200."

Silver said, "Sorry Dennis, for my smoke getting in your face. It's getting so we're not allowed to smoke in parks, restaurant patios or any public places.

"I nearly burnt my bed the other night. My mattress is on the floor. The end of my cigarette fell off and I guess it rolled under the edge of my mattress. I kept asking my roommate, 'Do you smell something burning?' I flipped over my mattress and there was a plate sized, smoldering hole. I got two or three pans of water from the sink and doused it. Then I had to sleep on the floor."

"Silver," said Outcast, "you're dropping ashes on Chester's backpack. Soon, it's going to be on fire."

"Chester," said Loretta, "Come over here and stand in front of me. I want to take off these long pants and put on my shorts. I'm too hot in these."

Outcast said, "I'm really being stupid. I have asthma, I'm smoking and I don't have my puffer with me. I've got lung problems too. Now, it's turned into cancer. In the 1980s I was working on the Post Office building, removing asbestos. We weren't wearing masks. We didn't even know it was dangerous back then. Of the twenty-seven guys I worked with only thirteen are still alive. The rest of us are still waiting for a settlement from the government.

"At least I have insurance so my kids are taken care of. My brother was a fire fighter during 9/11 in New York. His lungs are so badly corroded from the dust and the smoke that he can't do anything. I come from a family of eleven boys and one girl. I'm the youngest."

"That's a big family," I said. I turned to Silver.

"How was your weekend, Silver?"

Silver said, "I panned in my usual places on Saturday and Sunday, the big church and the little one. I worked four shifts from 10:00 am to 1:00 pm. I always do well there.

"This morning I went for breakfast at the Salvation Army. Mondays they always have a full breakfast. I had a three egg sandwich. They have really good sausages there. Tuesday, at the Mission, they're having their full breakfast.

"On Father's Day, the chicken man will be coming by. He came into a lot of money, now he's spreading it around. On Father's Day and on Mother's Day he gives away chicken and turkey hot dogs, and with them he hands out $5 bills. He must know we'll buy booze with the money. From the fumes of our breath alone, he could get drunk."

Barbecue

13 June 2012

Buck went on a run, leaving Dillinger with Loretta. "We've decided that Dillinger is getting confused with so many people telling him what to do, so only Buck and me are allowed to stroke him or give him commands. I don't even let Jake touch him, and I've known him for ten years."

Joy was feeling crowded, "This is getting a bit close for me," she said.

Deaf Donald said to Joy, "Loretta said that I'm not allowed to pat the dog."

Joy tried to explain, "Don't worry, it's not about you. They're trying to train him."

Donald said to Joy, "I'm having a barbecue at my place this afternoon. Do you want to come?"

"Sure, I'm up for it. Make sure you have some Imperial Sherry. I don't drink beer."

Silver said, "A barbecue sounds good. Me, I hate cooking. I like to put something in the microwave, go have a joint and when I'm finished, I eat. Right now, I have a joint rolled on my television set, just waiting for me."

Loretta asked, "Am I invited too?"

Donald didn't answer. When Loretta turned her back, he made a hand sign indicating that she talks too much.

Silver said, "I'll go along with that. In fact I'm going to sit beside Hippo to get away from all the racket."

Donald asked Jake, "Do you want to come to my place for a barbecue this afternoon?"

"Sure."

Andre said to Joy, "Do you know what's going to happen? At the last-minute he's going to tell Jake that he's not invited, so it will be just you and him. He did the same thing to me last week with Loretta."

"In that case, I'll give it a pass. I don't need any of that shit."

Today is Chester's 64th birthday. He was wearing a tee-shirt with a slogan, *I'm 29 (this is an old shirt).*

Loretta asked Joy, "Do you have any kids?"

"I've got five boys. They're all doing well, living in Montreal. They don't smoke, drink or do drugs. Three are working and two are still in school. I promised myself I wouldn't cry, but here I am crying. My youngest was the result of a rape. After my mother told him about it, he asked me, 'Why did you keep me?' I said, 'Your asshole father was just a sperm donor. I carried you, I nursed you, I raised you. Most of all I love you.' He was happy with that."

Loretta said, "I have a daughter who's sixteen now. She has the second highest marks in her class at school. I'm so proud of her. I had a tubal ligation. That hurt more than having a baby."

Joy asked me, "Are you cold?"

"No," I said, "I'm fine."

"Liar!"

"Really, I'm fine."

"Liar!"

"Okay, I'm a bit chilly."

"Here, put my sweatshirt on."

"No, I couldn't do that."

Andre said, "I'm not wearing my jacket. Here, put it on."

"Thanks Andre, I appreciate that."

Hobophobia

14 June 2012

"Where did you sleep, Hippo?" I asked.

"Behind the dumpsters in back of the coffee shop."

Andre said, "I woke up and one of the waitresses came out and asked me if I wanted a coffee. I said 'Sure.' "

Hippo said, "Andre and I both made our price (for a bottle of sherry) today."

"I'm still short a quarter," said Andre.

"Here you go," said Hippo as he handed him a quarter.

Andre said, "I've got a peanut butter and jam and a tuna sandwich if anybody wants one."

Joy said, "Neither of those appeal to me."

"Me neither," said Andre, "That's why I still have them."

"Hey!" said Hippo, "What about me!"

"Hippo," said Joy, "you're a human garbage can."

"I know."

Andre and Hippo wandered off, probably going to the park to relax and have a drink.

Joy said, "I wonder how long that tuna sandwich has been in Andre's backpack." She looked in her cap, "I've been here since 6:00 and I've made exactly $4.20. That's depressing.

"There goes Tim. He's the one with the sign that says, *Help Put an End to Hobophobia.* What does that mean?"

I said, "A homophobe is a person who doesn't like homosexuals. A hobophobe is a person who doesn't like hobos."

"Hobos?" asked Joy, "People like me?"

"Yes, a misogynist is a person who doesn't like women."

"That's Big Jake. I'll have to remember that.

"You have access to a computer, don't you? I'd like the address of Millhaven Penitentiary. I want to write Jake a nasty note using the word 'misogynist.'

"I'm trying to get Fran away from Gene. I said to her, 'Look at me. You've seen me with black eyes, a broken nose, cracked and broken ribs. I could hardly walk because of the chest pain. My legs have been black and blue, all because of Jake. I've seen you with black eyes. If Gene hit you once, he'll hit you again. I know what I'm talking about. If you're ever worried or in trouble, promise you'll phone me. Even if you just want to talk, give me a call.'"

Just then a pigeon, sitting on the roof of the library, shit. It landed on the knee of my pants. Joy laughed as she handed me some paper napkins and her bottle of water.

"That's considered good luck. I'm morbid, but it reminds me of a place I lived. There were two apartment towers, one higher than the other. Most of the tenants were elderly people. One day a friend and I were just leaving the building when I heard a 'thud' and noticed some blood on my leg. At first I thought I had scratched myself on something. Then I saw an old lady lying on the pavement. She actually lifted her head, then died. She'd jumped from the twenty-fifth floor. I guess she felt she'd lived long enough. Why would a person want to end their life like that? Her head made a dent in the pavement.

They had to scrape her face up with a spatula. That's really getting morbid.

"While I was living there, maybe five years, about fifty people jumped to their death. Usually they'd hit the railing. You can imagine what a mess that made."

I said, "That's like the subway jumpers. At least once a week the subway shuts down because someone leaped in front of a subway car."

Joy said, "One time I was waiting at the bus platform. There was a woman beside me who looked like she didn't have a care in the world. When the bus came, she threw herself in front of it. I can still remember the sound of her scream. She wasn't killed. They had to amputate one arm and one leg. I'm not sure what other injuries she had.

"I'm just babbling away here. I'm like dinner and a movie without the dinner. You can have this apple. I can't digest the skin. I've also got a banana. I don't eat much fruit. I'll probably give it to Jacques or Hippo."

This afternoon, at the park I talked to Rocky, "How are you feeling?" I asked.

"I'm okay. I have to see my probation officer at 1:00. I think he's going to breach me."

"Why would he breach you?"

"I was supposed to quit drinking and I haven't."

"Have you been in any programs to help you quit drinking, like Alcoholics Anonymous or the Wet Program at the Shepherd?"

"I'm banned for life at the Shepherd and the Mission. I have six tokens from AA."

"What are the tokens for?"

"They give you a token for every meeting you attend."

"Do you enjoy the meetings?"

"I do enjoy some of them. Some of the speakers are really good. Others take an hour and a half to say what should take five minutes."

"Have you been eating? Do you need money for food?"

"I had breakfast. It's Thursday, so the sandwich ladies will be coming by shortly."

"Hi Gaston," I said, "I visited your website and read about your drop-in center for victims of AIDS.

He said, "I've started two drop-in centers, one here, one in Montreal for children who have been physically or sexually abused."

"How do you go about starting a drop-in center?" I asked.

"First of all, I'm a very confidant person. Before starting any venture, I know I'll succeed. For funding, I approach groups such as the Wives of Lawyers Auxiliary group. I make my presentation to them and they convince their husbands to invest money."

I noticed that Andre was eating his peanut butter and jam sandwich (*pb & j was written on the plastic wrap*). "I thought you didn't like peanut butter and jam, Andre."

"I don't, but when I'm hungry, it's better than nothing. Here Shaggy, see if you like this?" Andre fed small pieces to Shaggy who, hesitant at first, decided that she liked it.

Millhaven Penitentiary

15 June 2012

Joy was quiet this morning, "I didn't have much sleep last night. Chuck had the television on loud until 11:30 pm. The crack heads next door were so loud that he phoned the police. He woke me at 5:00 am. I said, 'You didn't need to wake me. I've been awake most of the night.'

"He's getting lazier and lazier. He got the dog for exercise, but he hardly takes him out. I'll be damned if I'll pay for any dog food. He hasn't been doing any panning; he just lies on the couch watching TV. That means when I get home, I don't have any time to myself. He wants to have a barbecue tomorrow. His parents are coming over. I'll have to check with him later to see if he wants me to get any groceries on my way home."

"I tried to check on Big Jake," I said, "but the information is only available to immediate family."

"How did you check?"

"I searched on the Internet for Jake's name, but nothing came up. I searched for Millhaven and got a directory, but that's as far as I could go. They don't have any listing of inmates. They have instructions as to what to do if you want to visit."

"No, I don't want to visit. I don't want anything to do with him.

"Hippo and Andre were by earlier. They've been sleeping behind the dumpsters in back of the coffee shop. I guess Hippo had been panning across the street from Andre and had only made a quarter. He came over to get a cigarette. He saw a woman reach down toward his hat. He thought she was dropping money, but she took his quarter. They seem to have been eating pretty well according to what they tell me."

I said, "You mentioned yesterday that your youngest son is still in school. Who is he living with?"

"He lives with my oldest, who is 28. He takes really good care of him. The second youngest was adopted out. I guess I wasn't a very good role model. Of course, I didn't have good role models myself.

"Chester hasn't been doing too well lately. He had an inheritance of $8,000 and it was gone in a month. He asked me to do a run for him one time and gave me his bank card and number. I asked him, 'How many people know your bank number?' He said, 'I don't know.' He's been like that ever since he fell down that flight of concrete stairs and split his head open. He forgets a lot of things, and people take advantage of that."

Joy said to me, "My mom was sort of a swamp lady. She'd catch bullfrogs and deep fry them in batter. She'd also make squirrel stew. It tasted a bit gamey. We also ate deer, elk buffalo, bear, and rabbit— pretty much anything.

"Big Jake's parents never approved of me. We stayed at their cottage one time. They left to go back home, and we were to stay there and cut firewood for the winter. Jake got into his mom's codeine pills and spent all his time on the couch. I was the one who went into the woods with the chain saw, cut the trees, hauled them out, cut and split them for firewood.

"I said to him, 'What kind of support is that? I don't know what I'm doing up there. What if a tree had fallen on me?' "

Little Jake had staggered away to lie on the grass with his head on his backpack. Debbie said, "Joy, I've got lots of newspapers here. Why don't you sit on these instead of your blanket? I think Jake should have something over him."

"First of all, Debbie, this blanket is going home with me, to go on my bed. I don't want to be sharing it with Jake. Second, it's warm. He doesn't need anything covering him."

Debbie left to drape some newspapers over Jake. Silver yelled at her, **"Will you just leave him the fuck alone? Jesus!"**

Joy said, "Silver, you don't get your balls up very often, but when you do, it sure is entertaining."

Andre said, "Whatever kind of food I want to eat, that's the type of restaurant I pan in front of. Last night Hippo and I had roast beef, maybe tonight it will be sushi."

Algonquin Land

18 June 2012

"Hi Serge! How have you been feeling?"
"I've been feeling sick the past few days."
"What kind of sickness did you have?"
"Too much booze. I'm taking a break for a while."

Shaggy rubbed against me, slid her head under my hand to be scratched and stroked.

Ian was talking to Andre, looking very somber. He had been sitting with his girlfriend Marlena and had touched her breast. The police saw it and charged him. Ian handed Andre the summons.

Andre said, "I thought you just got a domestic. This says you're charged with sexual assault. You're fucked! If you go within fifty feet of her, you can be charged. Don't get me wrong, Ian, we're family. We know you didn't do anything wrong. We'll always have your back. It's just the police. You're a marked man. Even if she goes to court and tries to have the charges dropped, you'll have a stay on your record. If you get charged for anything else, you'll go straight to jail, and as a sexual offender, expect a lot of beatings. They'll probably put you in PC (*Protective Custody*), but even there you won't be safe."

Daimon said, "I've had domestics before. Even if you're just arguing with your old lady, they can kick you out of your house or apartment. They won't do a thing to her, but if you leave, they figure there's no more problem."

Andre said, "I've served twenty-five years in jail, in and out. If there's one thing I know, it's the law. Since it was the cops who laid the charges against you, it's them you'll have to deal with."

"I have witnesses too," said Ian.

"That could help. One time I was charged with uttering death threats against my wife, her parents and my kids — five counts I was charged with. I spent eleven months dead time before I went to court. When I finally got my court appearance, the judge said, 'Is there anything wrong with this picture? Here's a man pleading innocent after eleven months, and he still hasn't had a trial. I'm throwing this out for time served. Andre, you're free to go.'

" Six-up to my left." One male and one female bicycle police officers rode up. The female said, "Hi Andre, Ian. Are you guys keeping out of trouble?"

"You over there," she said to Outcast. "Did I just see you kick a beer can over the railing?"

"No, but I wouldn't be surprised if you find some empties down there."

"Shakes," she said, "you're sober. What happened?"

"What happened is you made me pour out all my booze last night. I have nothing to drink."

"I'm going to lay it out for you guys. If you're just up here shooting the shit, that's okay, but this is private property. Do you understand? If we see any liquor, you're going to be charged. You got that?"

"Yes, officer," said Andre. "You wouldn't happen to have a smoke would you?"

"No, Andre, I don't smoke."

After the police left, Ian said, "This is Algonquin land. I'm Algonquin. There's no way they can keep me off my own land."

Dennis Cardiff

Chili Beaten

19 June 2012

Joy said, "I was late getting down here because of the rain, but once it stopped, I hopped the bus. I was here about seven thirty. It was too hot for me to come out yesterday.

"We had a barbecue on the weekend with Toothless Chuck's parents. Chili had smashed some coke and was swinging on the pipes above Chuck's mom's head. Chuck was not impressed. He threw her out.

"She told us that Daimon and Lucy had jumped her for her drugs. Her eye is black and swollen now. I told her to keep away from people like that. Lucy is psychotic around women. The other day she saw my phone hanging out of my pocket and she asked to borrow it. I said, 'I have no time left on it. It isn't working.' Then, of course, it rang. She grabbed the phone, and we were struggling for it when Daimon came up behind me and smacked me in the head.

"Stealing from panhandlers is bad. Friends double teaming friends is just sick. I have to get away from people — into the woods somewhere."

I said, "Shark and Irene have mentioned vacationing someplace near the Bay. I think Anastasia also has a place on a lake somewhere."

"I'd love to go somewhere with Irene or Anastasia, but Shark and I would be at each other's throats after a few days."

"Daimon and Lucy are bound to be at the park today because this is the day that Shark gets his meds. I don't think that Irene will come down again. She's too scared."

"Shark said that Anastasia is a bit crazy."

"Irene and Anastasia like to drink together. Usually Anastasia has gone through a bottle of vodka before she even comes to the park. She's so pretty, but she can get weird."

Joy asked Chili, "Does it hurt when you smile or laugh?"
"Yes, it does."

Joy said, "One time I was on the floor when Jake hit me in the cheek with a billy club. I had a bruise in the shape of the letter L. The cops asked Jake if he had done it. He said, 'One of your finest did that.'

"I'm going to call Toothless to see if he'll change his mind about letting you stay at our place." She dialed his number.

"Hi Chuck, I'm sitting with Chili. She's sorry for what happened on the weekend. She knows she fucked up, but she has no other place to stay and I'm trying to keep her away from Daimon and Lucy. Chuck, don't hang up okay? Chuck…" She snapped the phone off. "He hung up. He's still pissed about that thing with his mother."

Chili said, "I know I fucked up."

Andre came over and gave the women a hug. "Andre," said Joy. "How can you sit with that pair of assholes after seeing what they did to Chili?"

"It's just that I've known Daimon for over twenty years. I used to hang out with his older brother who is three times his size."

"Has Daimon always been an asshole?"

"Yeah, he's always been the same."

Joy said, "Will you come with us to the bank? Chili needs to deposit some money, and she's afraid that Daimon and Lucy are going to jump her again."

"Sure, I'll ride shotgun."

"Thanks, Andre, you're someone I know I can trust."

Daimon and Lucy eventually walked away together.

Joy said, "I really wish someone would boot-fuck those assholes until they were just twitching. Then, maybe, we'd call 911 – sorry too late. I'm really the matriarch around here. Jacques and I are the last two left from the old group, now that Rip is dead."

Psycho

"Hi Joy, how did everything go after I left yesterday? Was there any more trouble with Daimon and Lucy?"

"No, Andre walked Chili and me down to where she had to go, then I took the bus home. When I was on the bus, I realized that I didn't have my phone. I had it tucked into the cuff of my jeans. It must have fallen out when I was helping Chili. I tried phoning the number and it sounded like a kid that answered. I said, 'Look, I've just gotten off the bus. I really need my telephone. Would you do me a really big favor and bring it to the mall?' Then the phone went dead. I tried calling the number later, but it wasn't in service.

"A guy gave me a phone, but I have to pay a $35 activation fee. I'm going to check around and see if I can get a better deal than that.

"I swear that I'm going to give Loretta a shot in the head today."

"What did she do?" I asked.

"She was panning in front of the coffee shop. I said to her, 'You can't stay here, you're cutting my grass.' I sent her over to see Silver. He sent her over to Hippo's spot. She probably only got about ten minutes before the woman from the hotel asked her to move.

"Chuck has been real pissy lately. He's always talking down to me. Last night when I came home, I still had a piece of steak in the fridge. I nuked it, then put it in a bun with cream cheese. It tasted just like one of those Philly Steak and Cheese sandwiches that you can get at that fast food place. I worked at one of those places one time. It was mostly a front for a drug operation. I left just before they got raided.

"Nicholas was really getting on my nerves. He just kept talking and talking about everything. He even followed me into my room. I said to him, 'Nicholas, you may know about some things, but you don't know everything. If you don't shut the fuck up, I'm going to do you right here.' "

" 'But I have a girlfriend,' he says.

"I said, 'I didn't mean that I wanted to have sex with you. I meant that I was going to punch you in the head.'

"Chuck was barbecuing and asked me if I wanted a sausage. I said, 'No.' He got all pissy about that and I really lost it. I packed all my things, put them in my bag and walked out. I slept behind the coffee shop. I had my blanket under me, a soft pile of cardboard underneath and another blanket that I pulled over my head.

"Hippo and Andre came by sometime in the night. Andre peeked under the corner of the blanket and said, 'Hey, it's Joy.' Later on he said, 'I may accidentally put my arm around you in my sleep.' The first time he did it, I just moved his arm. The second time, I gave him a shot in the head. I didn't want any spooning going on. I was all snugly. Andre and Hippo shivered all night. I don't know why they don't get some blankets or a sleeping bag. There are lots available now.

"Hippo had a shower the other day and he's acting all different like, 'I'm King Hippo.' He's still wearing the same dirty pants that are nearly worn through. He said to me, 'Joy we should go down to the park now.' I don't need him telling me where I should and shouldn't go.

"I have to see my 'probie' today. She wants me to move to a women's shelter. I don't even know where it is. I've talked to a few women who've lived there. They say there are a lot of rules, like doing daily chores, not coming in drunk, once a week having to cook a meal for the entire floor. I don't even cook for myself. If I can't throw it in the nuker, I don't buy it."

I said, "How about sharing a place with Loretta? You seem to get along fine with her."

"The only problem is that she's too far away. I don't want to stay somewhere it takes three busses to get downtown. The only person I would consider living with is Pierre. He's invited me over sometimes on the weekend. He has a twelve-year-old son that he talks to on the telephone. I hear him saying, 'I love you, son.' I can hear the son saying, 'I love you dad.' That's really special.

"Pierre says he's not interested in a relationship. He's interested in a friend with benefits. He's a bit older than I am, but it's something to think about."

I said, "I met Pierre yesterday. He seems nice. I think he'd probably treat you well. Why don't you give it a try?"

Before getting ready to leave, I asked, "So, what's going to happen with Daimon and Lucy? Are they going to just keep on jumping, beating and robbing people?"

"Yeah, until Daimon goes back to jail. I felt so bad when I saw that you weren't wearing your watch yesterday. It's really bad when friends can't visit friends without stashing their stuff." Before I left work, I had taken the precaution of putting my watch in my pocket.

I sat next to Hippo. Someone had found a newspaper photo of a hippopotamus. The photo was being passed around and someone was teasing Hippo that it was an image of his father. Hippo said, "Yeah, he's famous. He got his picture in the paper and he's being fed by a prince or something.

"I remember one time going to the Clayton fair. It's a tiny town, but they have a big fair. That's where I got driven over by a car. Another guy drove his truck straight into the swamp. He was just sitting there in the cab. He thought he was still driving. Somebody was there with a big winch truck. Nobody wanted to jump into the swamp to hook up the chain, so I did — *bloop*."

I was surprised to see Chili sitting next to Lucy and Daimon. Her bruises still haven't healed from the last time she was with them.

"We went to pan this morning," said Daimon, "There was a guy in our spot. I said, 'Get the fuck out of here! This is our spot.' He didn't move, so I kicked him in the head. Then he moved."

Hippo said, "I had to ask Loretta to move. She was in my spot."

"What if she hadn't moved?" asked Andre.

"Then I would have asked Lucy to move her."

Daimon said, "There is someone else that's looking for a beating. It's Alphonse and Magdalene."

Gene said, "Daimon could take Alphonse, Lucy could take Magdalene."

Andre said, "The problem is, Magdalene is five months pregnant."

"I don't have a problem with hitting a pregnant woman," said Daimon.

"It's a shame," said Gene, "that someone would beat and rob Shakes. All you have to do is ask him for something and he'll either say, 'Yes!' or 'No!' That's not complicated."

"If it's, 'No,' " said Daimon, "you can wait until he passes out, then take it... I was just kidding!"

No Matter Where We Go, They Tell Us To Move

21 June 2012

I sat down with Silver, then I saw Magdalene and Alphonse sitting across the street. It appeared that Alphonse had bought Magdalene something cold to drink.

"So, Silver, have you made a decision about moving out of your place?"

"I don't know. I've been there so long, over four years. There aren't too many crack heads. There are a few pot smokers down the hall. Everyone pretty much keeps to themselves. I like it that way.

"It's really hot for sleeping, even with two fans going. They just move the hot air around. I have to get a new mattress. I burned the last one and threw it out, so now I'm sleeping on the floor. I just keep tossing and turning.

"I got my last mattress from the Mission. I don't know where I'll get the next one. I'm worried about bedbugs. I don't have any now, but the landlord brought around some bed bug traps. I said, 'Oh no, not this again!' I hate bedbugs. It's people who bring them in, especially the ones who stay at the Mission or the Shepherd.

"Something really spooky happened last night. I usually leave the door to my room ajar, for air circulation. I woke up and my roommate was standing in the doorway. I jumped up and asked him, 'What's going on, man?' He was sound asleep. I shook him and he said, 'I must have been sleepwalking.' That could be dangerous. He could fall down the stairs. I said to him this morning, 'You really weirded me out last night, man.' He didn't remember a thing.

"After you left the park yesterday, the cops showed up again, a Sergeant and a rookie. He said, 'If there are more than four of you guys sitting around, we're going to ask you to move.' I said, 'What if there are a lot of groups with just four each? Is that okay?'

"He said, 'We'll be back. You'd better be gone.'

"I wandered over to the loading dock. I'd bought myself a big sausage sandwich and I drank my beer. I know all the guys there. They don't know that I panhandle."

I said, "I saw Hippo last night at about six o'clock. He was really drunk and said that he still had a bottle to go. He hadn't been eating."

Silver said, "He can really eat when he wants to. We went to a wake for Hobo at the funeral home. They put out six meals for us downstairs before we went to the service. Hippo stayed behind. When we got back, he'd eaten all six meals.

"Hippo really guzzles that sherry. I don't know why people drink that. It's killed so many of my friends, like Hobo and Rip — no, I think Rip's still alive. They have him under house

234

arrest. He wears one of those collars on his ankle. As soon as he leaves his front door, an alarm rings.

"He was nearly killed by a six-foot Amazon woman. I don't know what he saw in her. She was nuts. She pulled a knife on him. He tried to defend himself. He got a slash across the palm of his hand and a stab wound to the groin."

I was about to shake Wolf's hand when I saw that it was purple and swollen. He said, "I won't shake your hand today. I was feeding Bear and she bit me. It's Weasel's dog, he should be taking care of her, wherever he is."

Daimon and Lucy were just leaving with Shakes. "Are they heading off to work?" I asked.

Jake said, "Yeah, they're taking Shakes to his office. He's so drunk he couldn't make it by himself. I expect that his pockets will have been emptied before they leave him."

Gene said, "I'm going to have to go to work just to get a smoke and a drink."

Hippo had been drunk when I met him the night before. I asked him, "How are you feeling?"

"Hot!"

Andre said, "I was panning last night in front of the coffee shop. A guy dropped me thirty dollars. I thanked him and said, 'Don't forget my buddy across the street.' He walked across and dropped Hippo a twenty. We did a lot of drinking after that. I had the shakes so bad this morning, I couldn't do anything. I'm still feeling a bit rough, but I'll be okay. I'm just going to take it easy." He pulled out an egg salad sandwich from his backpack. He said, "I'd better eat this before it goes bad."

I said, "It's Thursday, the sandwich ladies must have come around."

"Yeah," said Hippo, "they were just here." He was sipping on a drinking box of apple juice.

Two bicycle cops rode up on the lawn, a male and a female. I had seen them there a few days ago. The female stopped to talk to Wolf's group. The male rode up to where we were sitting.

"How are you guys doing?"

"We're just enjoying the shade," answered Andre.

"Andre, are you sober?"

"Stone cold sober."

"Why is that?"

"I woke up with the shakes this morning and thought I'd better give my body a rest."

"Why did you have the shakes?"

"I drank too much last night." He held out his shaking hand.

To me the officer said, "Where are you staying, sir?"

"I live nearby."

"Why are you here?"

"Just visiting with my friends."

"You guys know that they don't want you here. Why don't you find another place that we don't patrol all the time?"

"No matter where we go," said Andre, "they tell us to move along. We're not drinking, there's not a big group of us, we're just enjoying the shade. Where do you want us to go?"

"I'll check with my partner."

I noticed that Wolf was being charged, probably with a liquor violation. After the officer finished writing the ticket, they both rode off.

Andre said, "I'm going to go pick some butts." Shortly after that I left. I met Andre coming back with a handful of cigarette butts.

Saint Nick

22 June 2012

I surprised Joy when I said, "Hello!"

"You scared me! I wasn't around yesterday. I was taken to hospital with heat stroke. I asked the doctor, 'How can that be? I've been drinking lots of water. I have two large bottles in my bag.' He said, 'Some people are more susceptible than others, especially if your immune system is low.'

"I hate hospitals. I couldn't wait to get out. When I was in there in November, I picked up some superbug, MRSA *(methicillin-resistant staphylococcus aureus)* or VRE *(vancomycin-resistant enterococci)*. That's why I was in so long. I could have died from that.

"When I got home, Chuck lit into me, 'Where have you been? I made supper for you!' I said, 'Before you get all wound up, listen to me. I've been in hospital. I had heat stroke and they kept me overnight.'

" 'Oh, I'm sorry. Anyway, there are a couple of pieces of chicken left in the oven,' he said.

"'Oh really? How long have they been in there? I think I'll leave those for you, Chuck.'

"He invited Nicholas and Corrine over for a barbecue yesterday. They were sitting on my bed. Chuck knows I don't like that. I asked him, 'Chuck, when am I ever going to get this place alone to myself?' He said, 'Maybe Sunday.' I've got to get away from here."

I told Joy, "I have the addresses and phone numbers for the YMCA. There is one a few blocks from here if you want to check it out."

She said, "The problem with the Y is they don't allow smoking, and you can't cook in your room. I can't imagine living in a place where I couldn't smoke or cook.

"Nick isn't with Trudy any longer. He said I could stay at his place for free. I could even have my own bedroom. He's a real sweetheart and he's quiet."

I said, "I've talked to Nick many times. I'm really impressed with him. He makes sandwiches and hands them out to homeless people. He's really a great guy."

Joy nodded. "So what's been happening at the park? What drama have I missed?"

"Chili is hanging out with Daimon and Lucy. That was a surprise! The other day she left with them. The three of them were heading downtown."

"That poor kid, she just won't learn."

I added, "The police were by yesterday afternoon. "The cop said, 'You guys know that they don't want you here. Why don't you find another place that we don't patrol every day?' "

"That's just it," said Joy, "they're talking about that place being private property. I've never heard that before and we've been going there for fourteen years. The other cop said we could stay there as long as we weren't in a big group, like twenty people. Otherwise we were okay."

I asked, "What kind of a beef do Daimon and Lucy have against Alphonse and Magdalene? A couple of days ago, Daimon said they were in for a beating. Andre said, 'Magdalene is five months pregnant.' Daimon said, 'I have no problem with hitting a pregnant woman.' "

Joy said, "I told those guys they should gang up, jump him and beat the shit out of him. I'd have no trouble one on one with Lucy and she knows it. The problem is Daimon. He can't just go around beating and robbing people. When the cops were by the other day, they were checking out some of the guys. I kept nodding towards Daimon and Lucy. They must have a breach outstanding somewhere. The cops just ignored them.

"Alphonse has always been a sweet quiet guy. I don't know Magdalene."

When I arrived at the park Joy was sitting alone. "I'm not being antisocial," she said. "It's just that the reflection of the sun from that building over there was shining in my eyes. I think it's moved now, so let's go join the group."

"Have you talked to Nick? Is everything okay about you staying there?" I asked.

"Yeah, I even asked him if I paid by the month, would it be alright if I moved in permanently. He said we could work out the details, but it was fine with him. I didn't want to talk too much. I don't want everyone knowing my business."

We joined the group and Nick said to Joy, "You come over any time you want – rain or shine. I don't want to see you sleeping outside again."

"I won't come unannounced," said Joy, "I'll phone first."

"Don't worry about that. I'm usually home."

"It's just that Chuck always has so many people over."

"I know, and who ends up funding these barbecues? You do."

"I just can't afford it." Said Joy. "Even around here — I bought a carton of cigarettes from Wolf and I had maybe a third of them. The rest went to Hippo, Little Jake and Andre. Chester hit me up for bus tickets. I know his leg is still hurting him, but I have to get home as well. I don't owe Chester anything. It's him that owes me."

Joy left to talk to Chuck. Nick said to me, "Every morning when I walk across the bridge, I'm surprised at who comes out. I have sandwiches that I distribute. I bought some of those plastic containers and filled them with stew. I gave out sixteen of them. I got one container back; the rest weren't returned.

"Sometimes, I'll meet someone and I'll invite them to come with me to a restaurant for coffee or breakfast. They might ask, 'Could you buy me a beer?' I say,' Coffee or food, but no beer.'

"I always have my Bible with me and I pray for people. We may not be the same religion, but it doesn't matter. I think it's of help to have someone pray for them."

Nick's phone rang. He talked for a while then handed the phone to Joy.

Joy said, "Hi Pierre, how are you? Are you pissed with me? I was in hospital. I had to stay overnight. I didn't have my phone with my contact list. I didn't know how to get a message to you. Am I still going to see you on the weekend?

Oh… I'll call you then. Bye." She handed the phone back to Nick.

"He's acting all pissy because he had invited me to his place for a barbecue and I was going to sleep over, but that was the day I went into hospital. I didn't have my phone. I couldn't contact him. He says that he has things to do on the weekend and he has a lot on his mind. His girlfriend is in Inuktuk with his year old baby. He's heard that it isn't his, but what's he going to do?"

I said, "It shouldn't matter to him whether it's his child or not."

"I agree; a baby needs love. It doesn't matter where it comes from."

It was time for me to leave. "It'll all work out, Joy. I see good things in your future. Have a good weekend."

I said goodbye to Nick. He hugged me and said, "I love you, brother."

I said, "I love you, Nick. We're on the same path."

Weasel in Hospital

25 June 2012

"Hi Andre!" I said, "How was your weekend?"

"My weekends are always good. Every day is good. I'm just a carefree, happy guy. I've already made my price and enough for another (*bottle*). I don't know why the Sally let me in last night, I was so drunk. I made my price, downed it, made my price again, downed that too. I was staggering from one side of the walk to the other."

Joy said, "I saw you last night. I said to you, 'Where's the real Andre?' I don't think you knew your own name. It's good that you left Hippo and Little Jake on their own. It'll show them how much they depend on you to get drops."

Andre said, "Yeah, Jake works hard, but he's got to open up more. Hippo does nothing. He has his legs straight out and his cup between them. People have to step over his legs to make a drop. Some people resent panhandlers taking up so much room on the sidewalk, especially when the walking traffic is heavy.

He continued, "I also try not to let people see me smoke. I'll hide the cigarette behind a column or behind my back. If they think I can afford to smoke, they think I can afford to eat. I was panning with a guy one time. He kept checking his computer pad. A woman was ready to drop him a five when she heard the guy's phone ring. He pulled it out to answer and the woman stuffed the bill back in her purse. She said, 'I can't afford a pad or a cell phone. You're better off than I am,' "

Joy said, "I keep telling Roy not to phone me here. He'll ask, 'What are you doing?' I'll say, 'What do you think I'm doing? You're spoiling my business. Phone me back after nine.' It's not that he has anything to say, maybe 'If you see Buck, get some cigarettes.' "

I asked, "Did you work things out with Nick, for a place to stay?"

"No, I'm going to stay with Chester. I spent the weekend there. He's still upset about Anne leaving him. He's kind of let things go. I spent most of Saturday cleaning. He has a beautiful place. I sleep on a pull out couch in the living room.

"Sunday we just took it easy. I had some money, so I bought chicken. We had it with mac and cheese. Chester's quiet. I like that. We just had a few drinks, a few joints. It was nice.

"When I got to Chuck's place this morning, all I could smell was V. There's nothing worse than the smell of a wet dog.

"Chuck had a bunch of people over for the weekend. All the food I bought last week was gone, and the place was a mess. I told him I was leaving. He said, 'You'll be sorry.' I said, 'Yeah, I'll be sorry alright. Sorry to have extra food in the fridge. Sorry to have extra money and cigarettes.' "

Loretta approached me and asked, "Dennis, can you spare me some bus tickets. I have to go to hospital. It's because of the car accident I was in a few months ago. I'm going to see a plastic surgeon. He's going to do more work on my face and my knee. As soon as my gums finish healing, I'll be getting a set of dentures."

"Sure Loretta," I said, "Here are some bus tickets."

"Thank you so much."

Wolf came over to me. I tentatively reached out to shake his bruised hand. "It's okay now, we can shake hands, the swelling has mostly gone. You can still see Bear's teeth marks on my wrist.

"Dennis, would you do me a big favor. I've been looking after Bear since the police took Weasel to hospital. The thing is, I just don't know what to do with her. I haven't heard from Weasel. I've asked people here with phones to make an enquiry about him at the hospital. He hasn't any friends. Nobody will make the call. Will you phone the hospital and see if he's still in there? If he is, try to find out if, or when, he's getting out. If he's been moved, try to find out where he is. Will you do that for me?"

"Sure, Wolf."

"I've cleaned my balcony and Bear's staying out there. She really made a stinking mess, but I cleaned that. She has a big pail of water to drink and she's used to living outdoors. Of course, when it is really hot, I bring her inside. Stella likes Bear and she'll take her to the farm, if that's what Weasel wants. I've taken good care of her, but when I tried to attach her leash, to take her for a walk, she bit my hand. I'm only starting to gain use of it again. I can't leave her alone with Shaggy because they don't get along. Shaggy is eleven years old. Bear could kill her. I don't want that to happen."

"I understand, Wolf. I'll phone the hospital and see what I can find out. I'll let you know any news tomorrow."

"Thanks, Dennis. I really appreciate that."

I questioned the man sitting beside Wolf, "How've you been, Norman?"

"It's Gaston, but that's okay."

"I probably called you Norman last Friday. I'm sorry; my memory for names isn't very reliable."

"I understand. I'm the same way. Often, I'll be in the middle of a conversation before the person's name comes to me. The message is more important than the name. That's been my experience. I study communication with people. I teach communication with people. If I could, I'd study at the university all my life. I'd love that.

"I also like working with people, sometimes at the Mission, sometimes at the HIV Clinic, sometimes here. What I've learned about homeless people, alcoholics and drug addicts is that they're not always connected to their true selves. They put up barriers. They lose control. A few beers or a few glasses of wine will give you a small buzz, but you're still in control. Drinking is more than that; it's the alcohol controlling you, not you controlling the alcohol. It's used to get away from memories that are painful. Memories of abuse and neglect. I've suffered from abuse and neglect.

"I went through years of university on heroin. I used very small quantities to give me a lift, just a pinch here, a pinch there. I've never come close to overdosing on drugs. Are you familiar with what an 8-ball is? It's an eighth of an ounce of cocaine. I've seen people do an entire 8-ball.

"There is an article in the paper about homelessness. They're going about it all wrong. Instead of dealing with the problem, they spend more and more money to inconvenience the homeless. This is a public park. The police have no right to ask us to move. Look how much time and money they put into that. What we need is more support for addiction facilities, better sleeping accommodations for the homeless, more access to food. I analyze all these things and try to come to some sort of resolution. Then I write about it."

On my way back to work, I saw Serge sitting in the bus shelter. "How are you doing, Serge? I see your eyes are black. Did someone beat you?"

"It happened right over there, where that person is sitting. My shoelace was too long. I fell on the sidewalk."

"I'm sorry to hear that. Are you feeling better now?"

"I'm fine. I've fallen before."

I phoned the hospital. By telling them I was Weasel's brother, Wolf, they put me through to him. I said, "Hi Weasel, Wolf asked me to give you a call. He was wondering how you were doing, when you are getting out and what to do with Bear."

"Tell Wolf I'm getting out right now. I'll be home in twenty minutes."

"I'll tell him that. I'm glad to hear that you're health has improved. I'll pass your message on to Wolf."

Silver and the Coffee Shop

26 June 2012

Sitting in front of the coffee shop, on a plastic storage container, I asked Silver, "You mentioned that you went to reform school when you were young. Tell me about it."

"I first went to reform school because I stole some money. I stole sixty dollars from one of my mom's friends. I didn't spend any of the money. I hid it in my sock drawer. The lady called the police. She told them, 'I'm missing some money and I know who took it.'

"I was coming home from school. I saw the police car and my sister was crying. The police said that if I returned the money, the lady wouldn't press charges. I said to my sister, 'Don't worry, I have the money. I can return it. Everything will be okay.' I went to my sock drawer and the money was gone. Somebody in my family found the money and took it. So, that's why I went to reform school. I did some other things, nothing very bad -- kid things. They seemed like good ideas at the time.

"Sunday I went to my church. Lately there have been a lot of new people panning there. They had every door covered. I said to one of them, 'You're in my spot.' He said, 'I've been coming here a long time. Do you know what time the service starts?' I said, 'You've been coming here a long time and you don't know what time the service starts? Yeah, sure!' It was a bunch of crack heads. There was no point in getting into a fist fight about it. I'll see if they're there next Sunday."

I said, "Gaston was at the park Friday. He seems like a decent person. Does he come by often?"

"Yeah, he and his friend are both quiet. They don't cause any trouble. They call him Bird. I don't know why."

"When I talked to him Friday, he was telling me about rescuing a skunk who had fallen into a ditch and couldn't get out. I know he has cats and a dog. I think he mentioned that birds come right up to him. I guess he likes birds."

"That would make sense."

I said, "Have you seen anything of Daimon and Lucy lately?"

"No, not since Friday."

"I don't get it," I said, "They want to beat up Alphonse and Magdalene. Alphonse is small and Magdalene is five months pregnant. They have no money, no anything, they're panhandlers. What do Daimon and Lucy hope to gain from that?"

"They're both psychopaths. What we should do is get a group of us together, jump them and beat the shit out of them. Then they'll get the message that they're not welcome."

"That was Joy's idea," I said. "How long have you been panning here, Silver?"

"I've been here about eleven years. I used to be where Joy is now. After she got out of prison, she said it was her spot. She gave me a couple of cigarettes for it. That was okay. I didn't like that spot anyway. I got a few tickets there for panhandling. For some reason they don't seem to bother Joy. When I was still with my ex, I used to pan on the other side of this column. It's a government building. They said that I was blocking their fire exit and asked me to move. If there had been a fire I wouldn't have stayed around to be in anybody's way. I'd have been long gone. Just to annoy them, I moved a few feet over. Now I'm in front of the coffee shop. I've talked to the owner. He doesn't mind me being here, he just asked that I don't open the door for the ladies. I said, 'That's no problem.' Now the ladies open their own doors.

"When I got out of prison I worked for a retired cop. I'd mow his lawn, dig his garden, anything that needed doing around the yard. He watched every move I made, as if I was going to steal something from his garden. Finally, I got fed up. I told him, 'With you watching me all the time it's as bad as being in jail.' I guess it gets in their blood.

"Hey Dora!" Silver yelled, "Where's my treat?" She came back a few minutes later with a toasted Danish. "Dora, I was just kidding."

"A customer left it on the counter. Don't you want it?"

"Of course I want it. Thanks, Dora!"

A man stopped and dropped a folded ten dollar bill in Silver's cap. "I've made forty dollars so far. It's just about time to quit for the day."

"Hi, Serge," I said, "How are your eyes today? Do you have any headaches? You didn't fall again did you?"

"No, I didn't fall again. Last night I slept in a park nearby. It was nice."

Andre gestured to a camp stool and said, "Have a seat. Gene gave this to me. Look down below." I looked. There were two zippered pockets. One held a plate, plastic glass and cutlery. The second was a cooler.

"That cooler will hold ten beers or four bottles of sherry. The cops won't even know I have any liquor. Yesterday I must have drunk, let me think… nine bottles of sherry. I've got a hangover now, so I haven't been drinking. See my hand shaking?"

I asked, "What's this carved wooden animal in your hat? Is this for good luck?"

"You don't recognize it?"

"It looks like a bear."

"It's a kitty cat. I call it my pocket pussy."

Gene commented on a German Shepherd that was being led on a leash by its owner. "That's a beautiful dog. It's well-groomed too."

"Yes, it's had a lot of brushing."

Gene said, "I used to have a dog just like that, a King German Shepherd named Chinook. He was a really smart dog. There are a lot of tests that you can put a dog through to determine its intelligence; putting food under an upside down cup, putting a blanket over the dog's head. He passed all the tests. He knocked the cup over to get the food, shook his head to get out from under the blanket. Some dogs would just sit there, like when you put a cover over a birdcage.

"We had a four foot fence around our yard. I had a problem with some neighborhood kids who were teasing and throwing stones at Chinook. I told their parents what was happening and asked if I could teach the kids a lesson. They said, 'Okay.' When the kids came over again, I went out and talked to them. I said, 'This dog is almost as big as you are. It has a gentle nature unless it's provoked. This dog could kill you. You think you're safe behind this fence? Watch this.' I gave the command, 'Chinook, over!' He easily jumped the fence and came to my side. He used to jump into the back of my pickup.

You should have seen the expression on those kids' faces. Their eyes were like saucers when they saw the dog up close.

"We had kids in the house at the time, so we didn't smoke or drink very much. It's a funny thing, but Chinook didn't like people smoking or drinking. It was alright if I was sitting at the table and had a few beers or a smoke, but if someone came to the door with the smell of alcohol or cigarettes on them, he'd get upset. He even growled at my mother-in-law. I asked her if she'd been drinking. She said she had. If I was sitting on the lawn with a beer beside me, Chinook would knock it over. He was great with kids. They'd pile on top of her, pull her ears. He wouldn't react at all."

Gene's cell phone began to ring. "I'm going to have to take this," he said. "I'm supposed to be working today. I'm a carpenter. My boss has my belt and all my tools. I can't contact him. I think he's at his cottage. If he didn't have any work for me, I could have found work with someone else... if I had my tools."

I said to Joy, "I talked to Weasel yesterday. He's been in the hospital since last Tuesday. He got out around four yesterday. I bet Wolf will be happy. He won't have to look after Bear anymore."

Joy said, "Wolf's hand still hasn't fully healed from where Bear bit him. I was thinking that maybe Weasel had died. If he had, I wonder how many people would attend his funeral."

Silver said, "That's a morbid thing to say, Joy."

"I'm not wishing he was dead, I was just thinking that it wouldn't be like the funeral we attended for Hobo. That was packed."

Steve said, "It looks like Bear has already started digging a grave for him here in the lawn."

"It's a pretty shallow grave," said Silver.

Joy said, "A shallow grave would be good enough. He's skinny. I'd be glad to throw in the first shovel of dirt."

Hippo said, "I'm getting pissed off with Jake. We've been panning together and he keeps saying stupid things like, 'This is my bridge.' It scares people away. If that's his bridge, then this is my park."

Pierre said, "I have to go home to feed my kid and me."
Andre said, "What's that?"
Joy said, "Pierre has a son. He has to go home and make his lunch."
"Oh," said Andre, "I thought he said, 'I have to go home to feed my kidney.' That just sounded wrong."
Pierre said to Joy, "Do you want me to cut the ribs?"
"Separate them; don't cut through the bone."
"That's what I meant."

Rocky arrived and said hello. "Hi, Rocky, how are you feeling?"
"I'm good."
"Is your stomach okay? Have you been eating?"
"I've been eating."
"Have you received any more information about housing?"
"I move July 15th."
"Do you know the location yet?"
"It's far away. To get here, I'd take a bus, a subway, then a streetcar. That takes about forty-five minutes. It's about half an hour to downtown."
"How did it go with your probation officer? You were worried about being breached."
"No, he didn't breach me. I've been going to my AA meetings."
"That sounds great, Rocky. It sounds a lot better than when you were throwing up blood in the bushes."

Andre said, "You know, I got five tickets the other day. I was sitting on the sidewalk with a couple of guys; actually it was Jake and Hippo. There was an open bottle in front of me.

The cop said, 'Whose bottle is that?' I said, 'I might as well own up to it.' He wrote me up. I said, 'Since I'm being charged, can I keep the bottle?' He said, 'I'll ask my partner.' His partner was my cousin. Of course he said I could keep it.

"He said, 'We're going to come back. If you're still here, you'll be charged again.' We stayed and we were charged again. I even got a charge for smoking within twenty feet of a doorway."

Outcast said, "Something similar happened to me. I was drinking a big bottle of beer. The cop charged me and I said, 'Can I at least drink the rest of this beer instead of dumping it?' He said, 'If you can down it before I finish writing up your friend, go for it.'

"Well, it went down in two seconds."

Wolf said, "I was talking to Francois the other day. Remember he and I got tickets? I said to the cop, 'It's my fault that he's here. Can you go a bit easy on him?' The cop wrote him up. I only found out today that he only got a warning. I got two tickets, $125 each. He has a driver's license, so he would have had to pay the fine before he could renew his license. For me it doesn't matter."

Daimon Gets Stomped

27 June 2012

Jou said, "I still haven't told Chuck that I'm moving, but I won't be giving him any rent money for July. I'll give him a hundred towards the cable bill. He's really been nasty to me lately. He phoned me at the park yesterday and asked, 'Are you coming home tonight?' I said, 'I don't know, maybe I will, maybe I won't.' 'If you do,' he said, 'bring me some pot.'

Andre came trudging up the sidewalk with his backpack, a raincoat and his folding stool. "I don't know what happened last night, but I found this in my cap." He held up a business card from a ninety-nine dollar hooker.

I said, "That should give you some clue."

"No, that's not in my price range. What really scared me is finding this rock in my cap." He held up a one pound rock. "This swung in my cap makes a mean weapon, just like a billy club. I vaguely remember saying to some guy, 'You want my money? Try and take it from me.' I don't know what happened after that. I went a bit haywire yesterday. I nearly got in a fight with Daimon. I said, 'Your brother is three times your size and I took him, so come and get it.' His brother is huge — twenty-two inch arms, about six-foot seven. He's a monster. He'd have to duck and go through a door sideways.

"I'm going to have to go to work. I need a drink." With that he left.

I asked Joy, "If Daimon just got out of prison, would he still be an addict?"

"It's much easier to get drugs on the inside than it is on the outside."

"So," I asked, "did I miss anything after I left yesterday?"

"No, it was pretty quiet. I waited for Pierre to come back. Then we watched a few videos. His son is 24 years old. He's autistic and has a mental age of about 12. We get along great. We were about to watch *Paranormal 2*. He said to me, 'You're going to be scared.' I said, 'I don't think so.' There is a part where this guy is being dragged off the bed by a demon. I jumped off the couch and ran down the hall. Everyone got a good laugh out of that."

"How are you doing, Serge?" I asked.

"I'm fine. I'm just going to the bench near the bank. I want to sit down before I fall down again."

There was lots of excitement in the neighborhood. Andre was swearing. He dragged Ian by the ankles for about twenty feet. Then Ian and Shakes started fighting, rolling around on the lawn.

I sat next to Joy and asked, "What's this about?"

"Ian is drunk and was being a dickhead to everyone. Andre had enough and went after him."

Ian eventually slunk back to the circle. "I don't know what I did wrong."

Andre answered, "Your woman screwed you over, pressed charges against you. Now you're drunk. You ask us for help. Sure we're going to help you; we're family, but don't act like a dickhead and treat us like shit."

I noticed that Shakes' leg was bleeding and that he had a burn scar near his ankle. "How did that happen?" I asked Joy.

"I'm not sure of the details. I don't think he remembers. Someone set him on fire. The same thing happened to another homeless guy sleeping on a park bench. Someone doused him with gasoline, then threw a lighted match. He was wearing a plastic raincoat and it melted into his skin. He was released from hospital and was staying at the Sally, but after three days of pain, he just gave up and died."

Joy asked Andre and Jake, "Where's your brother from another mother, Hippo?"

"He got money from his mother, now he doesn't feel that he should associate with the likes of us."

"He's being a real asshole, considering all you've done to help him. If he comes back to your place (behind the dumpsters in back of the coffee shop) you should lock him out."

"I'll do more than lock him out, I'll knock him out."

"Did everyone hear the good news?" asked Joy, "Rocky just told me that Daimon and Lucy got beat up by some black dude named Buddy. Lucy was knocked out. Daimon was stomped and has a broken leg. It happened last night. Rocky was there; I wish he'd caught it on video."

"I'm sorry to hear that," said Andre, "I was hoping to do that myself."

Gene said, "Daimon's not so tough. He kept bragging about his maximum security prison background, but I beat him one time. He sucker punched me on the side of the head. He was surprised that I came back with three punches. I knocked him into a closet. Then he ran away like somebody's bitch."

"When I was still with my Jake," said Joy, "Daimon came after me. Big Jake pushed him and Daimon bounced twice on his ass. Jake said, 'Don't even think of getting up.'

To me Joy said, "Chester says I can move in anytime, even if I haven't got my check yet. I hope that Chuck doesn't have a hissy fit when I tell him that I'm leaving. Maybe I should pack my clothes first. I don't want him throwing my stuff out the door or anything."

Okay, hire me!

29 June, 2012

I sat beside Shark. I asked him, "This is the weekend that Irene moves, isn't it?"

"No, a month from now, August first. She's on her own now. She invited me over to her place last night. I brought pork chops, potatoes, two bags of groceries. She said, 'Get out!'

" 'You mean right now?' I said.

" 'Get out!'

" 'Okay,' I said, 'I'm going, but don't expect me back!' I packed up the groceries and left."

"Had she been drinking?" I asked.

"Had she ever. She was into the lemonade coolers that are 7% alcohol. Then she added regular vodka which is 37%. These things taste so good that, on a hot day, you tend to drink them like water.

"She phoned me at midnight, one o'clock, two o'clock. She phoned Buck at three o'clock."

I asked Gaston how his life was going. He said, "My daughter is in Cambodia now. She's trained for eleven years to become what's called a medical engineer. That's an interdisciplinary degree applying principles of engineering, medicine and biology. Her husband is a lawyer. She's been there a week and says she feels comfortable living there permanently.

"I told her, 'Give it six months before you decide to buy a house, or take on any other long-term commitments.'"

I said, "The last time we talked you mentioned that you do some writing. Have you published any books or articles?"

"No, I have some started, but recently I've been attending a class in psychology and kinesiology at the university. I've previously taken them separately, but now they've combined them.

"I'm working on a history of my family, but many of the records were destroyed in a fire. That will be a long-term project. My father's family is from Sudbury, my mother's is from Val d'Or. Our family was living in Toronto, but went to visit family in Sudbury where I was born, January 1, 1950 – right on the dot of midnight.

"I have poor circulation. See the burst blood vessels in my ankles. I used to sleep with two pillows under my head and one under my feet. It's easier on your heart if your feet are elevated. I raised the bottom of my bed, now I'm able to get rid of one pillow."

Shark said, "I sleep with four pillows."

"Is that so you don't roll out of bed?" I asked.

"I still roll out of bed."

Gaston said, "I live near the university. I can remember when there were trees on each side of the street arching over. It was like driving through a tunnel. The city decided to widen the street so they cut down all the trees. About five years later, they came to the conclusion that there was too much traffic, so they narrowed the street again, but without the trees. It could have been done differently – circulating the traffic around the trees. We need the trees. They give off oxygen and take away carbon dioxide."

Andre had been sitting in a cross-legged position, sound asleep. When he awoke, he smiled and waved at me.

"So Shark," I asked, "you're not moving?"

"I've talked to my landlord. I'd like to get a two bedroom apartment. When one becomes available, he'll move me free of charge. We get along well."

Joy said to Gene, "No, Gene, I'm not coming on to your girlfriend, although I did have a wife for a year and a half while I was in prison."

Andre said, "That big cop does not like Little Jake."

"It's because he's always mouthing off," said Joy. "He's like a dog gnawing on a bone, he never quits. They have to be really careful with Jake because of his HIV. He always has open sores on his lips or scrapes where he's fallen down.

"Do you remember when there was the big Hep. C scare? I spit at a cop and got eighteen months for assault with a deadly weapon. I didn't spit anywhere near him. That could happen to Jake if he isn't careful."

Andre said, "I was panning yesterday. This suit passed me and said, 'Get a job!' I said, 'Okay, hire me!' He said, 'Bathe first!' You know, just because I don't have access to a shower, doesn't mean that I don't wash all over."

Joy said, "That's an image I don't want in my head."

"I'm just saying."

Cruising up the lawn on his bicycle, tattooed from head to feet, was our friendly neighborhood crack dealer. Time for me to leave.

July 2012

Fish Sticks

3 July, 2012

Shark said to me, "I lost my phone last night. The guy who found it had a heavy European accent. He must have gone through my entire contact list. I know he phoned my landlord, he phoned Irene, she said, 'Who are you and what are you doing with my husband's phone?' He finally called Jacques, who was with me at the time. The guy had an appointment at 10:45, so he asked if I could meet him at 10:40. It was good for me because I had to go to the liquor store anyway. So, I went there and got it back.

"I was going to get a new phone. The billing date for this one is near the end of the month. By that time, I usually don't want to spend money on a phone, I want to eat. If I get a phone with a billing date at the first of the month, I can pay it on check day along with my rent.

"I also got thrown in the can last night, charged with being drunk in a public place."

Shakes said, "Shark, we both arrived at the Shep at the same time. The Sally van dropped me off just as some fine piggies were throwing you out of a cruiser.

"I said, 'Hey, don't treat him like that! He's my friend.' They said, 'Stay back, Shakes!' "

Shark said, "They went through everything in my bag. I had a bottle of wine and five grams of pot in there. I showed the cop my license for medicinal marijuana. He said to the guy at the Shep, 'Don't give him the pot until he's ready to leave or else he'll smoke it on your property.'

"It's a good thing they didn't give it to me. There would have been a lineup of people wanting some.

"I phoned 311, run by the Salvation Army. They'll drive you home, provide you with a sleeping bag, or take you to any of the shelters. They close at 3:00. I guess I phoned at five minutes after. I just got a recording. It took me about an hour to walk home.

"Irene was pissed because I didn't take her home from Bingo, but I had to meet with George. By the way, do I have any dobber marks *(a dobber is like a big marker that Bingo players use to mark on their Bingo cards)* on me?" He took off his cap.

"Yes, you have one right on top of your head."

"Trudy, why don't you have any dobber marks on you?"

"I just stayed far away from the people with dobbers."

"This is my meds day," said Shark. "I have to walk to the clinic. That's where I get my morphine and marijuana."

"Andre," I said, "how was your weekend?"

"Good, great even! On Canada Day *(July first)* I was panning. There were a bunch of women around, so I started bellydancing. One woman gave me a couple of beer, another gave me some pot. I got drops of five dollars, ten dollars. It was great!"

"Shark," I asked, "How are you and Irene getting on?"

"It's iffy. You know women." Shark's cell phone began to ring. "She's just phoning me now. Here talk to her. Ask her if I'm a complete asshole."

I took the phone. "Irene, is Shark a complete asshole?"

"Shark, she says you're a partial asshole."

Shark shook his head. "Ask her if she wants me to bring her a lobster."

"Do you want Shark to bring you a lobster?" I asked Irene.

"She doesn't like lobster," I told Shark.

"I knew that. Ask her if she wants some shrimp. She hates shrimp."

Back to Irene. "How about shrimp?"

"No to shrimp," I relayed to Shark.

Shark said, "Ask her if she wants fish sticks."

"Do you want fish sticks, Irene?"

"Fish sticks are a go, Shark. Here she is. I'll let you talk to her."

Shark took back the phone. "Dennis, Irene asks if you're going to be here tomorrow."

"Only if she brings me some fish sticks."

Staggering Somewhat Straight

4 July 2012

"Hi Serge," I said. "How are you feeling? You still have bruises around your eyes."

"I'm okay."

"Did you see the fireworks on Canada Day?"

"I saw them, but I didn't stand up. I just watched from the bench here. You won't find anybody up top, maybe under the bridge."

"Thanks, Serge, you saved me a trip."

"I'll see you tomorrow."

"See you."

Bellydancing on YouTube

5 July 2012

Shakes was laying on the grass as usual. I bent to shake his hand, then noticed that he had a cigarette in one hand and a wine bottle in the other. "Don't bother shaking my hand, Shakes. I see your hands are full."

"Dennis," said Shakes, "do you know what a smoothie is?"

"You tell me, Shakes."

"It's when you're expecting a Hershey bar, and you get a squirt instead...ha, ha, ha."

"Now I know, Shakes."

"Thanks for not asking me to shake your hand, Dennis," he laughed hoarsely.

I asked, "Was anybody here yesterday?"

Andre thought for a while, "No, they turned the sprinklers on. That's one way to keep us away."

Charles offered me wild blackberries from a large plastic basket.

"I got those as a drop this morning," said Andre. "I was sitting in front of the coffee shop and this dude asks me, 'Do you want some fresh blackberries?' I say, 'Sure!' He goes into the back somewhere and brings this big basket of blackberries. He says, 'There's enough here to bake four pies.' I say, 'Thanks, but you're talking to a guy who lives on the street. I don't have a pot to piss in, let alone an oven to bake pies. I'll share these with some friends in the park. They'll enjoy them. Thanks again. I love blackberries.' "

It's Thursday, so the sandwich ladies had made their appearance. I saw juice boxes, a pair of white socks, and cellophane wrapped cookies. Larry unwrapped a sandwich and looked inside. "Does anybody want some of this?"

"What's in it?" asked Andre.

"I think it's minced ham, I'm not sure."

"I'll pass on that," said Andre as he pulled out a coffee shop bag. "We're eating high-class today!" He offered me part of a cheeseburger, but I had just eaten. Torn in four parts, he passed one each to Shakes, Larry, and Charles and saved the last for himself. Shakes passed around his bottle of wine. Charles sputtered and nearly choked.

Larry said, "Dennis, don't mind my brother. He gets silly when he's drunk."

"He's silly when he's not drunk," said Andre. "He's silly all the time."

Andre, who was shirtless, then demonstrated his bellydance. "I was doing this on Canada Day. One woman gave me a Sourpuss, one gave me two beer, one dropped five bucks and another dropped a knob of weed. She asked if she could videotape me and put it on YouTube. I said, "Sure!" I must be on there about ten times. There's one from St. Patrick's Day, 2010, labeled *bum fights*.

"It had over 700 hits the first week. Since then it's had over 20,000. I wish I was getting royalties."

Larry said, "One time I was sleeping under the bridge, around the time they were putting up the chain link fences. I was asleep in the corner when I heard someone rattling the fence. They said, 'Do you want a drink?' I was half asleep, so I didn't answer. Then they said, 'Do you want some bottles of wine?' My ears pricked up then. 'Sure!' I said. I came out and sure enough they had all these bottles lined up. They said there had been a wine tasting event nearby and any opened bottles had to be disposed of.

"A bunch of us met the next day and passed the bottles around the circle. Anyone who liked the taste, kept the bottle. If they didn't, they passed it on. I tried some Dom Perignon, but didn't like it. I know it's over $200 a bottle, but it tasted awful."

Andre said, "I had a job at a big hotel and when they had a function, any opened bottles, even if they only had an ounce out of them, were given to the staff. The full bottles I had to take down to the basement. When I was working down there, a huge mother of a bug dropped on my shoulder. I don't know what it was called, but it was about two inches across and had pincers, like scissors in front. I was wearing rubber gloves when I picked it off my shoulder and it nipped the end off one of the fingers. If I hadn't been wearing the gloves, it would have been my finger that was nipped off.

"Whenever I saw one of those bugs, I hit it with a shovel. I may have broken the odd bottle of wine, but I wasn't getting anywhere near those bugs.

"In the forests they also had wood-boring insects *(Mountain Pine Beetles)* that would drop from the trees, sometimes three or four at a time, and could bore into your skin. They would post signs advising hikers to keep off the trails at certain times of the year."

It was time for Andre, Shakes and Little Jake to go to work. Shakes was having trouble with his pants falling down. I asked Andre, "Are those new pants?"

"They must be," replied Andre. "They're clean."

"I'll get you fixed up, Shakes," said Andre. He tore a two-inch wide strip from a garbage bag in one of the sidewalk containers. He started feeding it through the belt loops, then he noticed that Shakes had a belt around his waist, but under his pants, over his underwear.

"It's alright folks, we're not doing anything disgusting here. We're just trying to help our buddy, so he won't do something disgusting all by himself." Andre fed the belt through the loops and Shakes was good to go. Unstable, but vertical and able to stagger somewhat straight.

Wolf Rants

6 July 2012

Another hot day at the park, 102 degrees. I shook hands with Larry, waved to Anne then extended my hand to Trudy. She hugged me instead. I extended my hand to Buck. He said, "What? I don't get a hug?" I hugged him and said, "Share the love, brother."

I walked over to Wolf who was talking to Debbie. He said, "Go away, I don't want to talk to you right now." I walked back to sit with Larry and Anne.

"Dennis," said Wolf, "I didn't mean to be rude. Well, yes I did. Anyway, I can't break my train of thought or I won't get it back again. I need to have eye contact. See, now Trudy is standing between us. Trudy, couldn't you go around the other way? Can't you see we're trying to have a conversation here?"

"I'm sorry, Wolf," said Trudy.

I moved closer so I could hear him better.

Buck said to Wolf, "Your German team didn't do too well in the Euro Cup."

"We didn't do well in the last two world wars, either."

"Dennis," said Wolf, "We're about the same age, so you know what I'm talking about. That murder in St. Isidore — that's what Debbie and I were discussing — have you been following that in the newspaper?"

"No," I said, "I don't know anything about it."

"Come on man, it was on the front page yesterday. You're smart. I thought you kept up with what's going on in the world. A 24 year old guy was murdered in St. Isidore. He was lured behind an elementary school by three girls, where he was stabbed and murdered by three boys. The oldest was twenty. The headline read, 'Seven Lives Wasted.' Can you imagine what those families are going through? Not only the family of the murdered guy, but the others as well.

"I have a son. I don't see him anymore. When he was 19 years old, he murdered someone. What's with these kids? There's no discipline, that's what's the matter. When I was a boy, I had to set the table, the knives would have to be just so, the forks over here, none of these people would know what I'm talking about. If I got something wrong, I'd get a smack across the back of my head. That's my Germanic background. Yours is similar, I think. What is it, Scottish? No, Irish. No, that's not it."

"Icelandic."

"Icelandic, that's it. Vikings, raping and pillaging, just like the Huns. Anyway, back to St. Isidore, the armpit of Quebec. What's with these kids? Did they think they would get away with it?

"That's one of the reasons I don't come here on weekends. You just never know what's going to happen. Hippo's been jumped. Rocky's been jumped. They're a lot bigger and tougher than I am. I've slept at the heater and I was darn glad to see Andre and Hippo come along. I was glad to have... what's the word I'm looking for?"

"Protection?"

"That's it, protection. When I'm anywhere in this area, I know I can call out and someone may come to my rescue.

"This heat is bad. When I cross that line of shade, where it meets the full glare of the sun, it's like walking into a wall. Shaggy's not going to be riding much today. Of course, she'll be in the cart going up the bridge."

I said, "Maybe you should get in the cart and have Larry push."

"That cart wouldn't hold me. It's meant to be pulled behind a bicycle. Jacques, big Jacques, you know how strong he is. He's fixed it a couple of times for me. That cart's getting old. Shaggy and I were hit by a car when she was three years old, so that's over eight years."

"I notice that the front has been changed. Don't these carts usually have wheels in front?"

"Yes, the wheels stuck way out in front. It was hard to turn. Jacques cut it shorter and replaced the wheels with the blade of a hockey stick. Now it slides.

"Anyway, on my way here this morning I stopped to buy Shaggy some dog food. She eats well. It reminds me of when Little Jake first got sick. I fed him well, maybe too well; it seemed to make him worse."

I asked, "How is Jake now?"

"I don't want to talk about Jake. Getting back to the dog food. I remember being at the counter and getting four five dollar bills as change. Later, I wanted to buy five grams of weed and I couldn't find my money. I had to take everything out of my pockets and at last, in this tiny little pocket of my jeans, I found the four bills stuffed inside.

"So, I talked enough. Do I rate a chapter in your book? Fuck off then, go away. I'm just kidding. But, seriously, it's time for me to go before it gets too hot."

I went back to sit with Larry, Anne and Trudy. I heard Larry say to Anne, "Chester asked me if I thought there was any chance of you and him getting back together. I told him, 'Ask her yourself. It has nothing to do with me.'"

It's like a daily soap opera, lives and loves exposed for all to see.

Sleeping Rough

9 July 2012

"Hello Serge, how are you doing?" I asked.

"You startled me. I didn't see you coming. I'm okay. I was feeling sick before, but now I've got my booze, I'll be fine."

I asked Joy. "How is everything going in your new place?"

"It's great. Living at Chester's is awesome. It's so quiet. I hear kids and cars, but nothing like the noise at Chuck's."

"There aren't the people coming in and out," added Chester.

"I've got the whole house cleaned," said Joy. "Now we're going back. I've got some laundry to do. I'll probably see you tomorrow."

"You're a good man, Chester. Bye. Bye, Joy."

"How have you been feeling, Jake?" I asked.
"My legs are sore."
"I notice you have a lot of bruises."

"Yeah, I've got bruises all over. I've been throwing up every morning, the dry heaves. I've been drinking a lot of water just so I have something to throw up. At Weasel's place the bathtub is really close to the toilet. Sometimes I've got it coming out both ends. I feel better now, though.

"I slept over there in the bushes last night, along with Weasel, Bear and Andre. I woke up next to Bear. I think I kicked her during the night. I was the first one up at about six. The sun coming up was orange. It was really picturesque. I went down to see Silver, but he wasn't there, so I panned in his spot. I didn't stay too long because I've got two charges against me. The cop, the big one with the tattoos — he's really got a hard on for me — he said that if I get caught again, I'll be going back to prison."

"Just ignore them," said Shakes. "I've got two charges as well. I was charged with vagrancy. When have you last heard of that charge, back in the sixties? They've been saying for ten years now that they're going to put me back in jail, but it never happens. Just go out there on the sidewalk and start panning. You'll see, nothing will happen."

"That area is a red zone for me," said Little Jake.

Shakes said, "Every street is a red zone. I slept in the bank last night. I just couldn't hold it anymore, so I dropped my pants and used the wastebasket. There was a garbage bag inside so I took it out, tied it up and placed it outside. The cops came by and said there had been a complaint that I had taken a dump in the bank. I said, 'Look officers, there's just me, my sandwich and a broken cigarette. I don't know what these people are talking about.'"

Jake said, "The cops came by yesterday and there was Shakes pissing through the rails of the fence. They said, 'Shakes, you just can't do that in a public park.' He didn't care."

Shakes asked Trudy, "Will you roll me a joint? My hands are too shaky."

"Sure, do you have papers?"

"Do you need scissors, Trudy?" asked Jake.

"No, this stuff isn't too fresh."

"I've had my first drink of the day," said Shakes. "Now, I'm going to have my first joint. Then, I can get my mind right."

Jake said, "You'll be able to stagger straight. Is that it, Shakes?"

"I'm leaving now," said Trudy. "They're having a memorial service for Alistair at the church. It starts at 1:00."

"Ask them to play some Ozzy for him," said Shakes. A soldier was passing. "Thanks for defending our country, sir."

To me he said, "I respect the military. One time I was at a bar and I saw an old veteran. I said to him, 'Come over and join us.' I had a 1942 penny in my pocket. I gave it to him. He started crying. He said, 'I was in the war then. That's the year my brother was killed.'

"Some people say that men don't cry. I can be arrested, beaten up, stabbed, shot and I'll never cry. But when it's something sentimental, like a memorial service or that old veteran bawling his eyes out, that makes me cry.

"I remember back at the Haven (*Millhave Maximum Security Penitentiary*), I was training this guy to box. I told him, 'I'll keep training you as long as you don't mess up. If you mess up, no more training.'

"Do you know where I learned to box? It was when I was six years old, on the farm. In the barn we had one of those heavy farm bags hanging from a rafter. My uncles showed me how to use it."

Buck was playing a scratch and win Bingo card. "I won," he said.

"How much did you win?"

"Ten bucks."

"I'll pay you for a card," said Shakes. He pulled out a plastic zip lock bag full of quarters. "Here I'll even pay you for one extra."

"This is a nickel, Shakes."

"How much do I owe you now?"

"One quarter."

"Okay, here's one quarter." To Jake he asked, "How much money did Joy say I have here?"

"fifteen bucks"

"Buck, can you go on a run for me and get two bottles of sherry?"

"Sure."

Buck left and headed toward the liquor store.

Jake said to Shakes, "Aren't you worried that he's going to head south with your money?"

"No, I'm not worried. I trust Buck."

He returned about twenty minutes later and handed Shakes two bottles of sherry.

Jake said to Shakes, "Don't forget you owe me twenty."

Shakes passed Jake a near empty sherry bottle. "That's great," said Jake, "He owes me twenty and he offers me a buck's worth of sherry."

Shark and Irene came by. Shark said, "Well, I got a new apartment, a three bedroom for $1100 a month, all-inclusive. It's really large. Officially, I move on the first of August, but the landlord said I can start moving stuff over beginning tomorrow. They've still got some repairs to do.

"I'm just moving across the parking lot. It's the same landlord. I've been with him a long time now. My present place and the one before were both with him. Now, we just have to arrange for a truck to bring Irene's stuff over."

I said, "Irene was concerned that, with your morphine and medicinal marijuana, the police may come over when you're away and she might be charged because the license is in your name."

"We'll have three bedrooms, one for me and one for Irene. The morphine and marijuana will be in my room. As long as it's in my room, they can't touch Irene. I can just get another license for when I'm not home."

Irene said, "That means we won't be neighbors any more, Dennis."

"Don't worry; it's not that far away."

No Dogs Allowed

10 July 2012

"Dennis," said Wolf, "I've got something to show you. I want your opinion on it. Here, can you read this without your glasses?"

"keep your pet away from fountains and shorelines"

(Pets are not allowed to be within 3 metres of any shoreline on City of Toronto land)

"What do you think of that? Be careful of what you say because Shaggy is listening. Does this mean that I can't take her in the river near my place? She's been going in there every hot day for the past ten years."

"That seems to be what it means."

"Do you agree with that?"

"No, they don't do anything to prevent wild animals, such as otters or beavers, from going in the river. Why would it be different for dogs?"

"That was my thinking as well. I talked to about ten women about it and they said, 'You'd let your dog go in that dirty river?' They weren't dog owners.

"I even think that on these days where it is over 100 degrees that Shaggy should be allowed to go into the fountain to cool off. What harm is there in that? Are they afraid that she's going to steal some pennies?"

Andre said, "I've noticed that some store owners are putting dishes of water out for dogs and other animals."

Buck came by and Wolf asked him, "Would you go on a run for me? The problem is I only have $10. Can you spot me the other $10.50?"

"Sure."

Conversations With God

11 July 2012

"I was talking to one of my private clients," said Gaston." We have been working with her a long time doing odd jobs, anything she needs help with. She has houses in Arizona and California. We've been invited to come down and manage one of her houses. All of our expenses will be covered. She'll even arrange for a maid service to come in while we're away, to handle our existing clients who need their houses cleaned."

"That sounds great, Gaston," I said.

Larry and I discovered that we were both born and raised in Saskatoon. "I lived there for seventeen years," he said. "After that we moved nearby. I wasn't with my real mother and father, but lived with a foster family. I always felt bad that other kids had parents but I didn't, but that's the way it was. I stayed with that family until I saw the guy hitting his wife. Then I moved out. I went to Winnipeg where I grew up quick." He lifted up his tee-shirt and pointed to his ribs, "This scar is where I was stabbed, a souvenir of Winnipeg. Then I went to prison.

"I had a wife. We split up, but we have a son. Whenever I'm straight and sober, I visit him. He's 17 now and he loves me. I've never had anyone love me before. We're neighbors. My ex-wife's boyfriend doesn't like me to come around. He probably thinks that we're having sex together.

"I'm educated. I used to be a very religious person, went to church every Sunday. Man, I really jumped in with both feet.

Then I had an epiphany. It was a dream or a vision where I saw two books on a table, one white, one black. I kept trying to reach for the black one –the Bible is usually black — but I was guided to the white one. Shortly after, I came across the book *Conversations with God* by Neale Donald Walsch. It's a book where the author asks questions of God and God answers. It opened my eyes. Previously, I felt guilty all the time. Now, I feel free. I can create my own destiny."

Larry had been teased about his moustache, so he shaved it off. "Now I remember why I stopped shaving," he said. "I must have cut myself three times. That's what happens when you use those cheap disposable razors they give you at the Mission. I think they get them at a discount because the blades have nicks in them. I remember using one of those to shave, and I don't mean my legs. It made a bloody mess. If I buy one of those five-blade razors, it will last me three months."

Loretta said, "Do you see the self-mutilation job I did to myself?" Her legs were covered with bruises. "I've got other bruises on my ribs. Larry and I and some others were going to Blues Fest, but we had some booze to drink first. We walked across the black bridge. I'm afraid of bridges anyway. We were on our way back, nearly across the bridge, when I lost my balance and fell over the edge. I landed in the river on some really sharp rocks. I could have killed myself. Larry helped me to get out of the water."

"How many lives is that you've used up?" asked Larry.

"Two. I have seven left."

Bear Gets a Ticket

12 July 2012

I could just barely see Joy's cap and her two feet sticking out behind the concrete partition. "Hi, Joy."

"Hi, Sunshine, how are you today?"

"I'm great. How do you like staying at Chester's place?"

"I like it. He's quiet, not like Chuck. I have the house all cleaned and it'll stay cleaned. There's no dog tracking in mud all the time. The fridge is full of food. We had bacon and eggs this morning. I have all my laundry done.

"The only thing I'm waiting for is my GST (*Goods and Services Tax*) check from the government. I don't think Chuck would hold that back on me. He says he hasn't received his yet either."

I said, "I haven't seen Silver or Hippo lately? I heard that Silver is panning near the Mission."

"That's strange," said Joy, "I can see Silver going to the Mission for meals, but he's had his spot for over ten years. He has regulars that come by. One that drops him a twenty. I can't see him sticking his nose up at that to pan near the Mission. As far as Hippo is concerned, I think he's probably visiting his folks.

"Another couple of people I don't expect to see are Daimon and Lucy. He wouldn't dare come down on crutches. He'd be too vulnerable and he's made a lot of enemies. I think he's going to be lying low for quite a while.

"I have an appointment to see my probation officer today. On the card she gave me, the date reads Thursday, July 11. The 11th was Wednesday, yesterday. I just noticed it this morning. There shouldn't be any problem. I'll tell her I was going by the day of the week, not the date."

I said to Hippo, "You look all cleaned up; you've shaved. Have you been home visiting your folks?"

"No, for the last week I've been staying at the Center (*The Detention Center*)."

"Hippo, did they remove your stitches while you were there?" asked Andre.

"Yeah, the nurse took them out."

Shaggy was contentedly eating dog treats and licking Joy's toes. "I'm not sure I like her that close," said Joy, "Last time she bit my ankle, and drew blood."

Danny said, "One time, when I had my work boots on, Shaggy bit my boot. Her teeth went through a quarter of an inch of leather and left a mark on my foot."

"Did you hear that Bear got a ticket?" said Wolf. "Can you imagine giving a ticket to a dog?"

"I can imagine it," said Andre, "She's going to defend herself, your honor."

"Why would they give her a ticket?" I asked.

"Maybe because of the holes that have been dug in the lawn," said Wolf. The cop asked me if it was Shaggy that dug them. I said, 'No, it was the black one, not the white one.'"

Andre said, "You should have seen the breakfast I had this morning. It was all stuff I got while I was panning last night. I had calamari, octopus, all kinds of seafood, nachos and fajitas. I was at the Oven and the owner pumped up the tires on my bicycle. I was holding the bike; my hat was on the ground. Some women came by and asked me, 'Do you think the man who was here would mind if we left him some food?'

"I said, 'No, ma'am, I'm sure he wouldn't mind. He would probably appreciate it. I'll guard it until he comes back.' "

Joy said, "I walked by you guys around six this morning. Ian was asleep and his pecker was out of his pants, just blowing in the wind. What a revolting sight first thing in the morning."

Ian said, "I must have gotten up in the night to pee and forgot to zip up. I was really wasted."

Andre said, "I was drinking with this guy last night. We were sharing my bottle. After it was finished, he brought out a bottle of his own.

"I said, 'Now you bring out your bottle? You can be sure that we're going to stay up until this is finished. If you fall asleep, I'll finish it myself.' "

Joy was having trouble with her phone. "This is useless," she said. "I've got the phone plan that Jacques recommended. For one thing, I only have free-calling after six at night and on weekends. I never phone anyone on the weekend, unless it's seeing if any of you guys are down here. If you're not, I don't come. The rest of the time, I have to text. I don't know how to do spaces, so everything comes out as one garbled line.

"I just got a text back from Glen. He says, 'Who the fuck is this?'

"I texted, 'Joy.'

"He understood that."

A woman walked toward the group and spoke to Jake. He put on his backpack and walked away with her.

"Who was that?" asked Danny.

"That's his social worker."

"You mean a social worker will come looking for her client?"

"Not many will, but she does."

Ian The Mooch

13 July 2012

"Today is so hot and humid," said Anastasia. "I can't wait until Buck arrives, then I'm going to meet some of the others at the river, near Jacques' place. It's always cooler there. I love being by the water. My mother has a cottage on the Bay. I'm going there this summer, but I can't afford it right now. I'll have to wait until my check arrives, August 1st. It doesn't have running water or electricity. I love to relax in nature. I also paint, mostly landscape scenes and rocks. I paint in oils, I love the spontaneity. My daughter — she's thirty — just got engaged. They've bought a house. It's going to be a bit more difficult for me to visit her.

"Here comes Buck and Dillinger. I'll be off now."

Andre said, "I had a good time last night. I was riding my bicycle and saw a woman asleep on a bench. I thought to myself, 'I know that ass.' I peeked under her cap and recognized Betty. We were making out on the bench until about midnight. She handed me her apartment keys and said, 'I've got some things to finish up, but go to my place, have something to eat, have a shower. I'll be there shortly.'

"I fried a pork chop, some potatoes. Had a great meal, but what I really loved was the shower. It had a lot of pressure. I washed my hair twice. The first time the lather was black. When Betty came in, she opened the fridge and plunked a bottle of wine in front of me. We had a great time."

Hippo said to Buck, "How much do I owe you from yesterday?"

Buck checked on his smart phone and said, "Eight bucks."

"I thought it was seven."

"No, eight."

"Well there's no arguing with a computer. Can you add another ten on that?"

"Sure."

Jake said, "I wondered where everyone was last night. I'm not used to sleeping alone. I worry about panhandling, now that I have two charges against me. I've got one coming up on the 20th and one August 5th. I get sentenced September 15th. I'm sure I'm going to get jail time.

"I'm trying to decide what I'll have to eat. I think I'll to go to the store, steal some smoked oysters and crackers. I'll pay for a bag of chips.

"I owe Buck $56, but other people owe me $50. If they'd pay me, I could pay him off. I didn't see Ian last night. He owes me $10, Hippo owes me $10, Wolf owes me $10 and this guy owes me $20. **SHAKES, YOU OWE ME TWENTY BUCKS**." Shakes slept on. "And I haven't even had a drink yet!"

"That got his attention," said Andre. "He made $80 at the Jazz'n Blues Festival last night. I think he drank most of it already."

"Hippo, throw me that bottle," said Jake.

Hippo threw to him a half full, plastic wine bottle, but it hit his radio. The radio, playing little more than static, got worse. Danny fiddled with the dials to try to get better reception. Nothing he did made much improvement.

Jake said, "There's a difference between a bum and a mooch. I'll bum smokes off people, but I pay them back. Sometimes I've even paid a debt twice. When I ask someone how much I owe them, the nicest thing to hear is, 'It's okay, Jake; you've already paid me. I hope Shakes doesn't think that by giving me a drink every now and then, it's going to erase the twenty bucks he owes me."

"No way, man," said Andre. "If you borrow cash, you repay in cash. If you get someone drunk, they're expected to do the same for you in return."

Jake said, "Every time Ian comes around he's mooching cigarettes, money or booze... mooch, mooch, mooch. He never comes around when he has money of his own. We're going to have to put him straight on that."

Danny said, "I saw Shakes at the Blues Festival last night. The police were harassing him. There was a couple sharing a drink on one side of the road. The cops ignored them, but they crossed the road and ordered Shakes to dump his bottle. It should be the same law for everyone."

'Shrooms

16 July 2012

Chantal was squatting beside Joy programming her telephone. "There," she said, "now you have my phone number and I have yours."

"Thanks, I'm so bad at keeping track of phone numbers." They both promised to keep in contact. Chantal left shortly after.

"This phone is useless," said Joy. "As soon as my billing period is over, I'm getting a different phone that plays music as well. I need my music."

I asked, "How has it been living with Chester?"

"He's a sweetheart, except when he's drunk. He'd keep asking me, 'Is everything alright, Joy?' over and over again. He even yells up the stairs at me. Then he'll start crying, 'I miss Anne, I miss Ipeelee.' Now he's met a woman who speaks French and drinks like he does. I'm so relieved.

"Yesterday I barbecued some ribs with a sweet and sour sauce. We also had boiled potatoes. Chester wanted them mashed, but I told him, 'If you want them smashed, you smash them with your fork.' When I was getting the ribs ready — I boiled them first, then put them in marinade — Chester came down. Since I was already in the kitchen, I asked him if he wanted me to fix him something to eat. 'Sure,' he said, 'I'd like a fried egg, bacon and toast.' I had in mind to make him a sandwich.

"We don't have air conditioning. You'd think that in a building for seniors, they'd have air conditioning. I have a door to the balcony, but it only has a screen at the top. I leave the door wide open to catch any breeze. The only problem is the mosquitoes. As long as I can get to sleep before they start biting, they can feast to their heart's content. You can see I have a few bites on my legs.

"Chester asked me why don't we have Jacques over.' I said, 'Because he has bedbugs.' He sleeps on his kitchen floor because that's the only place there is no carpet. Bedbugs love carpet. I'm sure they can walk from the carpet to go over and bite him. They must be in his bed as well. They can hide in a pant cuff and lay dormant for eighteen months, then they drop a bunch of eggs. Soon, you've got ten thousand of them."

I asked, "Isn't there any way of getting rid of them? Aren't there sprays or something?"

"There are sprays. You have to use them over and over, and the bugs can be anywhere. You never kill them all. The pest control company sells a mattress cover that they can't chew through, but that means that any that are in the mattress are going to be crawling around under the cover. That gives me the creeps. The best way to get rid of them is to rip out all the carpets and throw out the mattresses."

"How about foam mattresses?"

"They can get into everything. Some people think they are safe if they use goose down pillows, but they get into them as well."

I said, "I haven't seen Silver for a while."

"I've heard," said Joy, "that he's been panning down near the Mission. That's crazy! The spot he has here is a gold mine and he's been here over ten years. I think he's smoking crack again. People have seen him sitting with the crack heads down at the Mission."

I said, "It must be hard to get off that stuff once you've started."

"I was fine when I was just dealing it, but when I started to smoke it, I was hooked. What got me off it was my mother threatening that, unless I quit, I'd never see my kids again. I quit right away, no programs or anything. I used to be a lot heavier. When I quit the crack, I also stopped eating so much. When my mother saw me losing weight, she thought I was back on drugs. I just didn't want to be fat anymore.

"Wolf and Weasel are both crack heads. I don't know why Wolf puts up with the abuse that Weasel gives him. Wolf always gives him a place to stay. He even has a sign on his door that says, 'gone fishing', which is the same as saying, 'fuck off', but Weasel will just keep hammering on the door. One time he kicked it in."

I said, "That was the night that Wolf and Shaggy slept at the heater. Wolf said he was so glad to see Andre and Hippo, just for protection."

Joy said, "Shaggy would never let anything happen to Wolf. I was over at his place with Outcast. It was an absolute mess. Wolf said, 'Don't lecture me, Joy. I know it's a mess. I'll get around to cleaning it.'

"I remember one time I was running from the cops. In my building they used to have crash doors. I didn't know they had changed them. Anyway, I was running down the hall, lickety split, hit the door and knocked myself out. I woke up at the cop shop. I said to them, 'Okay, you caught me, write me up and I'll get out of here.' They let me go and I went right back to doing what I was doing before.

"I went to the Women's Center to see about my identification. They said, 'We're sorry, Joy. We've run into a bit of a snag, but we should have your papers shortly.' It's as if I don't exist, but I get my GST check. See here it is."

"What does the K. stand for?"

"Kathleen, well actually, Kathlee. My mom ran out of room on the birth registration form. I thought that Kathlee was kind of neat; it was original, but people kept adding the 'n' anyway."

Serge Beaten Again

17 July 2012

This morning there was a brief shower. Joy was partially protected by the overhang of a building; just her feet were getting wet. I held my umbrella over her. She said, "Don't worry about the umbrella. I don't mind getting wet. It's better than the heat. When it's hot, I have trouble sleeping. I'm on a foldout couch in Chester's living room. Sometimes, I take the mattress off and put it next to the open balcony door. If Chester wants to watch TV late at night, I put the mattress back.

"I don't know why he doesn't get air conditioning. It would only cost an extra $25 a month. I told him, 'We can afford it.' He said, 'No, no, it's too much money.'"

"I've noticed a lot of fat people lately. I was fat for most of my life. Kids especially, but adults as well, can be really cruel."

I asked, "What caused you to lose the weight so quickly?"

"I was gutted with a saw-toothed machete. They put a cage to hold the parts of my stomach together. They also made it smaller. For a long time all I was allowed to eat was baby food. I tried eating scrambled eggs, but I threw up so violently that I pulled out some of the staples, so back to hospital. I still have to be careful about what I eat. I hate any pureed food."

I said, "I had a long talk with Gaston yesterday. He seems very intelligent."

"Yeah, he's a nice guy. We live right across the street from him. I'm not sure if he has full-blown AIDS or not. He's opened an HIV drop-in center, even some in other cities."

"How are you and Pierre getting along?"

"I don't know. He's such a drama queen. One day he just wants to be friends. The next day he gets all hissy if I don't text him. He said, 'I'm going away for a few days, so you'd better collect your pot.' Well, it's been a few days and he's still here."

Hippo stopped by. "We got soaked last night. The puddles were about two inches deep. There was me, Andre, Jake, Weasel and Bear. At noon we're going to some church. They put on a free meal. We can get free haircuts and other stuff. After that I guess I'll just go back to the hole."

The garbage man stopped by. "Hi, handsome," said Joy. "I don't know how you can do that job with all the smell. What does your girlfriend say when you get home?"

"Right now, I'm just working with cardboard and paper. That's not too bad. I tried the regular route. I was lifting a garbage can over my head and some of the liquid waste spilled on my face. It was awful. I quit right away. I can't even work with the recycled bottles and cans. The leftover liquid goes bad and smells like rotten fruit."

"Bye, handsome."

She turned back to me, "I took another look at Serge's eyes. There's no way that he got those bruises falling off a bench."

I said, "He told me that he tripped over his shoelace."

"There you go, he's lying. I said to him, 'Serge, I've been beaten enough times that I can tell the difference between a bruise caused by a fist and one caused by a fall. You were beaten, weren't you?' He said, 'I don't want to cause any trouble, or have anyone come after me.' "

I was walking along and I heard someone shout, "Hey!" I looked around and saw Serge sitting on a park bench in the shade.

"Hi, Serge," I said. "I didn't see you there. Your eyes are looking better. How do you feel?"

"I'm just waiting to get my booze."

"How was your weekend?"

"I forget."

I asked Hippo, "Did you go to the church to get your haircut?"

"No, we didn't make it there, maybe next year."

Andre rode up on the lawn on his bicycle and handed Shakes a brown paper bag. Shakes took out the bottle of sherry, unscrewed the cap, filled the cap with sherry and threw it on the lawn. Then, he passed the bottle around. When it got back to him he poured the remainder into a plastic drinking bottle. He threw the empty bottle to Wolf, who put it in Shaggy's cart.

Andre asked Wolf, "So that's forty cents you got?"

"No, I only get twenty cents a bottle."

"Yeah, but you got one earlier."

"I know I got one earlier. That was twenty cents too. I didn't know you were asking how many twenty centses I had. I've also got a bunch of beer cans."

Shakes asked Wolf, "Can I buy a smoke off you?"

Wolf said, "Now, where, on my way home, am I going to find a place to buy more smokes? Yes, Shakes I'll sell you a smoke. Here's two, just give me a quarter."

Hippo was smoking. Jake asked him, "Can I have a drag?"

"Sure," said Hippo, "Lay back and I'll drag you around the park. What did we eat last night?"

Andre said, "We had double cheeseburgers and fries."

Hippo said, "I was wondering what I pooped this morning."

I said to Andre, "I heard you guys really got soaked last night."

"Yeah, Hippo was the first to wake up. He was just standing over his bag saying, 'Oh fuck, oh fuck!' He didn't bother to wake us up or anything; he just kept looking at his bag."

Jake said, "I thought it wouldn't last more than a few minutes. I just pulled my sleeping bag over my head and planned to wait it out. Almost immediately, I was soaked. We went over to where Weasel was sleeping; at least it was partially covered.

"I can't wait to find out if my housing is approved. I was shown a place this morning. It was fabulous. It's on the second floor. All the way up the stairs are Maple Leafs posters. I was wearing my Leafs shirt."

I asked, "When will you find out if you get it or not?"

"It depends on my worker. There are other people interested in that place. I don't know how they come to a decision."

"Your worker seems really nice," I said.

"She's super!"

Shakes said, "I was talking to Lucy today. She said, 'Shakes, I tried drinking and smoking while lying down like you do, but I would either spill my drink or drop my smoke. I don't know how you manage it.'

Andre said, "I fell asleep with a smoke in my hand last night. I always keep my hands crossed on my chest, that way if I fall asleep I'm the one that gets burned. You can see the mark right here."

Tempers were getting short. "I must have told him six times," said Shakes, "I don't have any wine."

"I wasn't asking if you had wine," said Andre, "I asked if you have any cigarettes. If you want one, I got some."

Shakes said, "Andre and I went to the Jazz'n Blues Festival last night. Andre rode his bike and I walked. I arrived a few minutes before he did. I met an old friend there. He said, 'Let's get together around 11:00.' I said, 'Okay.' We got together sometime between 11:30 and midnight. We went to his place. We had some beer, some wine, some pot, did some lines, ate some 'shrooms. I woke Andre at 8:00. I said, 'Let's have some LSD.'"

Andre said, "I partied with the band last night. All I had to do was show them some of my bellydance and I was in."

Little Jake Ticketed Again

18 July 2012

"How do I get to the river?" asked Loon.

"Fastest way," said Andre, "is to take any of the long busses. Make sure you don't try to jump any of the short busses."

Loon said, "What if I take the streetcar? Won't that take me there?"

"For one, "said Andre, "The streetcars are harder to jump. Two, it's a $250 ticket if you get caught."

Jake said to me, "I can't panhandle anymore."

"Yeah," I said, "You told me that yesterday."

"No, I got charged again last night. I don't know why they have such a hard-on for me, but I was at my usual spot and a cop car pulls up. He writes me a ticket and says, 'This is the last time, Jake. I know that as soon as I'm gone you're going to be panning again. I won't be back, but the next time I catch you, you're going to jail.' "

I asked, "Was anyone following him?"

"No, not as far as I knew. It wasn't ten minutes before a cop on foot patrol came and wrote me up. He said, 'Next time, Jake, you're going to jail.' Now, I'm on probation and have two breaches against me. I'm going to start fighting back."

"What are you going to do, Little Jake?"

"Spit on them!"

"Don't do that Jake," I said, "You've got AIDS, and the charge will be assault with a deadly weapon. Because of Joy's Hep. C, she did eighteen months for spitting near a cop. It didn't even hit him."

"What am I supposed to do? It's still two weeks to check day, and I've got no money. None of us have been doing very well, except at the Jazz'n Blues Festival. I've got a hearing tomorrow. That'll just be in and out. Then I've got a court appearance on the 29th, I think. I've got it written down someplace. I'm going to fight it."

Hippo said, "When you go to court, Jake, ask for Legal Aid. At the Legal Aid office, get an appointment with Sherry. Tell her you're an alcoholic and that you're living on the street. She's an alcoholic herself."

Andre said, "I don't know why they bother you guys. I'm at my usual spot in front of the coffee shop. I've got some regulars. One buys me a large coffee every morning. Today, I shared it with Hippo. There's another who buys me a bagel or an English muffin. A cop came by and asked me what I was doing. I said, 'Officer, I'm eating my breakfast.' He said, 'You've got your hat out.' 'Yes I do,' I said, 'I live on the streets. What else am I supposed to do?' He left me alone.

"I worked at this bar in Calgary once. I was the cook, the maintenance guy, the bartender and the bouncer. When customers would come in, I'd tell them, 'We only got one rule here: don't piss off the cook. If you piss off the cook, you won't get anything to drink, and you'll be thrown out."

Danny said, "I have a regular who brings me heart-shaped cookies every morning. She calls them love cookies. This morning she said, 'I've never given you money before, so take this.' She dropped a twenty. She's cute too.

"I found a lot of booze at the Jazz'n Blues Festival. I brought my flash light to look for empties, and I came across a bag behind a curb. In it was half a twenty-six of cognac. It wasn't anything special, but it sure was good. I almost threw the bag out when I noticed this can of weed. I also found sixteen full beer cans that people had stashed in the bushes and the hedge."

Andre said, "Shakes and I didn't make it through the gate until the last night. It's a bit harder when you're riding a bicycle. You can't just jump the fence. Anyway, we were coming by one of the back trails and I saw an empty bottle of vodka. Nearby was a water bottle, but it had something orange in it. I thought to myself, 'That's odd, what do people usually mix with vodka?' I put two and two together and took a sip. It was powerful."

Jake said, "People think I'm lucky because I get to sit in the sun and get a good tan. The only reason I do is because I have to sit for hours in the sun waiting to get my price."

Andre said, "I've still got a full bag of food left over from last night. I've got a slice of pizza, some steamed rice and half a sub."

"I'm getting hungry," said Hippo. "I'm going to have to make another trip to the grocery store. Yesterday, I got seventeen bucks worth of food and only paid a dollar for a bag of chips. That canned ham I brought over last night, that's where I got it."

Jake said, "I don't have any batteries for my radio. I'm going to have to steal four double A's."

"You really are in a hurry to go back to prison," said Andre.

Gene Goes to Prison

19 July 2012

"You're looking good, Joy," I said.

"Thanks, it was too hot to drink yesterday. I didn't sleep much. The people downstairs were out on their balcony talking loud. They were also smoking pot."

"Are they the neighbors directly below you?"

"Yes."

"You could always spill something on them."

"I thought of that. Chester's also being a real pain, especially when he's drunk. I was doing the laundry yesterday; he came in and said, 'I'm hungry. Will you make me something to eat?' I said, 'Dude, you know where the fridge is, make something yourself.' I'm not his housekeeper.

"Outcast was over last night. He brought twelve beers and gave Chester six. After a while Chester came to me and said, 'I want him out of here, and he's not sleeping over.' 'Look dude,' I said, 'If you want him out, you tell him, and tell him why.'

"Later on he said to me, 'Joy, will you sleep with me? I won't do anything. I just want to be close to you.' 'Chester,' I said, 'We've been over this before. I'm not sleeping with you. It's not going to happen, not now, not ever.' Guys always try that. They say they just want to sleep next to you, then they start touching you. I hate that."

"You can see why Anne left him," I said.

"I sure can, but he still goes on about her, 'I miss my Annie,' he says. She's never going to take him back."

"There's nothing worse than jealousy to spoil a relationship," I said.

"That's for sure. Outcast isn't getting along with Debbie. She wants to up his rent because her daughter is pregnant again. Why that should affect his rent, I don't know. I told him that if things with Chester get any worse, we could find a two bedroom somewhere and share it.

"I saw Jake this morning; he's over at Silver's spot. He's got a huge bump on his forehead. Fran's new boyfriend head butted him last night. Jake was wasted, and he doesn't know what happened or why."

"Fran's new boyfriend? Isn't she with Gene anymore?"

"Gene is in prison. He jumped Fran and she has two hairline fractures in her back. The doctors are going to monitor it for a while to see what happens. She may need surgery. This new guy may be the father of one of her sons. He's a big guy. Sounds a lot like Daimon. I can't wait to meet him to see how tough he is."

"How is it going with Pierre?" I asked.

"I don't know. He sent me a text at 11:30 last night. I just read it this morning. He says he won't be coming by the park. I know why he hasn't been coming to the park, it's because he owes Outcast $100.

"I also saw Weasel this morning."

I said, "You know why Silver hasn't been using his spot, don't you?"

"Yeah, because Weasel accused him of stealing two beers from him. Weasel is a real mess. His eye and the whole side of his face is a massive bruise, with strange marks across it. He said he was boot-fucked. He doesn't remember who it was, or why. Probably some of the crack heads at the Sally Ann."

Sitting on the curb near the park was Levi from Arizona – just passing through. Andre arrived on his bicycle shortly after. Hippo said, "Six up, coming up the hill." I turned to see two bicycle patrol officers stopping.

One of the officers asked, "What are you people doing? Just congregating?"

"Yes, officer," said Shakes.

"Does anyone have any booze?"

"We can't afford it," said Shakes.

One of the officers got off his bike. I could read his name tag, Budmiester. He walked around the group and noticed an open can of Old Milwaukee behind Serge. He picked it up and emptied the contents on the sidewalk. "I'm going to have to charge you with this. What's your name?"

"Serge Martin, just like Steve Martin. You can write me a ticket, but I'm not going to pay it. You might as well save the paper. I'll just throw it out."

"You can do as you wish, but the courts have been giving thirty-day jail sentences, depending on how many outstanding charges you have."

Andre said, "I'm looking at your name tag, does it say Budweiser?"

The other officer said, "We've had a complaint. You're going to have to move somewhere else."

We all stood except Jake who said, "I'm supposed to stay here to meet my worker. I have to appear in court this afternoon."

"On what charge?"

"Panning."

"You'd better appear then."

We walked to the far end of the park and sat on the grass. It was still damp from the sprinklers. Andre reached into his backpack and pulled out a bottle of sherry and threw it to Shakes who opened it and passed it around. When it got to Levi, he said, "I don't drink, I only smoke." Shakes reached into his pocket and pulled out a small round can. He threw it to Joy. Andre handed her a rolling paper. Soon, a joint was being passed around.

Levi asked, "What are the laws concerning marijuana in Ontario?"

Joy said, "It all depends on the cop who stops you. You just saw Serge get a liquor violation ticket, while Shakes had a bottle right in front of him. Jake got a ticket for panhandling; I've been panhandling for fifteen years and never got a ticket.

"If a cop stops you and you've got five grams of weed, he'll probably just throw it out on the ground and grind it with his heel. He may give you a warning; he may give you a ticket."

"Dennis," said Jake, "What time is it?"

"12:45."

"Court starts at one, my worker hasn't shown up. I'm never going to make it. It's all the way across town, even if I took the bus I wouldn't get there in time."

"Sounds like a failure to appear," said Joy.

Poster Boy

20 July 2012

"Hi Joy," I said, "Did anything exciting happen after I left yesterday?"

"Yeah, there were cops all over. You saw the one who pulled up as you were walking down the sidewalk. I was standing at the curb and he said, 'Am I too late for the party?'

"I said, 'Yeah, and I'm not even drinking.'

Joy continued, "I walked to the bus shelter to catch a bus or a streetcar and on the way I met Weasel. We sat down and he pulled out a beer. I took a sip and right then a cop car pulled up. He wrote us each a ticket for $125. After he left, we tore them up and put them in the trash barrel. The cop must have just driven around the block because he stopped and charged us again. He said to me, 'You have some outstanding arrest warrants from Montreal.' 'Yeah,' I said, 'I keep meaning to go back there to take care of those.'

"I saw Outcast last night. I told you that he and Debbie aren't getting along too well. He came right out and said, 'Joy, I love you. I've always had feelings for you.' I like him too. He's not bad looking, we're the same age. Right now he's looking for an apartment for us. I told him, 'I want a room of my own.' He said, 'Yeah, I understand. We'll take things slow and see what happens.'

"Then Debbie came home. She had a really sour look on her face. I guess she thought that Outcast and I had been fuckin' around. I felt really flustered because of what we were talking about.

"I told her, 'Don't get the wrong idea. I don't like men. I'm more into women.' She hugged me and kissed me on the cheek, then kissed me again closer to my mouth, then just at the corner of my mouth.

"I said, 'Whoa, I've already got a girlfriend, and I should be getting home to Chester.' I nearly bolted for the door. I talked to Outcast on the phone.

After I left, Debbie said to him, 'I think Joy really likes me.'

"The boys took Levi out to show him the ropes. I don't know how that's going to work out. He seems like a sweet kid. I gave him a joint before I left. I said, 'This is just for you.' 'No, no,' he said, 'I'll share it with everybody.' I think he's a bit naive. I hope those guys don't roll him for his gear."

Chantal came by. Joy said, "Was I supposed to phone you, or were you going to phone me?"

"What's best for you?"

"It's best if you phone me because I only have service after six and on weekends."

"Okay, I'll phone you. Maybe we can get together." Then she left.

"She's such a beautiful person. Did I tell you about how we first met? I was sitting here, and she stopped by and said, 'Is everything alright? You look as if you've been hurt.'

"I said that my boyfriend had been beating me, then I just burst into tears. I still had pneumonia then. When I started crying, I started coughing. She placed both hands on my chest and it felt like electricity going through me. After she removed her hands I could breathe better.

"Chester's done that as well. When I was having trouble with my knee, he rubbed his hands together really fast, then placed them on my knee. It felt better after that. Chester always wants to put his hands on me. I don't like it."

David said to me, "I found my car. I'd lost it for two weeks. I couldn't remember where I parked it. It was in front of the beer store, right where I left it. It's in the market now. Last night I was too drunk to drive."

I sat next to Wolf and Shaggy. "Finally," said Wolf, "someone to talk to who can talk back to me. I've had a run in with nearly everyone here this morning, but when I talk to you, I can see the wheels turning. It's not just going in one ear, out the other.

"This morning, as usual, I took Shaggy down to the river. You know where I live. The river is shallow, so Shag can go out twenty feet, lay down, and the water is still just up to her neck. There are rocks there that are just the right height for me to sit on and have my feet in the water. It works for both of us.

"Anyway, I stopped in at the beer store to buy a six pack. I tied Shag to a post outside. The beer store guy asked me where I'd been. I pointed to Shaggy, who was still dripping water. 'Where do you think I've been?'

"He told me a sad story. He said that someone had been walking in the river a while back, they tripped and drowned. I hadn't heard about it or seen it in the paper. It takes the beer store guy to tell me what's going on in my own neighborhood. A guy would have to be falling down drunk to drown in that shallow water. I guess if he hit his head on a rock, he could drown. Anyway, that's the end of my story.

"I was playing with Shaggy this morning, roughhousing, like we always do and she bit me. She's never done that before. She's bitten lots of other people, but not me."

I asked, "What books are you reading now, Wolf?"

"One of those Ken Follett books. I have a friend who gives them to me every once in a while. I like it because it has large print. It's easier on the eyes. I've been thinking of getting some reading glasses, the kind they sell in the drug store. Do you think they're any good?"

"Yeah, I've used them. They worked fine for me. Do you go to the library? They have a whole section of large print books."

"No, I owe them money. I lost some books, so I owe them $32. I checked with them five years ago, and they still had it on their records. I don't think they forget about things like that.

"How do you like my new shoes? Well, they're new to me. A friend gave them to me. He gives me lots of stuff; he works at the Sally Ann.

"Anyway, I'm walking down the street and this kid says to me, 'Hey, Mister, you're wearing skateboarding shoes and shorts. Are you a skateboarder?' I can barely walk and he thinks I'm a skateboarder. I thought it was odd that the shoes had so much padding. That's the reason."

A man and woman stopped by and introduced themselves as Noel and Jennifer, Salvation Army Housing Outreach Workers. Wolf said, "I got my apartment through you guys. I was a poster boy. They photographed me and Shaggy on the balcony of my apartment. It's right over the front entrance."

"What's your name?" asked Joel.

Wolf thought for a moment whether or not to give his real name, finally he did. Noel said, "My boss, Gavin, has been trying to contact you. It's a matter concerning your rent. I guess that's a sensitive subject."

"I haven't seen Gavin for a long time."

"He's in management now, so he doesn't get out much."

"Yeah, I'll stop in and see him."

I said, "He probably wants to tell you that your rent has been reduced."

"No," said Noel, "I don't think that's the case."

After they left, Wolf said to me, "When I first moved in there my rent was $650 a month. After a year, they increased it by eight dollars. I know they're allowed to raise the rent, but I refused to pay the increase. I kept sending them checks for $650. They called me to a tribunal. As soon as I got there I said, 'What's the idea of raising the rent on that bug infested crack house?' The lawyer said that they should drop the matter, so they did.

"The next year, they sent me a notice saying the rent was going to be raised by eight dollars a month. I sent the checks for the original $650. It's three years now that I haven't been paying any increase, so that's eight, plus eight, plus eight. I don't know how much that works out to, but it's a lot of money. Long story short, that's why Gavin wants to see me."

Cops Go Easy

23 July 2012

"Silver's back," Joy said to me. "I asked him where he'd been. He said, 'I was just tired of Weasel's bullshit.' I said to him, 'Weasel said that you'd stolen two beers from him and were

292

hiding.' Silver said, 'That's a story I haven't heard before.' I said to him, 'Why don't you just punch him? You're bigger than him and probably stronger.' He said, 'I know, I just don't want to cause trouble.' I said, 'I know, you're not a fighter. Anytime you want me to fight him, just let me know.' He said, 'You'd do that for me?' 'Sure,' I said.

"I guess Andre laid into Weasel and Jake on the weekend. Weasel called Andre a goof and Jake backed him. Andre gave them both a backhand. Weasel said it again, so Andre punched him on his already swollen cheek and broke a couple of his ribs."

Andre stopped by and said, "I'm so pissed off with Hippo. We were supposed to meet an hour ago. He's just showing up now and he's wasting time chatting with Silver. I checked and both of our spots are taken. I know the guys that are there, it's not their fault, they were there first. I haven't made a cent this morning and it doesn't look like I'm going to."

Joy said, "Silver doesn't like people hanging around when he's working. You guys are helping Hippo; he's lost on his own. He's like a little kid."

"When he's panning," said Andre, "he just sits there with his cap out. He doesn't smile or greet people. If you give him shit, he just gets that pouty look on his face."

Joy said, "He only comes around when he needs something. When he gets money of his own, he's nowhere to be found."

Andre left on his bicycle, what he calls his 'granny-cycle.' I've never asked how or where he acquired it. I expect he just found it somewhere.

Joy said, "Chester is going to be away for two weeks visiting his family. I hope he leaves me a key. I have the apartment key and the garbage room key, but I don't have the electronic key to get in the building. He said that I could come with him, but everyone in his family would be speaking French, and watching French television, the same as Chester does here. I know that he doesn't want me to have anyone stay over, but I don't do that now, so why would I do it while he was away? I'll just have to wait and see what he's going to do. I may have to find a place to stay for a couple of weeks. This afternoon I meet with the housing worker from the Salvation Army. I told them I want an apartment downtown, but not a crack house."

As I approached the park at noon, I was pleasantly surprised to see that our benches and garbage container had been returned, freshly painted and varnished. Silver had watched the reinstallation and said to the workmen, 'While you're at it, would you mind leaving a case of beer as well.' They said, 'We can't go that far.'

I asked Silver, "Do you have any plans to move from your place?"

"Nothing definite," he said. "It wouldn't be anytime soon, not in winter either. I'd want a place that had no needle pushers, no pill poppers, no one using crack or rock. The problem is, you don't see it during the day, but at night, they run up the stairs, down the stairs, up the stairs. It never stops."

A man with white hair, white moustache and goatee came across the street. The guys all knew him. He said to me, "My name is Brian Cherry, sometimes they call me Grapes. I was at the bank all morning. I even had the manager called down. I was having trouble with someone dipping into my account, so I put a stop payment on them. Now, I have a new account, but they haven't closed the old one."

Brian asked Andre, "Where are you staying now?"

"Second dumpster down, in back of the coffee shop. There's me, Hippo, Jake, Weasel and his dog Bear. All our valuables we store at the far end beside Bear. Last night I was asleep, but I sensed something, so I opened my eyes. This dude was looking around, but as soon as he saw that I was awake, and there were four of us and a dog, he backed off. I watched under the dumpster to see where his feet were going before I settled back to sleep again."

Andre was watching a crane operator across the street lift some concrete panels to the top of one of the buildings. "What a sloppy job that guy's doing. Look at the angle on that load. I used to do that at a steel plant. I'd lift it, weigh it on the scale, then lift it into place. I was working one of those trombone cranes. That was a good job. I was getting twenty bucks an hour. My buddy, who I'd been getting a ride to work with, punched the boss in the face. I lived thirty miles from work. The next day, I tried hitchhiking to work. It was the middle of winter and I nearly froze. I had to phone the boss and tell him I had no way to get to work. He'd probably hire me again. He said that I learned in three weeks what the former guy had taken three months to learn. He wanted me to work for him.

"The cops have never bothered me panning. I'm always honest with them. I said to one of them, 'I'm just trying to get three dollars for a hamburger, then I'll be out of here.' He said, 'Okay, but don't stay too long.' "

Silver said, "Joy's never been bothered either, but one day, after she had left, I panned in her spot. It wasn't long before the library security guard came out and said I had to move. On my birthday, Jacques had given me a huge bottle of his homemade wine, and it's good. I hadn't drunk more than about three fingers when this female cop came by on her bicycle. She said, 'Silver, you're going to have to dump that.' I said, 'It's my birthday.' She said, 'In that case I won't charge you, but you'll still have to dump it.'

"Another time, the same lady cop came by just as I cracked a beer. She told me to dump it, then asked, 'Do you have any more in your pack?' I said, 'Yes.' I wasn't going to lie to her. She could have searched it anyway. She said, 'I'll let you keep them as long as you don't open them here.'"

Gravy Stains

24 July 2012

This morning Joy was sitting in her usual spot. Butcher was leaning against the railing talking to her. He was looking very dapper in his Hawaiian shirt and khaki shorts. I couldn't take my eyes off his tattoos that stretched from shoulder to wrist on both arms. The design was an intricate west coast Haida motif.

Joy said, "I was surprised to see Hippo at 6:30 this morning. I asked him where he was going. He said, 'To work!' I've never seen him start that early before."

I said, "I think that Andre had a talk with him."

"I think so," agreed Joy. "One morning he'd only made a quarter. He came across the street to bum a smoke. He saw a lady bending over his cap. He thought she'd made a drop, but she'd taken his quarter."

"You'd think," said Butcher, "that a person whose sole occupation was to collect money, would know enough to take care of it."

Joy said, "I saw a guy this morning with two twenties hanging out of his back pocket. I shouted at him, but he didn't hear me."

"When I was in Israel," said Butcher, "I saw a number of people with wallets half out of their back pockets. I was walking with a friend and he saw a twenty on the ground. He bent down to pick it up and a guy yelled at him, 'That's mine; it's there for a reason.' My friend said, 'Okay,' and backed off. I guess it was part of a sting operation to catch pickpockets. The guy you saw this morning was probably there to lure pickpockets. You don't see it too much here, but in Montreal and New York there are guys who are so smooth they can grab your wallet and watch without you knowing it. I know; it happened to me. That's why I don't wear a watch."

I said, "Did you notice that we have our benches back in the park?"

"Yeah," said Joy, "I watched them putting them in. I said to one of the workmen, 'You could have wiped them off before you reinstalled them. One of them has pigeon shit on it already.' He said, 'Sorry ma'am, we don't wipe benches.' Why would they? We're just skids.

I asked Joy, "Did you speak to the housing people from the Salvation Army yesterday?"

"No, I left early."

Chester stopped by. Joy said, "Okay people, I'm too popular. I've only made four bucks this morning. I don't know what happened to my money. When I got home last night, all I had was a quarter."

I decided to leave to let Joy get on with her panning. "I'll see you at noon, Joy."

At noon Hippo said, "I made a buck twenty-five and I started work at 6:30 this morning."

Andre said, "I made the price of a bottle and lent Joy three dollars and change so she could buy a bottle. It's the first time I know of that Joy's had to borrow money to buy a bottle. On top of that, I got a sixty-five buck ticket for panhandling. I saw the cop coming, so I scooped the change out of my cap. He pulled up at the curb and asked me what I was doing. I said, 'Officer, I'm just eating my breakfast and drinking my coffee. He said, 'Why is your hat out?' I said, 'My mother brought me up in a Christian home and insisted that we always remove our hats before eating.' He said, 'I'm going to write you a ticket for panhandling. What's your address?' I said, 'I'm not panhandling, officer. There's no money in my cap. I'm homeless, I have no fixed address, but I'm staying at dumpster number two behind the coffee shop.' He said, 'You're not going to pay this ticket are you?' I said, 'No sir, I'll probably use it as a fire starter for my barbecue."

Shakes had gone to the store to use the bathroom. When he returned he said, "Dennis, see these pants? Yesterday they were white, then someone gave me a plate of roast beef and gravy."

Andre said, "Yeah, Shakes ate all the roast beef and what gravy he didn't spill all over himself, he gave to me. I love that dark chicken gravy, but it doesn't agree with me. I had the shits and the farts all night. I was wearing this same tee shirt. See, no gravy stains, it all went in my beard.

"Weasel and Jake were both being assholes. Weasel kept calling me a goof and Little Jake backed him up. With the back of my hand, I hit them both with one swat. Weasel said it again, so I got him in a headlock and let my elbow do the rest."

I said, "I remember the video of you on YouTube – St. Patrick bar fights 2010. I saw that you used some karate moves."

"I know karate, tai kwon do, tai chi. I use them all. That video was taken at the club. There was a line up to get in, so I was panning the line. I think I must have made $400 that night. There was one asshole in line that was making trouble for everyone. He was loud and swearing. I went up to him and said, 'There are ladies here, they shouldn't have to put up with language like that.' He took a swing at me and missed. I knocked him down four times before he stayed down.

"The owner called me over. I thought I was in big trouble then. He said, 'I saw what you did. That guy has been causing us trouble all evening. We've got a VIP area inside and I'd like you to be my guest. Just stick your hand up when you want a drink. It's all on the house.'"

Shakes said, "We should have gone to that club we were invited to by the guy from the Jazz'n Blues Festival."

"Yeah," agreed Andre, "the vodka got in the way. A guy named Rob, a friend of mine who just got out of jail, swiped two bottles of vodka from the liquor store. That's funny, Rob robbed the liquor store. Anyway, we started on the vodka. I had a couple of 7.1% beers, then Rob brought out a bottle of Captain Morgan. I don't know how I rode my bike back that night."

Shakes said, "I don't know how I walked to my daughter's house that night."

Andre said, "It reminds me of a time a buddy and I were driving past a beer store in his pickup. There was a semi backed up to the loading dock, but the store was closed. I guess the driver arrived too late to unload. There was just enough room for me to squeeze between the truck and the dock. I jimmied the lock and couldn't believe my eyes – wall to wall beer. We filled the pickup with all it could hold. I think we had twenty-seven two-fours. We were tempted to unload and go back again, but you never return to the scene of the crime. We sure had a party though."

Shakes said, "If you get greedy, that's when you get pinched."

One Week Sober

25 July 2012

This morning, Joy seemed a bit down. I asked her about it, "It's just one of those days." she said. "I didn't get much sleep last night." I noticed that she had a wrapped candy in her cap. "Did someone drop you a candy?"

"No, I picked it up at Outcast's yesterday. Debbie still thinks there's something going on between me and him. She asked, 'Do you like me?' 'Yeah,' I said, 'you're okay.' 'No, I mean do you really like me? You like women, right?' Yeah,' I said, 'you're just not my type.' She said, 'I have a friend, Meg, I'd like to introduce you to.' 'No, thanks,' I said, 'I already have a girlfriend.' She's probably one of those bull dyke types.

"I was supposed to stay for supper, but then Outcast and Debbie started arguing. I didn't need to be in the middle of that, so I said, 'I've got to go. I've got things to do.'

"Andre and Jake got into it again this morning. Jake sent Andre on a run. He gave him a five dollar bill and a dollar. I guess the guy didn't charge Andre. Anyway, he brought back the food. Later, Andre pulled out a five and Little Jake got all pissy about it and asked for it back. Andre decked him.

"Yesterday, Andre, Jake and Hippo were standing near me. They reeked. I said, 'Guys, would you mind moving down wind. I know you've got no place to live but water is free, so use it.'

"Hippo was going on about, 'I only made a buck twenty-five and I've been working since 6:30.' His worker had to come down to take him to an appointment with his probation officer. It's only a block and a half away, in the courthouse. I can see Jake's worker coming to take him to court. Otherwise, he just wouldn't go. Andre said he's going to grease Hippo off, let him see what it's like to be really on his own."

I said, "I noticed yesterday that neither Andre or Shakes were sharing their bottle with him. He said, 'It's okay, I decided not to drink today.'"

"He's got to learn. I'm tired of supplying cigarettes to him and everyone else. We all do the same job, and I'm paying rent to Chester. There's no reason for me to be supporting them, just because they drink more than I do. When Andre came to see me yesterday, he had his bottle right out in the open. My regulars were staring at him. It's no wonder these guys get charged.

"Earlier, there was a guy across the street just staring at me. I gave him a friendly wave. He looked around as if to say, 'Are you waving at me?' I pointed at him, 'Yes, you.' Humans, you just got to wonder about them sometimes. If you shoot them, you go to jail. What are you supposed to do?

"I haven't seen Jacques for a couple of weeks, not that I miss him. I like to stay well away from people who have bedbugs. Maybe we get sand fleas from putting our bags on the ground. They can be nasty.

"When I went into hospital, I lost a lot of my winter gear. Big Jake didn't bother picking it up from our apartment, then the landlord threw it out. I had a pair of army pants and a really heavy army coat. With two pairs of long underwear, I was really toasty. I had a black backpack with the khaki in front and the black on my back. The guys said I looked like a Ninja Turtle. They'd say, 'Hey, Turtle, which one are you?' I'd say, 'Michelangelo!'

"Are you going up to the cabin on the weekend? Maybe you could sneak me in your trunk. I could hide in the woods and you could say to your wife, 'I found this wild creature in the woods. Can we keep it? Can we?'"

I said to Joy, "I'll let you get back to work."

She handed me a granola bar. "Do you want this? Otherwise, it'll be squirrel food. Stella should be coming by today, she comes every Wednesday, so maybe I'll see you in the park. It should be a full house."

"Hi Serge," I said, "How is everything going today?"

"Every day is a good day."

"That's a good attitude to have."

He asked, "Are you taking a vacation?"

"Yes," I replied, "I'll be away next week. I'll be sitting in the shade by the lake drinking beer."

"That sounds good."

"You're looking a lot better today."

"I feel fine."

"I'll see you later, Serge."

"See you."

At the benches were a half dozen of the regulars. On a bicycle was a stranger who was saying to the group in general, "If you see Lucy, tell her that I want my watch and my cell phone back. The watch isn't so important, but I need the phone. If I don't get it back, she's going to be in big trouble." Then he rode off.

"Andre," said Joy, "if you let your hair grow any longer, you could have dreadlocks."

"Lucy already pulled half of it out. She just grabbed me by the back of the neck then pulled. If she was a guy, I would have belted her."

"Why do you guys put up with shit like that? Just kick her. I can't wait until she tries something like that on me. I'll show her."

Andre said, "She says she's going to get Daimon after me. I can't wait for that."

"Daimon doesn't dare come down here with a broken ankle. After an ankle is broken once, it breaks really easy the second time. I know. I've had both of mine broken. After that, the bone sort of crystallizes. It gets brittle. You can break it just by stepping off a curb."

I asked, "How did you break your ankles?"

"I'd had enough of my husband, Delbert. I had my bags packed. I'd phoned a cab and was carrying our son in my arms. Delbert pushed me down the stairs. I made sure I didn't land on the baby. The cab arrived, I went to my mother's, and she looked after our son while I carried on to the hospital. They took x-rays and told me I was pregnant. I said, 'How can I be pregnant? My last baby is only five months old.' I was only two weeks along. I had my fifth, then got pregnant again. This time I had an abortion and had my tubes tied. No more baby nappies for me.

"I just about made the price of a bottle today. I had to borrow thirty-five cents. I haven't opened it yet. I'm still working on the one I started yesterday."

Andre said, "I think Shakes and I have gone through four so far. Soon, it'll be time to go back to work."

I asked Shark, "How is the move to your new apartment going?"

"We're doing most of it on Saturday. Danny is helping me take my stuff across the parking lot. Irene has a truck from the Salvation Army coming to move her stuff."

"It sounds like a nice place that you're moving to."

"It really is."

Joy asked Irene, "How are you making out with your Risparidone?"

"I'm taking 1 tablet, 100 milligrams, but it doesn't seem to be doing much."

Joy said, "I usually chew about four of those tablets before I go to bed. I need that much so I don't dream. Poor Chester, once this week I woke up screaming. He came running in saying, 'Joy, what's wrong? I thought someone was trying to kill you.' 'So did I, Chester,' I said, 'but it's okay now.'"

After Shark and Irene had left Joy said, "They both have been sober for a week now. It doesn't sound like much, but for them it's a big deal.

Cirrhosis

July 26, 2012

Silver said to me, "I haven't seen Joy. I don't know if she's coming down or not. Today might be check day for her, so she may be waiting around for that."

I said, "I heard her mention that she'd have to go to Chuck's to see if she has mail, so that might be what she's doing. What did you think of that guy who rode up on his bicycle looking for Lucy?"

Silver said, "He also came back later. I said to him, 'I saw her earlier at the Mission.' I was there later and saw the guy riding around on his bicycle. I went in for dinner and Lucy was there. She was drunk, or loaded to the eyeballs on something. She kept falling out of her chair. I didn't offer to help her up.

"I don't want to seem mean or anything, but I really hope something bad happens to Lucy and Daimon for what they did to Shark and Irene; not once, but twice. They were after Shark's medication."

I was introduced to Joanne, a regular of Silver's. She said to him, "Would you like coffee and a muffin?"

"Sure, thanks." While she went into the coffee shop, Silver said to me, "She's a jogger. I took a break from here for a couple of weeks and saw her running along the bicycle path. She's offered to bring me some of her husband's shirts, but she said they'd hang on me like a tent. He must be big."

Joanne returned with coffee and a blueberry muffin. She chatted with Silver for a while then went on her way to work.

"She's a nice lady," said Silver.

I said, "Shark and Irene are all set to move on the weekend."

"Are they moving in together?"

"Yes, they've got a three bedroom apartment. One room is just for Shark when he wants to get away to play his video games. I think he can lock himself in."

"He'll need that. I went out with Irene for eight years. She can be really nice sometimes, then she snaps. That's when you don't want to be around her. She's just a small woman, but if she hits you right, she could break your nose. I hope Shark knows what he's getting himself into."

I said, "He's told me of times when he'd brought over groceries to make supper. Before he had a chance to sit down, she told him to get out. I'll let you get back to work, Silver. I have to do the same."

I was pleased to see Magdalene. When I saw her last, she was five months pregnant. Now, her baby, named Alphonse, is seven weeks old. They are living near the hospital where

Magdalene had her baby. Social Services arranged accommodation for them. They pay ten dollars a day.

Magdalene said, "Alphonse is my second child. I have another named Jean-Guy. He's six years old." She showed me a tattoo on her left shoulder. It was the head of a wolf and under it was written Jean-Guy. "The wolf mother will always protect her young. She can be vicious if anyone comes near her babies. I speak French, my English isn't too good. Can you understand me?"

"There are a few words I might miss, but yes I understand you."

Andre said, "When Magdalene first came to town, I was the first person she met. I said, 'I'll show you the town,' and I did. We partied for three days and she doesn't remember any of it."

I asked, "Do you remember any of it, Andre?"

"No."

Magdalene said, "We didn't sleep together or anything, he's just my best friend, like a brother."

I said, "He's like a brother to me too."

"Shakes," I asked, "How did it go in court this morning?"

"I was late, but my lawyer took care of everything. They set a court date of August 28th."

Inusiq said to me, "I forgot your name. What is it again?"

"Dennis, and your name is Inusiq, right?"

Shakes said, "His name is Nuisance, ha."

A Salvation Army van stopped across the street. A male and a female worker came over. They offered bottles of water to everyone and asked if anything was needed.

Hippo said, "Do you have any tee shirts? I could use an extra-large."

The male worker came back with two shirts, "I've got white and blue. Who wants what?"

Magdalene said, "I'll take one. This one I'm wearing says 'Hug me I'm Irish.' I don't like to be hugged by people I don't know." She tried on the blue shirt. "It's too blue," she said and took it off.

Andre said to the female worker, "You're new, aren't you? I don't remember seeing you around."

"I came from Alberta."

Andre said, "I know Alberta, which part do you come from?"

"Near Red Deer, I was in prison there."

"Right on!" said Andre, "We all know what that's like."

I asked Irene, "How is everything going for your move on Saturday?"

"Everything is arranged, but I'm not ready. I'm glad we have some young people to help us carry things upstairs. Shark is going to help me take apart my futon. I'll just put the mattress on the floor and sleep there tonight. This afternoon I have to go see my doctor."

I asked her, "Do you have to go to get your white blood cell count? Is it affected by your medication?"

She said, "I've been feeling sick. My stomach has been bloated. Even the water pills aren't working."

Shark said, "We both have cirrhosis. Our livers won't produce enough red blood cells. That's why our white cell count has to be monitored."

Irene said, "We've both been sober for over a week. We're not going to be able to invite any of these people over to our new place. We can't even invite Shark's brother. If we take one drink, we'll be right back on it."

"Congratulations," I said, "What you're doing is really difficult. I'm proud of you both."

Trading Pants

27 July 2012

This morning I visited with Silver in front of the coffee shop. It's interesting, the looks I get, especially when he has to leave for a few minutes to use the washroom. Some people look away, but one lady dropped me a dollar. Silver offered to split it with me, but I told him to hang on to it.

Silver said, "I remember one time, when I still had my big beard, I went into the coffee shop for a coffee. Jody served me; I'd known her for years. The woman behind me said to Jody, 'You serve people like that?' Jody said, 'Sure, he's a paying customer. Why wouldn't I serve him?' I didn't say anything. What am I going to do, spoil my meal ticket?"

I said, "Andre told me that he's on good terms with the owner of the coffee shop. The owner told him that he's welcome to stay in back as long as he keeps it neat. Andre goes out of his way to make sure all the trash is picked up. It works out for everyone."

Silver said, "I'm waiting for Chester. He gets his check today and he said that he'd lend me fifty bucks. I've borrowed from him before and I always pay him back on time, not a week late or a day late, as soon as I get my check.

"I miss a lot of people who used to be around here, like Trash and Craig."

"I remember Craig," I said. "He used to sleep by the library in mid-winter. I'd bring him a coffee in the morning and peek under a corner of his sleeping bag, just to make sure he was still alive. Sometimes he'd grumble, 'Just leave it there, bro. I'll have it later. I'm not awake yet.'"

Silver said, "Craig lived at the hotel for a while. He got an inheritance of $8000. He got people to do everything for him. He never left his room. Soon, it started getting bad. He'd shit all over the floor. We'd say to him, 'Craig, the bathroom's just down the hall, use it.' He got moved into a program at Addiction Recovery for detox.

"Chester's usually here by now. He comes down early to do a butt run, but since he's getting his check today, I guess he doesn't need to."

I said, "Joy told me that Big Jake is scheduled to get out in October, but since he refuses to do his programs, for alcohol recovery and anger management, he won't be out until spring."

"I never liked that guy," said Silver. "It was his eyes. I could never trust the look in his eyes."

"I find Daimon the same way," I said, "but with the broken ankle, he'll always have a weakness. Joy broke both of her ankles and she said they've been fragile ever since. She could break one by stepping off a curb. Daimon would go down with a kick to the ankle."

"Yes, but which ankle? What if I kicked the wrong ankle? I think it's better if I just run — *whish* — I'm out of here."

At noon Outcast said to me, "Dennis, you have to go take a look at Jake. You won't believe it. One night with Debbie and he's a new man."

"Here comes Jungle Jim. He probably dropped some crack with Jake." A man with a long beard, wearing a tank top, and a tall slender woman, were walking towards us.

Joy said, "The last time I saw her she passed her hand over the spikes in my hair. I jumped up and punched her in the back of the head."

Outcast said, "Honestly, Dennis, you have to go see Little Jake." I walked up to the lawn and hardly recognized him. He was shaved, his hair was washed and stylishly trimmed. Also, he was wearing clean clothes. I introduced myself to him and he laughed.

I turned to Shark. "Hi Shark," I said. "So, tomorrow is the day for your move."

"It's Monday. Irene's at home making some phone calls. That's why she's not here. I just came down to meet Buck."

Andre shook my hand then fell asleep against the shoulder of Shakes. He awoke briefly to ask for a drink. Shakes handed him the bottle and Andre slowly nodded off. Just as he dropped the bottle, Shakes reached over and caught it.

"You know, Dennis," said Shakes, "I may be a drunk and a stoner, but I have some scruples."

"What scruples do you have, Shakes?"

"I'm kind to children. I have a grandson and some granddaughters. Do you know what I don't understand?"

"What's that Shakes?"

"I don't understand parents who take children to restaurants and drink in front of them. That sets a bad example."

"Did your parents ever drink in front of you?" I asked.

"No. I drank in front of them, but I did it discreetly."

Inusiq's arm was in a sling. "How did you hurt your arm, Inusiq?"

"I fell off a ledge. I dislocated my shoulder. I had to go to hospital. I didn't do it with these guys. I did it by myself. What's your name again?"

"Dennis," I said.

"Do you remember my name?"

"Nuisance," I said.

"See Shakes, he remembers my name. And your name is Dennis the menace, right?"

"Shakes," I said, "your pants look cleaner. Did you wash them?"

"No, but we got some laundry detergent. Dennis, can you do me a favor? There's a clothing store going out of business. Everything is on sale. Can you get me a pair of track pants?"

"What size do you wear?"

"My waist size is twenty-eight. The length would be thirty two or thirty four."

"I can't get them today, Shakes, but perhaps on the weekend."

"In that case, can we trade pants?"

"Shakes, if we were to trade pants, I'd have to roll them up three times at the bottom. My pants would come to your knees. Can't you get pants at the Shep?"

"They're closed."

"How about the Mission?"

"I'm barred for life from the Mission."

"How about the Sally Ann?"

"I'm not barred from the Sally Ann, but they wouldn't let me in with alcohol on my breath. They'd throw me out."

Inusiq said to me, "You and I could trade pants, then I could trade with Shakes."

"That's a nice thought, Inusiq, but as nice as your pants are, they wouldn't conform to the dress code where I work. We have a Friday Jeans Day, but no Track Pants Day. I don't think trading pants would work."

Shark came by and said, "Has Buck been by? I've been waiting for him. Did Joy, Outcast and Chester leave? Do they know something I don't? I guess I'll hang around a while longer. Right now, I'm going to McDonalds to buy an iced tea."

"Shark," asked Shakes, "could you buy me one of those Sausage McMuffins?"

"They close those off at 10:30."

"Then how about a cheeseburger?"

"I'll see what I can do, Shakes."

To me Shakes said, "I have to eat something. I bought a cheeseburger this morning, but we split it three ways."

Inusiq said, "He has to eat something. I have to eat something. You have to eat something."

It was time for me to go. I shook hands with Shakes and Inusiq. Andre was still asleep. As I was leaving, Inusiq said, "Txin yaxtakuq."

I asked, "What does that mean?

"I love you."

I replied, "Txin yaxtakuq, Inusiq and Shakes."

Part of the Family

After eighteen months of daily conversations with people living on the streets, in shelters or sharing accommodation, I have made the following observations. A full-fledged member of the street family is one who has been with the group for over ten years. Jacques and Joy are the patriarch and matriarch. Everyone else is a newbie — on probation. To gain acceptance one must be vouched for and have proven themselves not to be an asshole.

The group expects honesty and sincerity. That may seem strange when you consider that most of these people have prison records. Many have been involved in scams of one sort or another, but if you're family they expect the truth. How else, they explained, can they help you?

They'll share with you what little they have, even the jackets off their back. The same is expected in return. The people who come around only when they're in need of money, cigarettes, booze, drugs or food are soon put on notice. On check day, all debts are paid in full.

Continue reading *Conversations with Street People*

Gotta Find a Home: More Conversations with Street People, Book 2
Gotta Find a Home: Further Conversations with Street People, Book 3

Read about Joy, Shakes, and all the others in real time on Dennis' blog <u>Gotta Find a Home</u>.
http://gottafindahome.wordpress.com/

A generous portion of the proceeds from the sale of these books goes towards helping the homeless.

You can help in this goal by leaving a review wherever you purchased this book, by writing a review or mentioning Dennis and his work on your blog, or by spreading the word about *Gotta Find a Home* on your social media networks.

Thank you so much!
Dennis Cardiff, author and Karen Hamilton Silvestri, editor.

Ottawa Innercity Missions, Street Outreach Program

I can't do much for these people except to show them love, compassion, an ear to listen, perhaps a breakfast sandwich and a coffee. I want to do more. To know them is to love them. What was seen cannot be unseen. I thank my publisher, Karen Silvestri for helping to realize my dream.

All profits from the sale of these books will be used to support the *Ottawa Innercity Missions, Street Outreach Program.*

OIM's *Street Outreach* teams come to walk alongside the poor and homeless in the downtown core. Volunteer teams provide relief provisions, pastoral care, crisis intervention and referrals.

Street Outreach is the main component of OIM's work. Through *Street Outreach* our trained volunteers meet men and women living on the street, create trusting relationships, and can work to filling both physical and personal needs. Last year (2012) OIM connected with 7,672 individuals on the street in downtown Ottawa, 2,735 of whom were youth.

The Red Vests
If you see two or more people walking down the street wearing a bright red vest with the OIM logo on it then you have run into one of our mobile outreach teams!

OIM's *Street Outreach* volunteers are out meeting with people and handing out snacks and toiletries six days a week.

We have teams on the street Monday to Thursday nights (7pm – 9pm), including late Wednesday (9pm-Midnight).

Additional teams are out during the day on Wednesdays & Saturdays (10am-1pm) and Thursdays & Fridays (1-3pm).

You may donate directly to *Ottawa Innercity Ministries* by clicking on the following link: CanadaHelps.org https://www.canadahelps.org/GivingPages/GivingPage.aspx?gpID=36449

Interview With Dennis Cardiff

What Might Creativity Achieve for Others?
by Jeff Lee
(originally posted at Recent Items, September 8, 2013
www.recentitems.wordpress.com)

Giving time to other people's stories is a gift in a world increasingly built around attending to the self. Dennis Cardiff gives his time to people who aren't normally given time – namely homeless people – listens to what they have to say, and then considers this important enough to take further time in organising and sharing it.

There's an honesty in his description of their lives that's frequently unsentimental. Yet there's more to this than mere warts-'n'-all shocks. In one dialogue, the talk includes where to get the strongest free Wi-Fi signal for listening to the radio on a mobile phone. If these narratives are anything, they're an education.

Dennis's education is primarily in art, poetry and creative writing, and he's three and a half years into an honors degree in Theory and History of Art. Unsurprisingly, he's done care work with seniors through an outreach centre so that they could remain in their own homes rather than move to a care facility. He's also been a professional portrait painter for over forty years and worked in art galleries in a variety of assistive and educational roles.

But this interview is about Dennis's writing practice. In all the time and space he devotes to others, he's almost an absent figure, as though his process necessitates a kind of self-abnegation. Unsurprisingly then, even when discussing his practice, he does so through discussing others. The questions thereafter move further towards those others. Finally, there will be some concluding remarks about the implications of Dennis's work.

Is there any 'ultimate goal' in writing about homeless people?

My goal when I started these interviews was to investigate the ultimate cause of homelessness, to find a possible solution. I haven't found any solutions, but have encountered as many reasons for homelessness as there are people sleeping on the streets.

I spoke to Joy [a central contact in Dennis's befriending] about my interest in writing a story about her and her friends. She thought that was a great idea. I discussed with some of her friends my intention of writing a book from the point of view of homeless people. I asked them, 'What would you guys like the general public to know about your situation?'

'I'll talk to you' said Darren [a college graduate and Gulf war veteran]. 'First of all we aren't you guys, we're not a group, we're individuals. We come from different places, different backgrounds, in some cases different tribes. Some of us don't even like each other, but we congregate here to have a beer, smoke a joint, to be with others who don't judge or verbally abuse us. We accept everyone here as they are.'

How do you practically go about writing the conversations? I'd imagine that recording devices could ignite some people with mental health conditions and/or addiction problems. Is it all recalled from memory? If so, do you go about this as soon as possible, or do you wait a while?

I have never used any recording device. If I were found with one, my life could very well be in danger. Every day I hear about thefts and witness minor crimes, mostly the sale of illegal cigarettes and dope deals. I know the dealers and turn away when business is being transacted.

I pay particular attention to accents, manners of speaking, unusual phrases, and general topics being discussed. Now that I know these people, as long as I can remember the topics, I can reconstruct how they would respond. I also seem to have a particularly good memory for dialog – very little else. I jot notes in my journal as soon as I can and type the conversations later.

What does the technology of blogging bring to this writing? Do any of the homeless people read your blog?

Blogging, especially on WordPress, has brought me encouragement and support. Many homeless people, or people who have, at some time in their lives, experienced homelessness, have written to me about their experiences. Psychologists have given anonymous accounts of child neglect, physical and sexual abuse and how these can lead to homelessness in later years. Very few of my homeless friends know how to use a computer. Since my blog is still a rough draft, I haven't brought it to their attention.

My blog is a workspace, part of my editing process. The dates referred to jump back and forth from 2012 to 2013. I do this in order to be able to post each day. I still haven't completely edited 2012. If I had, I would post it as a chronological set of entries as I have for 2010 and 2011. There is still much editing to do. I use Scrivener for that.

The people in your stories often sound like teenagers. There's little indication of their ages and so on, so the suggestion is that they're adults who have had developmental problems in their youth.

Actual ages vary from early twenties to senior citizens. Most of them have suffered physical and sexual abuse from early childhood. Parents were often alcoholic. Some babies were born with fetal alcohol syndrome. Some were physically injured while still in the womb. Some have very little education, while others have university degrees. Most of them have mental conditions such as bipolar disorder and agoraphobia. They also have physical illnesses such as HIV/AIDS, cancer, fibromyalgia, kidney malfunctions, cirrhosis of the liver and heart conditions.

I notice that you concentrate on the events of each person's day rather than their histories. Is this a conscious move, and if so, why?

I try not to ask directly about a person's history, although bits and pieces do come up in conversation. I hope to compile these bits and pieces together as I edit the book.

I concentrate on the events of each person's day because I want the individuals to come through in their own words. I don't want to influence or edit, in any way, what is being said. There are often contradictions between what is said one day and what is said in another. I will leave it to the reader to take from these conversations what they wish.

Do you have any background of political activism (on any subjects) or is what you do now down to that first chance meeting with Joy?

I have no background of political activism or political interest, although my political leanings have always been to the left. It was my meetings with Joy, Antonio and Craig that sparked my interest in homelessness. Also, I was reading books on Buddhism at the time, and committed to informally follow 'the path of the Bodhisattva.' This entails, among other things, to open one's heart and to practice generosity: having the will to dedicate body, possessions and merits to others.

My brother-in-law works at a treatment center and hostel for homeless alcoholics. His involvement aroused my interest and led me to apply to The Shepherds of Good Hope, where I volunteered. I stopped working there due to back injury.

There's something chaotic about the conversations you've written; for example, this one jumps from topic to topic without any apparent structure, nor is any point being worked towards. How much of this chaos is a reflection of their lives, and how much of is it reconstructive work at the writing stage?

My original blog was at Writing.com. It was written in blog style so that the latest entry would always appear on top. If it were to be printed it would come out chronologically backwards.

I endeavor to post to WordPress every day, so on weekends or rainy days, when none of the panhandlers are out, I refer to entries from 2012 [panhandling = slang for begging (with or without a pan)]. In the final book everything will appear chronologically, names and places will be changed in the interests of privacy.

A typical day for me involves taking the bus and walking two blocks to work. I pass Joy's spot every day. I usually sit and talk with her for twenty to thirty minutes. Chester and Hippo may drop by to chat. Joy generally doesn't do Mondays – days immediately after receiving her monthly check – nor does she do rainy or very cold days.

Most afternoons, depending on weather, I walk two blocks to the park where the group of panhandlers varies in size from two to twenty or more. They don't panhandle at the park. Like a soap opera, every day is different; some scenarios will carry over a few days or weeks. People will disappear for weeks or months due illness, rehab programs or incarceration.

These two situations could develop into two different books: Joy's biography, and a collection of the stories I hear at the park. By writing two books, […] I could avoid some of the redundancy of explaining where each story was taking place. I have no idea how they will end.

Do you plan on bringing the subject of homelessness into your paintings?

I hope to draw or paint portraits to accompany these stories. In this way I could subtly alter individual facial features to maintain privacy, yet still include the details of dress and surroundings.

I have photos, but for reasons of privacy, I have been told that I cannot use them, nor can I use real names. Even if I was to have signed publication releases, they would not hold up in court, due to the fact that many of these people are not of sound mind and are usually drunk.

Does your writing process provide anything for you that you can't get from the world of work or consumer leisure?

Writing about the homeless, and helping the homeless, has given my life a purpose that it didn't have before. Documenting their stories will, I hope, introduce them to the public in a non-threatening way. Some panhandlers look intimidating, but that disappears when one sees them laugh.

I'm also encouraged by the number of comments I get on my posts. I didn't know that there was so much interest. This also bolsters my resolve to bring this project to completion.

Would you go so far as to say that this is a life-changing event? Is there a Dennis' 'life before' and 'life after' the conjunction of those first meetings with Buddhism? Or is this all simply a continuity from things you'd already involved yourself in throughout your life?

I have always read books on Buddhism, Sufism and New Age books on love forgiveness and relieving stress through meditation. When I met Joy I was going through an emotional crisis. Meeting her and her friends – worrying about them and whether or not they would be able to eat and find a place to sleep – took my mind off my problems, that then, seemed insignificant. It was truly a life changing experience.

What kinds of changes have visitors told you that your blog has made for them and/or what they've brought from your blog to the world beyond themselves?

Many visitors have told me that, after reading my blog, they want to be more active in helping the homeless, either on their own or through their church. Many say that my writing has opened their eyes to people they would otherwise have ignored.

What have people who are professionally or voluntarily involved in dealing with homeless people in their day to day lives said about your blog? I use the term 'dealing with'

rather than 'helping' because I'm not assuming that everyone who comes across your blog is necessarily sympathetic.

The reactions are mixed. I have been told that I am wasting my time, that addicts and alcoholics can only be reformed if they want to quit; that they are manipulators and that my efforts, although altruistic, will simply lead to these people buying more alcohol or drugs.

I respond by saying that I am not trying to reform either alcoholics or other addicts. Most of my friends have terminal illnesses, cancer, HIV/AIDS, cirrhosis of the liver and kidney failure. My intent is to make their last months or days less stressful. With a meal card and bus fare they have the means to eat and get back to where they are staying. I realize that these things can be traded for cash to buy alcohol, but that is beyond my control.

Most psychologists, health workers, social workers and church officials who provide meals for the poor, commend my efforts.

So too do I, though maybe for reasons they wouldn't give. His use of writing stands out in a number of ways. It centers on, as already suggested, his attention to others. The self-publishing revolution, for all that it's done to help aspiring authors, has in its very name the emphasis that its industry puts on so much of its endeavours: the self.

It's understandable that the democratisation of creativity by technology is individualistic. Computers as we understand them today have that spirit in their very name: they're personal. It seems a pity then that global interconnectivity doesn't do more to help us work towards goals beyond building our personal profiles and wealth. How many times have you been advertised at with a slogan such as 'it's all about you'?

So what do I mean by goals beyond personal profiles and wealth? I'm not referring to the ubiquitous propagation of religion on the Internet. Many religious people will go about this propagation in any medium. And though it's true that Dennis has some religious feeling in what he does, his writing is no doctrine. As he says, his interest is in the experience of homeless people in their own words, however mixed-up that is. Just read his blog to see for yourself how he desists from judging them.

Of course, we have only his account of their account to go by. I'm not suggesting that he's some kind of paragon of moral creativity. I'm not sure he would either. This is ultimately a matter for his readers to decide on. What I do propose though is that his work (in writing and beyond) raises important questions about what creatives want to achieve and for whom.

There are all kinds of causes that people are passionate about. There are all kinds of changes in the world that people would like to see and make happen. Yet self-publishing seems to be dominated by escapist novels. Why on earth is that? Is this a good use of talent and energy? The nearest that authors usually get to causes greater than the self is when writing about events in their own lives that may touch others. Why then is a practice like Dennis's so much the exception?

Perhaps the Internet distracts people from causes greater than the self by generating anxieties about how to get the greatest possible audience? There seems to be no end of advice available about how to do this. Perhaps pursuing a cause feels too niche to apply some creativity to? Yet the web is surely a great medium for both collecting the interested everywhere and adding to their number? Or perhaps there are other reasons? Perhaps for some people it's all a bit like 'do-gooding' (as opposed to what, do-badding, or even doing nothing)?

Where can anyone go for intelligent discussion and information about directing our creative interests into causes greater than ourselves? And are the practitioners of an other-oriented art the last people to ask because it would mean expounding on their experience?

So many questions. And these are the kinds of them that Dennis' practice and his comments about it leave me with. All this, and without even getting into the expectations we might realistically have about how much creativity can achieve for other people. And is the real creativity, in his case, more in the befriending than in the writing? Hopefully I'll return to Dennis with these and other questions at a future date. In the meantime, my thanks go to him for taking the time for this interview.

Jeff Lee

Connect with the author:

Email Dennis Cardiff:
dacardiff@gmail.com

Follow Dennis Cardiff on Twitter:
https://twitter.com/DennisCardiff

Follow Dennis Cardiff on Facebook:
https://www.facebook.com/gottafindahome

Subscribe to *Gotta Find a Home* blog:
http://gottafindahome.wordpress.com/

Follow Karenzo Media on Twitter:
https://twitter.com/kathamy

The Usual Suspects

People come and go on a daily basis on the street, so this list only includes 'the regulars' – the ones that Dennis refers to as 'the usual suspects'. This list will refresh your memory on their approximate ages and who their 'partners' are.

Alphonse – age 40, with Maggie

Anastasia – age 60ish

Andre

Angela – Joy's probation officer

Anne – with Chester and Nick

Bear – Weasel's dog

Bearded Bruce

Bettie – daughter of Shakes

Big Jake – Joy's boyfriend

Bowser – Shakes' stuffed dog

Buck

Chantal – the 'religious lady' to stops by to chat

Chester – with Anne. Joy's 3rd roommate.

Chili – age 21

Chuck (Toothless) – Joy's 2nd roommate

Daimon – with Lucy-in-the-Sky

Deaf Donald – age 35

Dillinger – Buck's dog

Debbie- with Outcast

Fran – daughter of Shakes

Gaston

Hippo

Ian – with Marlena

Irene – with Shark

Jacques

Little Jake – age 41

Joy

Luther

Lucy-in-the-Sky – with Daimon

Maggie (Magdalene) – age 22, with Alphonse

Marlena – with Ian

Metro – sells newspapers

Nick – with Anne. Pans to make money to help out his street friends by making them sandwiches.

Outcast - with Debbie

Raven

Roy – Joy's first roommate

Rocky

Serge

Shakes – age 46

Shaggy – Wolf's dog

Shark – with Irene

Silver

Toothless (Chuck) – Joy's 2nd roommate

Two-four – sells newspapers

V – Chuck's dog

Weasel

Wolf – age 57

www.ingramcontent.com/pod-product-compliance
Lightning Source LLC
Chambersburg PA
CBHW072338090426
42741CB00012B/2827